WILD WATERCOLOR

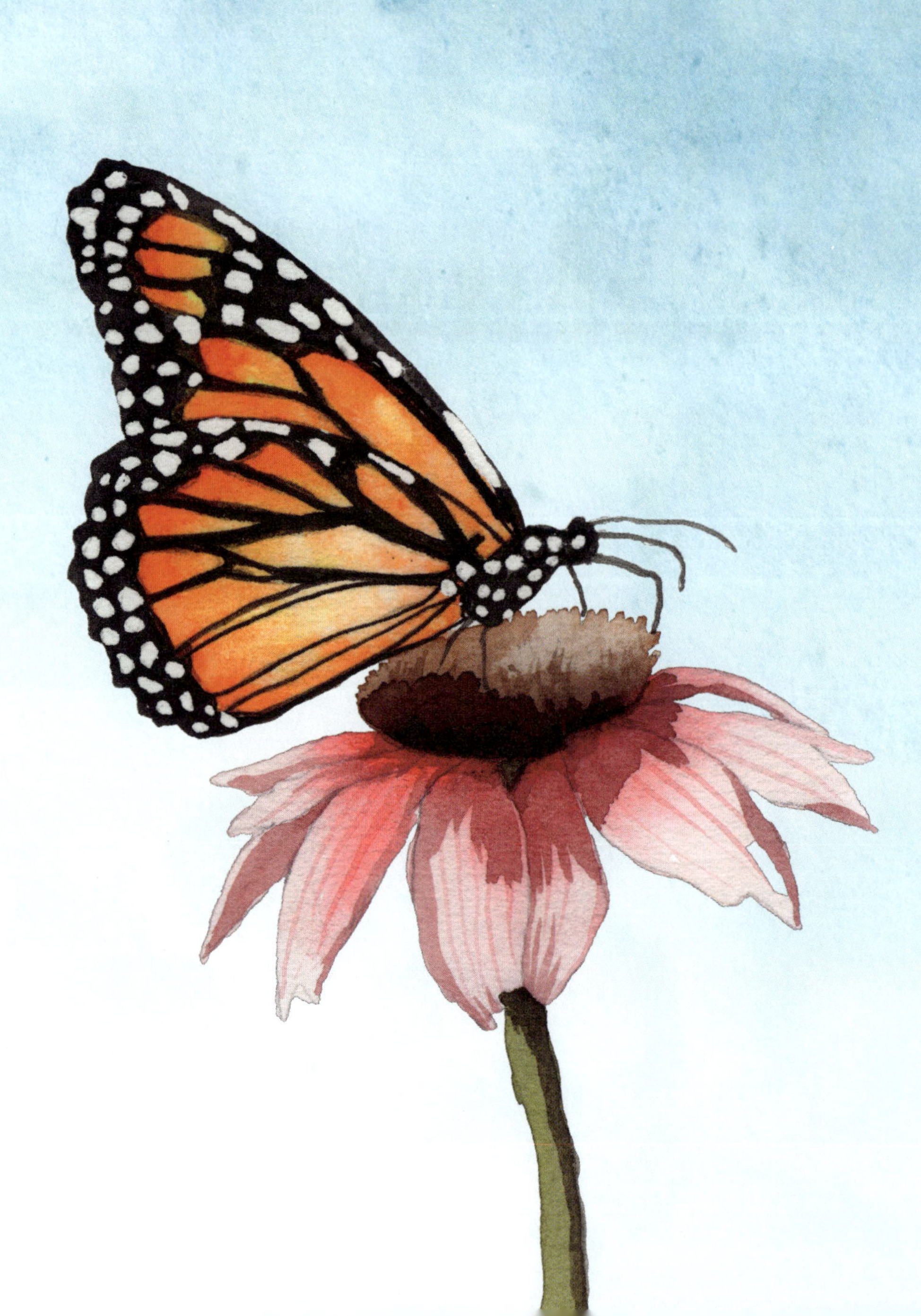

Wild WATERCOLOR

Weekly Lessons and Techniques for Stunning Creations

Karen Elaine

ZEITGEIST · NEW YORK

Zeitgeist™
An imprint and division of Penguin Random House LLC
1745 Broadway, New York, NY 10019
penguinrandomhouse.com
zeitgeistpublishing.com

ISBN: 9780593885864

Manufactured in the United States of America
2nd Printing

Illustrations by Karen Elaine
Art on pages 3 and 4 © by Shutterstock.com/merrymuuu,
pages 13 and 16 © by Shutterstock.com/Liudmila Kopecka,
and page 15 © by Shutterstock.com/illustratordreamer
Book design by Emma Hall
Author photograph © by Karen Elaine
Edited by Angelica Martinez

The authorized representative in the EU for product safety and compliance
is Penguin Random House Ireland, Morrison Chambers, 32 Nassau Street,
Dublin D02 YH68, Ireland. https://eu-contact.penguin.ie

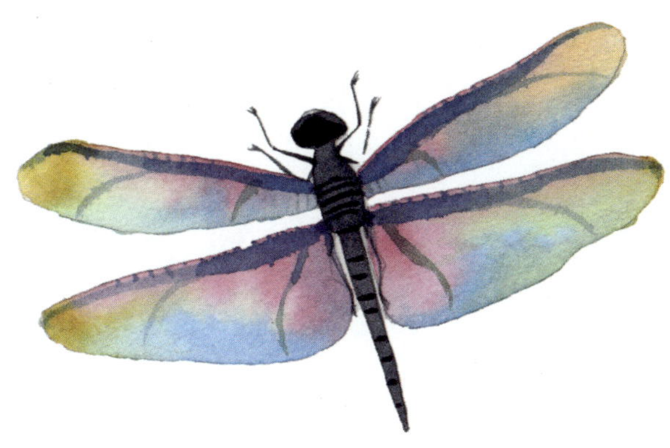

To the memory of my friend and
soul sister, Linda Gray

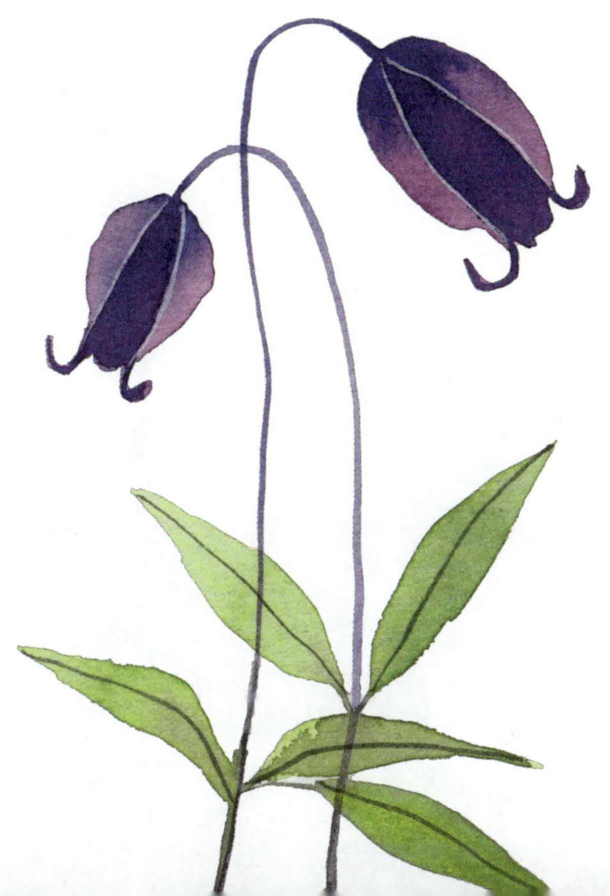

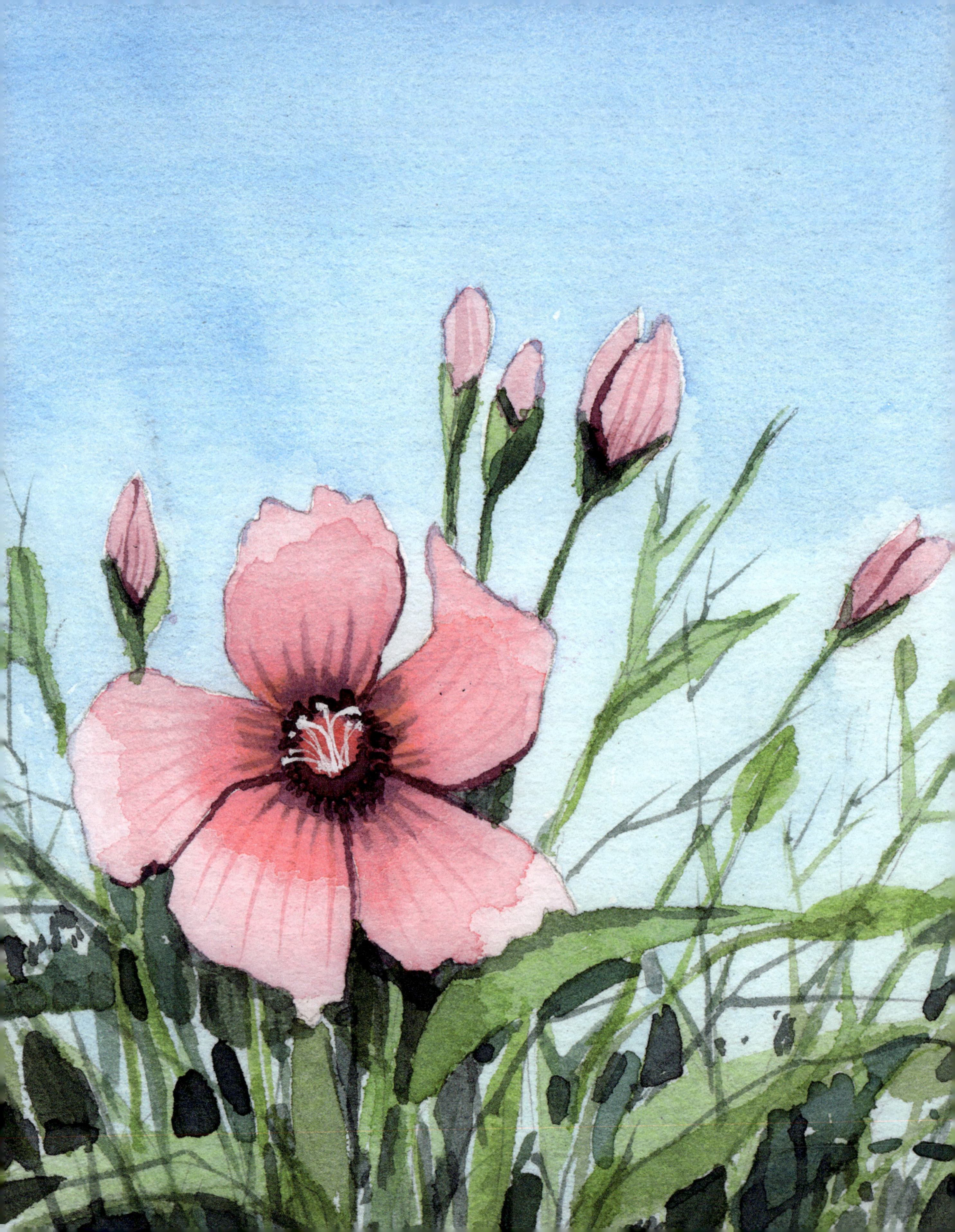

Contents

Projects

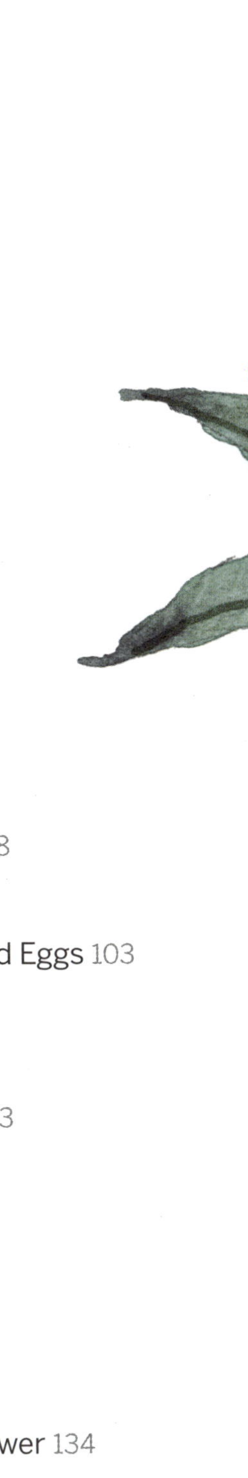

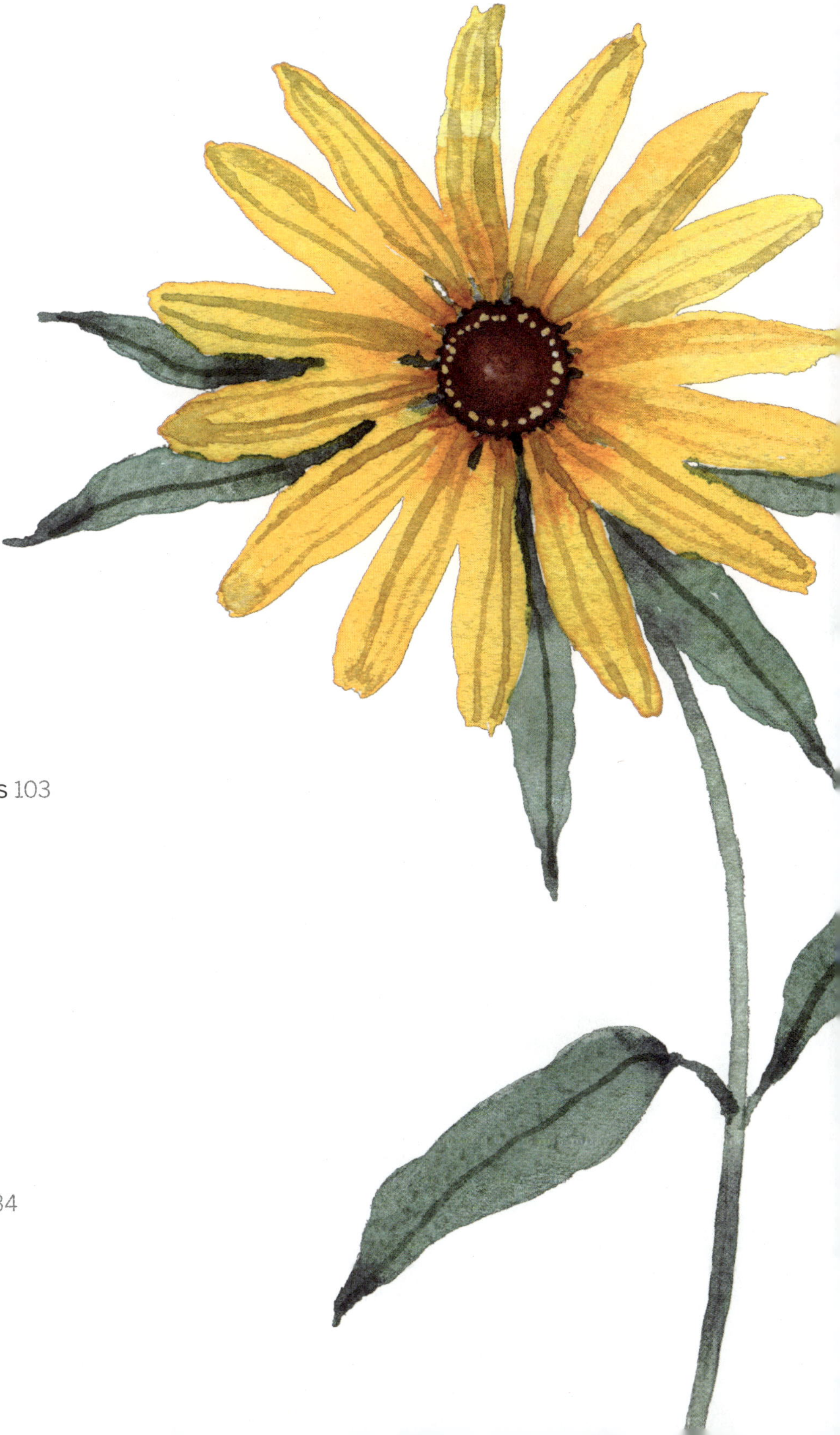

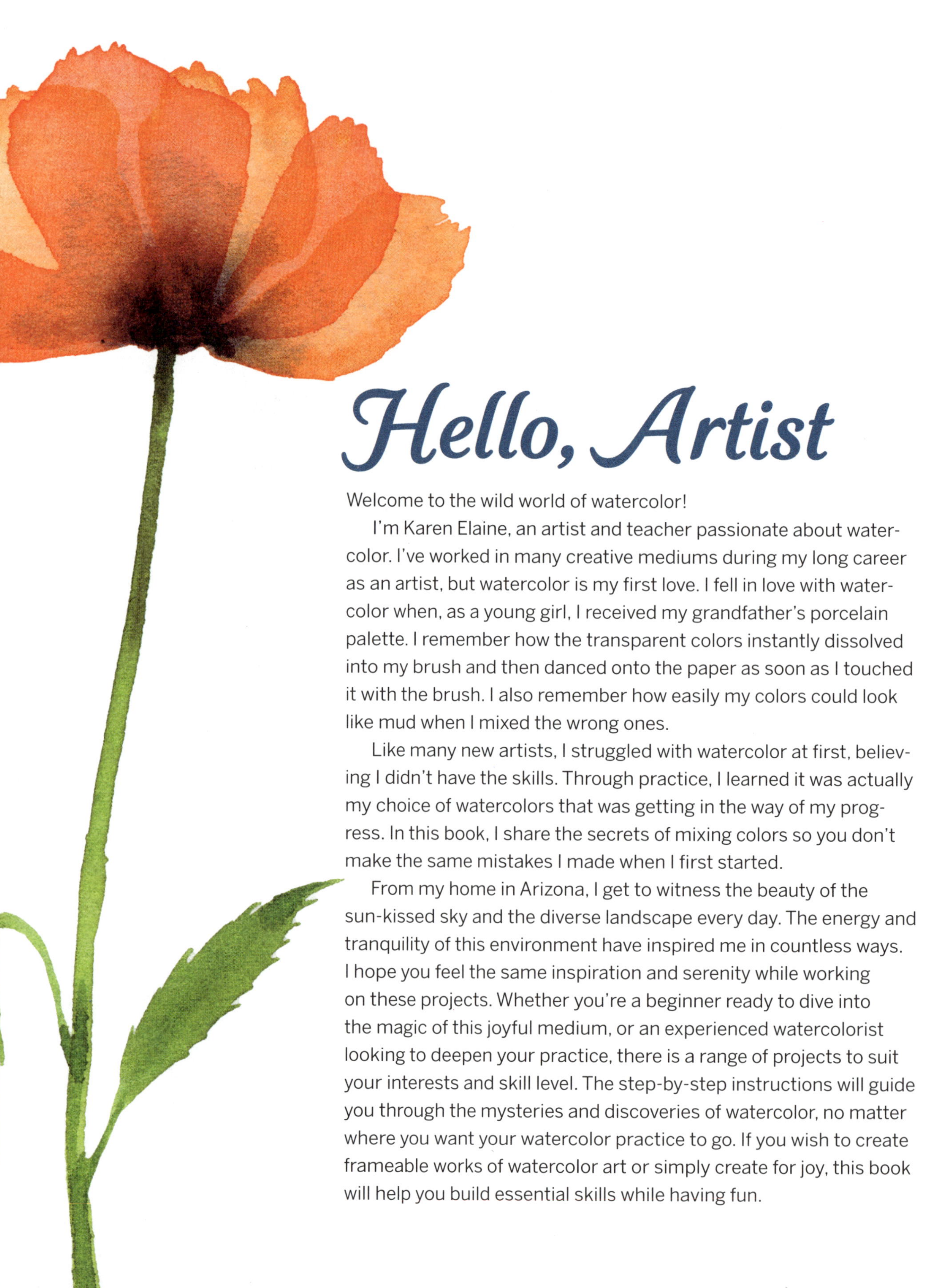

Hello, Artist

Welcome to the wild world of watercolor!

I'm Karen Elaine, an artist and teacher passionate about water-color. I've worked in many creative mediums during my long career as an artist, but watercolor is my first love. I fell in love with water-color when, as a young girl, I received my grandfather's porcelain palette. I remember how the transparent colors instantly dissolved into my brush and then danced onto the paper as soon as I touched it with the brush. I also remember how easily my colors could look like mud when I mixed the wrong ones.

Like many new artists, I struggled with watercolor at first, believ-ing I didn't have the skills. Through practice, I learned it was actually my choice of watercolors that was getting in the way of my prog-ress. In this book, I share the secrets of mixing colors so you don't make the same mistakes I made when I first started.

From my home in Arizona, I get to witness the beauty of the sun-kissed sky and the diverse landscape every day. The energy and tranquility of this environment have inspired me in countless ways. I hope you feel the same inspiration and serenity while working on these projects. Whether you're a beginner ready to dive into the magic of this joyful medium, or an experienced watercolorist looking to deepen your practice, there is a range of projects to suit your interests and skill level. The step-by-step instructions will guide you through the mysteries and discoveries of watercolor, no matter where you want your watercolor practice to go. If you wish to create frameable works of watercolor art or simply create for joy, this book will help you build essential skills while having fun.

How to Use This Book

Flip through the pages and get a glimpse of what you'll be creating. I suggest you work through this book from the beginning, as the projects are designed in sequence to grow your skills as a watercolor artist. You will progress through a total of 36 projects, week by week, but you are welcome to go at your own speed and do as many projects in a week as you wish. Try to take your time and enjoy each step of your watercolor journey.

LEVEL 1: BEGINNER

In the beginning, you will discover the joy of color mixing while learning water control and fundamental watercolor techniques. You will practice wet on wet, glazing, layered and graded washes, and color mixing using a limited palette. Projects include simple landscapes and skyscapes as well as leaves and flowers while you become familiar with the materials.

LEVEL 2: INTERMEDIATE

In this section you will learn how to create smooth and dynamic watercolor washes for beautiful backgrounds. You will practice painting nature-inspired motifs while developing your sketching and observational skills.

LEVEL 3: ADVANCED

By the time you reach this section, you will have built the confidence and skills to create wild landscapes, florals, botanicals, and animals. You will continue to practice the basic skills and discover new skills as well as essential composition fundamentals.

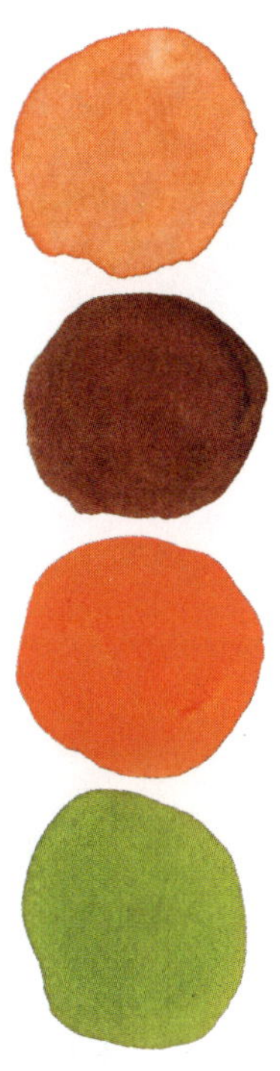

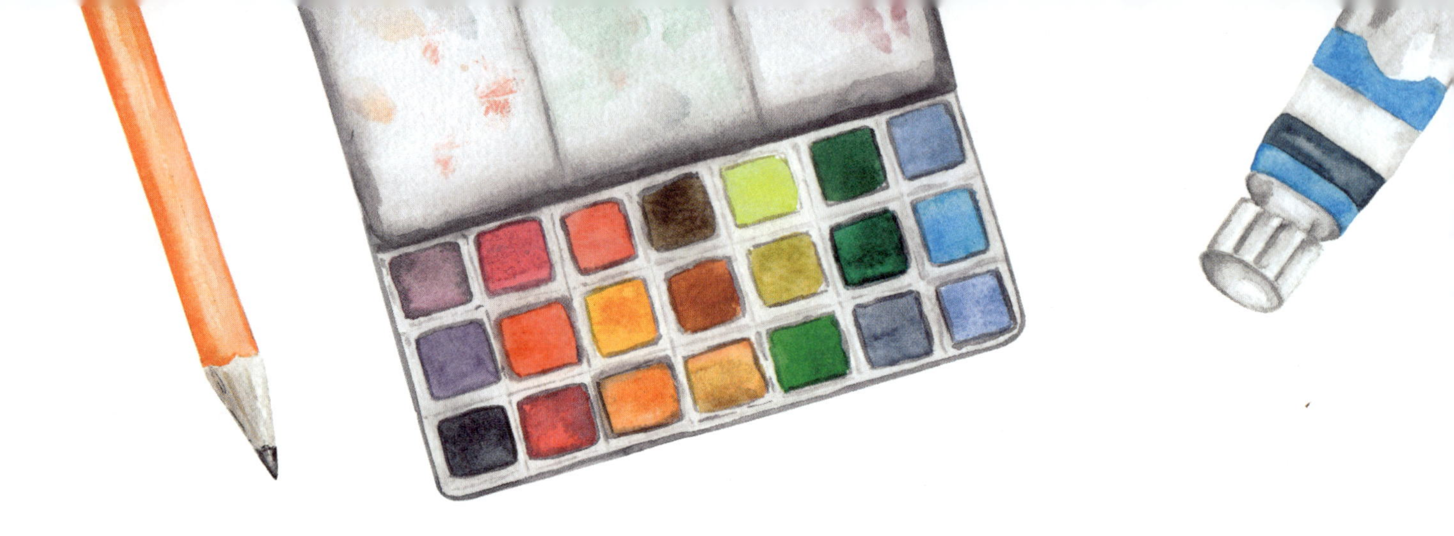

Getting
STARTED

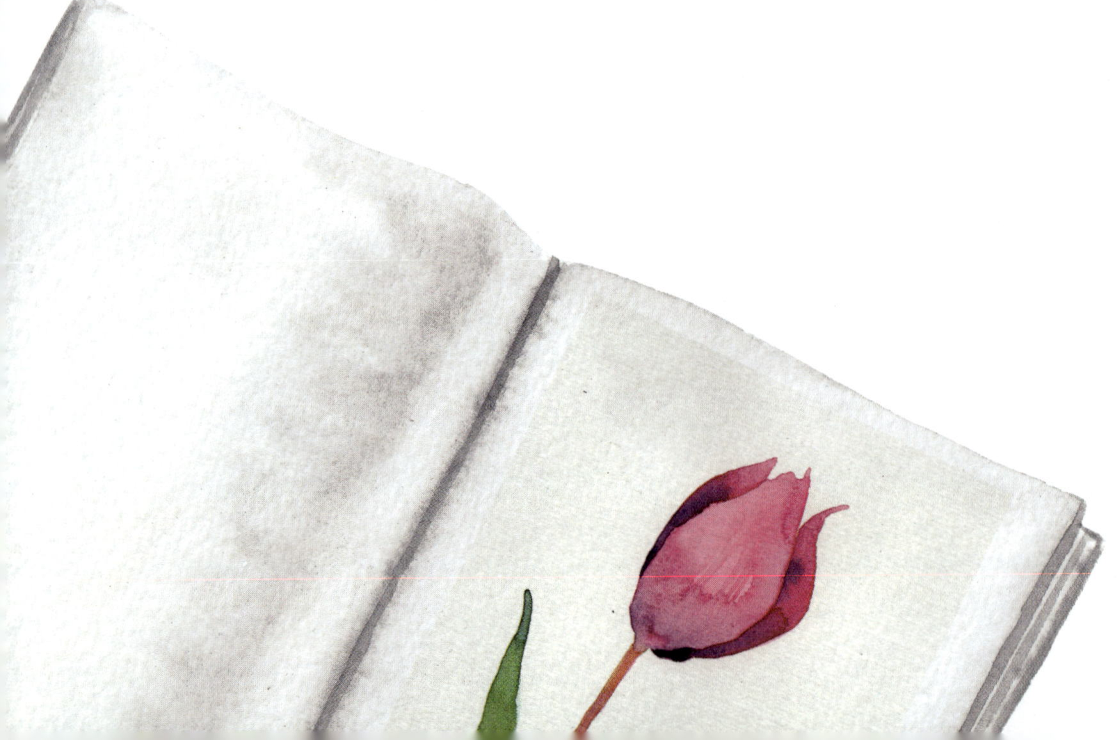

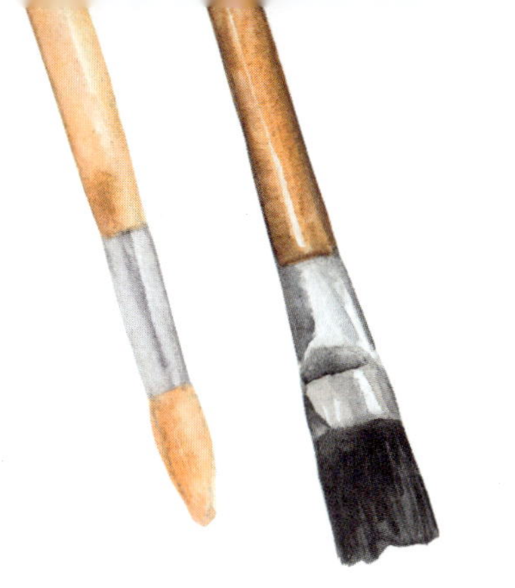
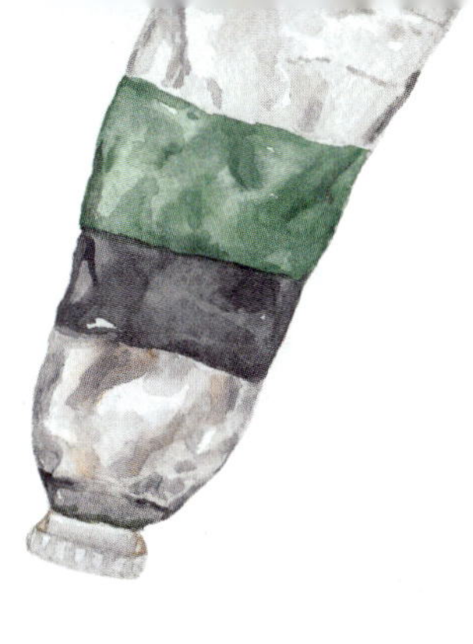
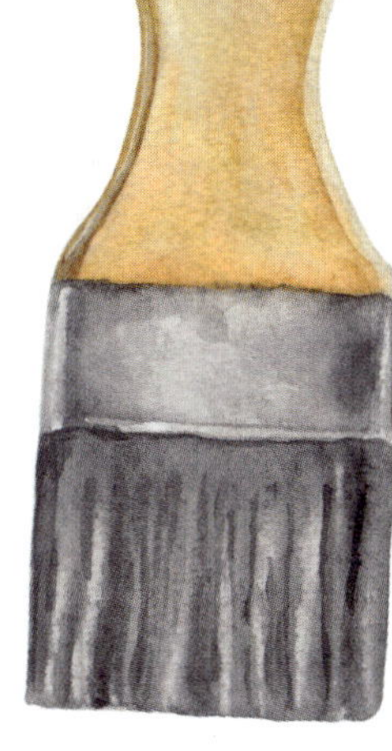

Wild Watercolor is about taking inspiration from nature and using the tools and skills you're building to bring your paintings to life. Find a space in your home to set up a watercolor painting station. It can be on your desk or a small table where there is good lighting. Make it inviting and easily accessible so you can get right to painting when the urge hits. Are you ready to explore the joyful world of *Wild Watercolor*? Let's dive in!

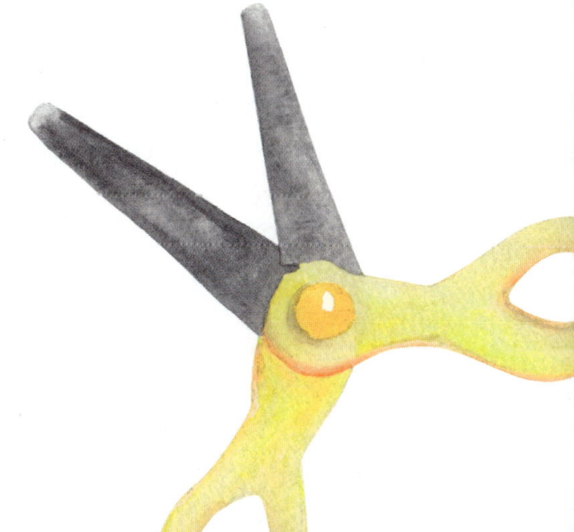

Tools and Materials

Having the best quality paint, paper, and a good-performing brush or two will give you the best possible results and the most stress-free experience. I learned a long time ago that having a basic four-color palette and using the highest quality materials was the best way to create brilliant, luminous watercolor paintings. The pigment, the paper, and the brush are all equally important to each other, and water is the catalyst.

Watercolor Paint

For the beginner-level watercolor projects, you will need only four professional-grade watercolors in your palette: CMYK mixing colors. CMYK stands for cyan, magenta, yellow, and key (black), which are the four primary colors in the color process. Buy the best quality paint in these four colors you can afford. That way, you'll be able to create any color from these CMYK colors, which is much more affordable than buying a ton of different watercolors. I recommend choosing from the brands listed, but you can use any brand of professional watercolors that have the same pigment names, and you can mix brands as well. The paint can come in tubes, half pans, or full pans.

CYAN: Phthalo Blue (Green Shade) by Daniel Smith, Helio Cerulean by Renesans, or Phthalo Blue by Qor

MAGENTA: Quinacridone Red or Quinacridone Rose by Daniel Smith, Quinacridone Red by Renesans, or Quinacridone Magenta by Qor

YELLOW: Lemon Yellow by Daniel Smith, Transparent Yellow by Renesans, or Hansa Yellow by Qor

KEY/BLACK: Lunar Black by Daniel Smith, Mars Black by Renesans, or Ivory Black by Qor

Another alternative is the Niji Artist Watercolors set. It contains all the transparent colors you need for mixing and is reasonably priced.

As you progress through the projects, add new colors to your palette, choosing colors you love. Additional colors to consider are Ultramarine Blue, Cerulean Blue, Quinacridone Gold, and Payne's Gray.

Paper

It's important to have high-quality watercolor paper
for successful watercolor painting. My favorite brands
are Niji, Fabriano Artistico Extra White, and Arches.
Canson, Strathmore, and Hahnemuhle make great
papers as well. Different brands and qualities of paper
accept the watercolors differently and you may soon
discover you prefer one brand over another.

You will be working on small sheets of watercolor
paper for the projects in this book. I like working small
because it's less intimidating than a large sheet and it
makes it easier to commit to daily painting. I will always
suggest the ideal paper size for each project, but if you
don't have the exact size listed, feel free to cut your
paper with scissors or an X-Acto knife (and a cutting
mat, so you don't cut into your table!).

Overall, I recommend using 140lb cold pressed
watercolor paper made of 100 percent cotton for the
best results. Twenty-five sheets (individual sheets or
in a block) no larger than 9 × 12 inches will provide
enough paper to complete all the projects. You can opt
for a cheaper brand for the Beginner and Intermediate
lessons or use the best paper possible for all projects.
Either way, just make sure you're not working on regu-
lar printer paper.

Brushes

A brush designed specifically for watercolor is essential, but it doesn't have to be expensive. Watercolor
brushes can be made with synthetic or natural hair and
must hold a lot of water and come to a sharp point. For
most projects in this book, you will need a medium- to
large-size round brush at least ¼ to ½ inch in diameter
(size 8 or 10), a small flat wash brush at least ¼ inch
wide, and a fine-line brush. I found the Yasutomo Fusion
brush assortment to be the most economical and best-
performing brush set with a wide variety of sizes. Silver
and Princeton Brush offer excellent brushes at reason-
able prices as well.

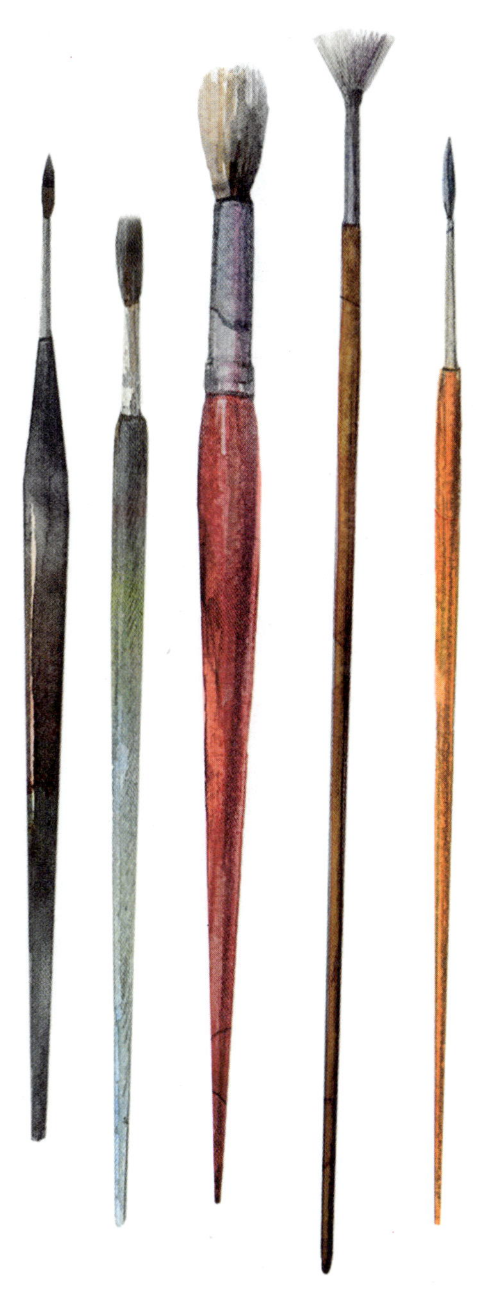

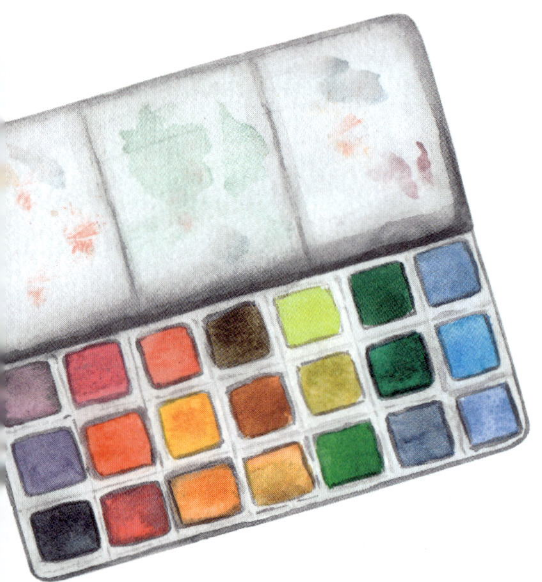

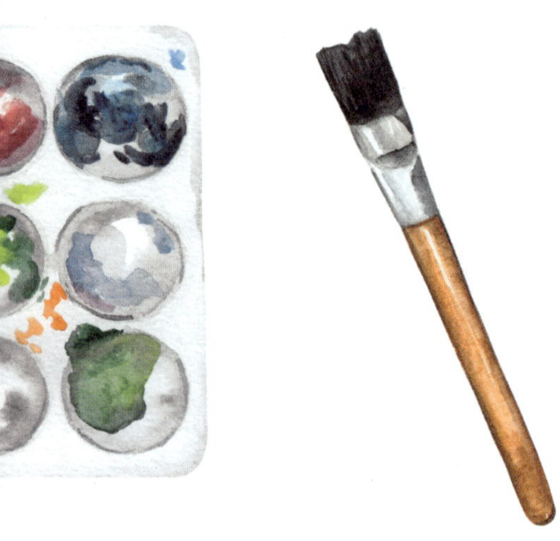

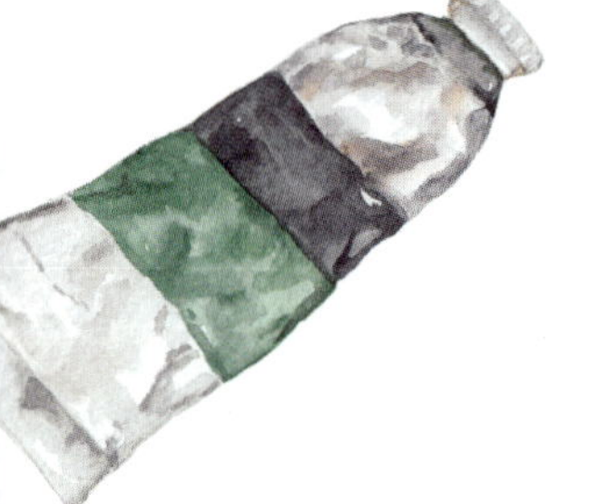

Other Supplies

Now that you've got your paints, paper, and brushes, you're almost ready to begin. There are a few extras I always recommend artists have handy, especially for more advanced projects. You may find many of these things in your home already, whereas others may require a trip to the art supply store.

- 2H lead mechanical pencil (0.5 mm)

- Cotton swabs

- Facial tissue

- Fine-mist spray bottle

- Kneaded eraser

- Large cup, to hold water

- Markers: Black fine-tip (micron 0.5 or smaller); white opaque fine-tip

- Masking fluid or masking fluid pen

- Paint palette

- Rags or paper towels

- Ruler or measuring tape

- Scissors

- Small natural sea wool sponge, or any small sponge with texture

- Thin Masonite panel

- Masking or washi tape

- X-Acto knife and cutting mat

- Water

Skills and Techniques

In this section you'll learn the basic watercolor techniques that will help
you build valuable skills and confidence for your watercolor painting
journey. You may be tempted to skip this part, but these techniques are
fundamental for successful and joyful watercolor painting. Feel free to
return to this section anytime you need to practice your skills.

Water Control

"Water" is watercolor's first and most important word. One of the most
common challenges for beginners is knowing when they have too little
or too much water on their brush. Many people use too little water when
starting out in watercolor. Mastering water control takes practice; using a
paper towel or cotton rag while you paint will help soak up extra paint or
water as will knowing your brush's capacity for holding water. Worry not: As
you move through the lessons in this book, you will become more familiar
with water control.

Color Mixing

The primary cyan, magenta, yellow, and key (black), or the CMYK colors,
will allow you to create an infinite range of colors. Adding black darkens the
color and changes the *value*, which refers to the lightness or darkness of
a color. Add more water to create a lighter value and less water for a more
saturated value. Having a good understanding of color mixing will help
avoid the pitfall of muddy colors. Your watercolor paintings will be more
luminous and more interesting. See the exercise at the end of this chapter
to practice color mixing, which is the best way to master this skill.

Brush Strokes

Round and flat watercolor brushes are most commonly used, and there are specialty brushes, like triangle and oval wash brushes, for creating various strokes and shapes. Round brushes allow for a variety of thick to thin strokes just by pressing on the belly, or underside, of the brush. Try practicing thin lines by holding the brush loaded with watercolor at an angle and touching only the tip while painting the line.

Practice a thicker line by pressing the belly (underside) of the brush loaded with watercolor onto the paper while painting the line.

Practice a varied line by touching the tip of the paper with the loaded brush while painting the line, then pressing the belly (underside) of the brush onto the paper while painting the line.

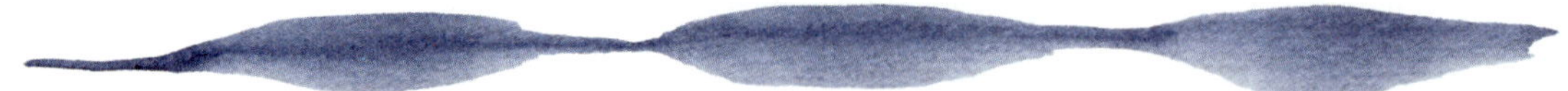

You will be using mostly medium round brushes, a flat wash brush, and a fine-line brush in this book but feel free to try other types of brushes for creating interesting marks and strokes for your watercolor painting.

Washes

Applying a "wash" simply means applying a layer of paint diluted with water to achieve a slightly transparent effect on the paper. Usually, a wash is used as a background for your painting, to build layers of color, and to give it a particular value.

To achieve a smooth and uniform result for your washes, it's important to brush watercolor washes quickly and evenly across the paper's surface. Mastering washes can be challenging, but it's a fundamental technique in watercolor painting. With practice and by following some basic methods, you can successfully paint beautiful washes. There are a few different types of washes, including:

FLAT: Even, uniform color and value all over

GRADED: A gradual, smooth change in value from dark to light

VARIEGATED: Different colors and values in various places on the paper

Glazing

This technique involves applying multiple layers of paint to add depth and complexity to your artwork. To use the glazing technique, you paint a shape, let it dry completely, then paint a new shape over the previous color. Because watercolor paint is transparent, the new brush marks allow the previously painted layers to show through. Combining two layers of paint produces a new appearance with a modified color and a darker value. Glazing produces a more desirable result and looks more luminous instead of applying a thick layer of paint to achieve a darker value.

Masking

Masking is used to retain details or to keep areas of the paper white. To create masking, a masking fluid, masking tape, or masking paper is applied to an area of the paper to prevent the watercolor from going there.

Color Lifting

This technique can be used in an area where a color has already been applied to "lift" it, or lighten or brighten the area by blotting the area with a tissue or sponge. You can also lift color by touching the tip of a clean damp brush into the area you wish to lighten. Staining watercolors do not lift, so this technique works only with non-staining colors—always test the lifting properties of any color on a separate sheet of paper first.

Wet on Wet and Wet on Dry

These techniques describe how paint is applied to the paper.

In the wet-on-wet technique, the paper is already wet before applying the paint, creating a soft and blended effect.

Wet-on-wet swatch

Wet on dry involves applying paint to dry paper, allowing for more precise and controlled brushstrokes.

Wet-on-dry swatch

Practicing these two essential techniques will help you achieve beautiful backgrounds, especially landscapes.

Troubleshooting Tips

Creating a beautiful watercolor painting may seem challenging at first, but with practice it can become effortless. Here are some valuable tips to address two common watercolor painting challenges.

1. Streaky, uneven washes and hard edge marks: When applying a watercolor wash, it's common to notice a streaked appearance, which becomes more visible as the color dries. To avoid this, make sure to mix a sufficient amount of paint for your wash. Also, use well-loaded brushes for each stroke and work quickly to prevent the paint from drying between strokes.

2. Watercolor blooms and backruns: Blooms and backruns are dark, feathery patterns that occur when wet paint is added to a drier wash. To prevent this, absorb the excess fluid on the paper with a clean, blotted brush before a backrun or bloom has time to form.

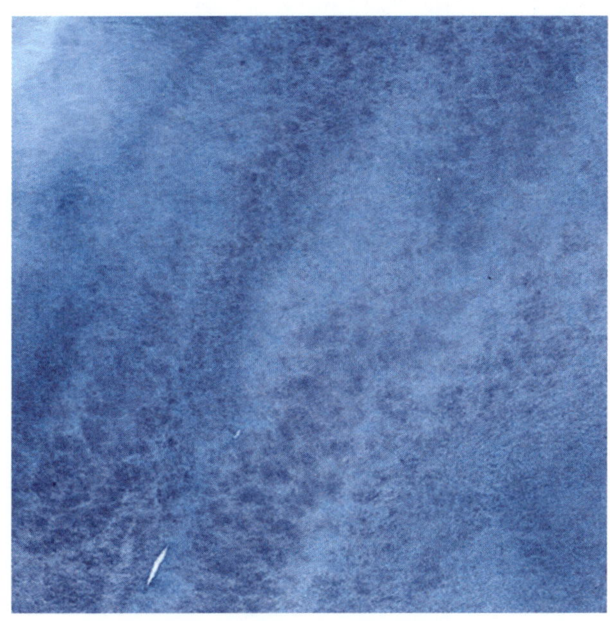

Uneven wash

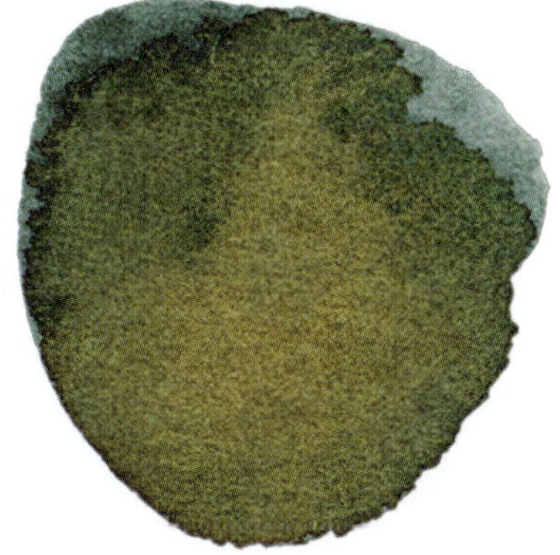

Bloom

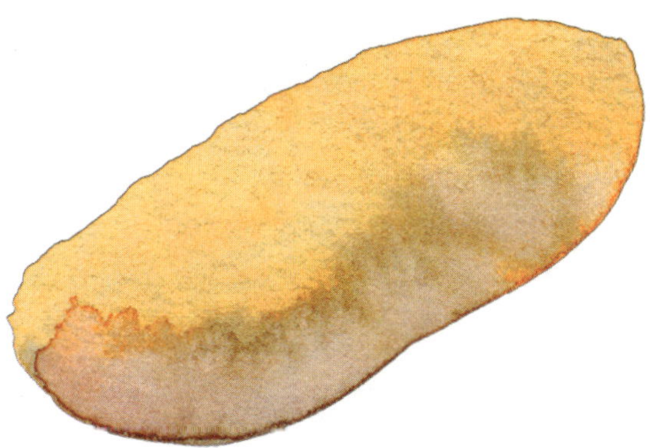

Backrun

Color Mixing Exercise

Before you begin your first project, it's helpful to experiment with color mixing. To prepare, squeeze a small amount of each CMYK color onto a palette and have a sheet of cold pressed watercolor paper, a small round brush, and plenty of water ready.

STEP ONE

At the top of the paper, paint medium-value swatches of all four colors. I used Phthalo Blue (Green Shade), Quinacridone Red, Hansa Yellow, and Lunar Black. I like Lunar Black because of its granulating properties that give more texture and interest. For a smooth watercolor mix, use Ivory Black instead. Use any combination of colors, as I mentioned before.

STEP TWO

Below the CMYK swatches you'll paint additional swatches. Mix blue with magenta to make a medium-value purple; yellow and blue to make a medium-value green; equal parts magenta and yellow to make a "primary" red; add more yellow to the red mix to make orange; and add black to the orange mix to make brown.

STEP THREE

Now add another row of swatches, this time in green hues. Add some yellow to the green mixture for one swatch; add more yellow to the same green mixture; mix some black with the green mixture; and add some blue to the green mixture. You can start to see the variety of colors you can create with just four colors.

STEP FOUR

Fill the page with as many color combinations as possible. Make a note of your favorite color combinations and try this exercise with any watercolor in your collection.

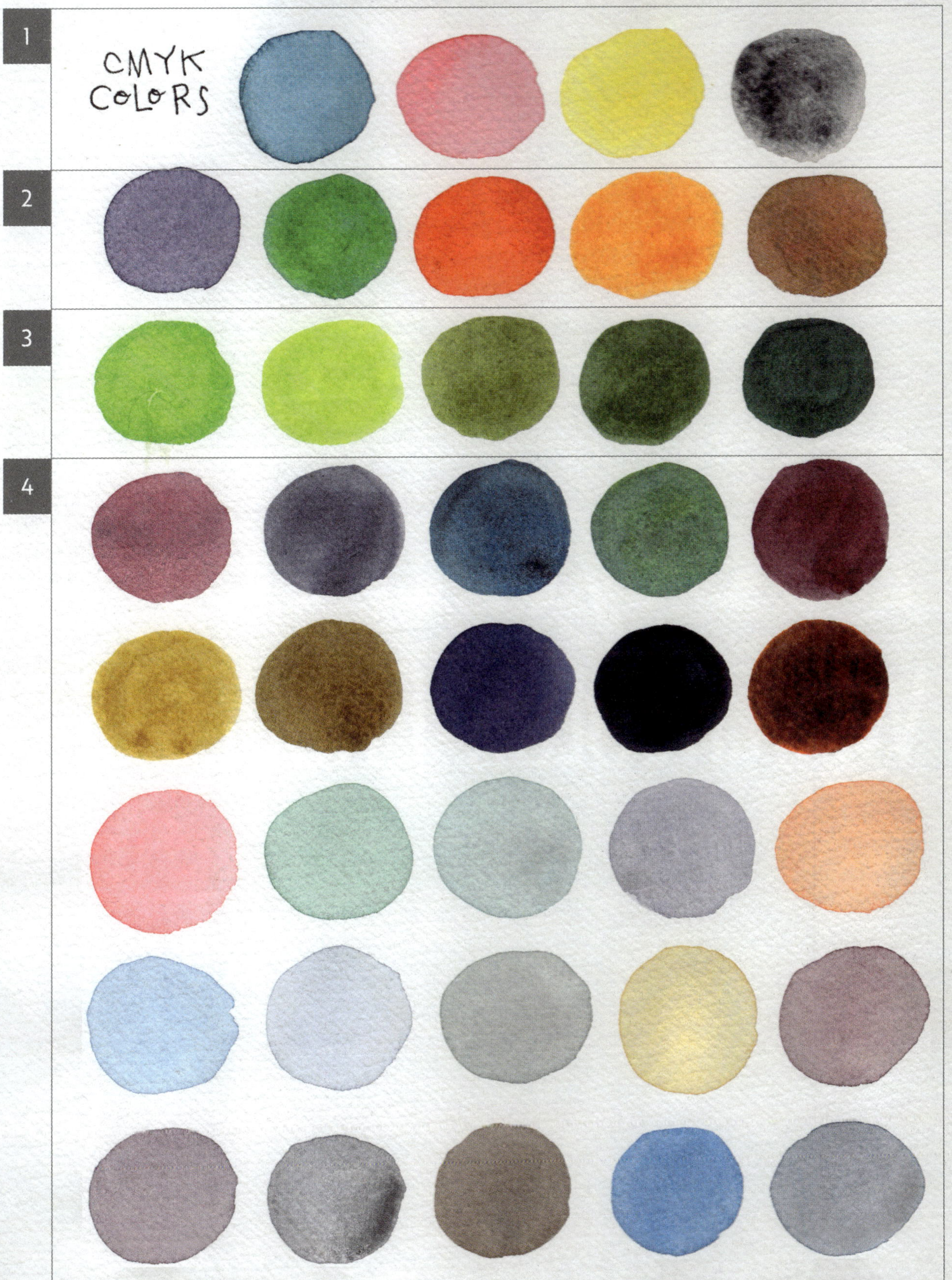

1
CMYK
COLORS
2
3
4

Weeks 1–12

Beginner
WATERCOLOR PROJECTS

Let's begin with some easy projects for
you to build your skills and learn the basic
techniques. The projects in this section
are designed to help you get to know your
materials, learn color mixing, water control,
and other techniques so you become
confident in your watercolor painting. They
are also designed for you to have fun! The
most important thing to remember is to enjoy
the process and not worry about the outcome.
Let nature inspire you to take a pause, be
present, and enjoy the journey.

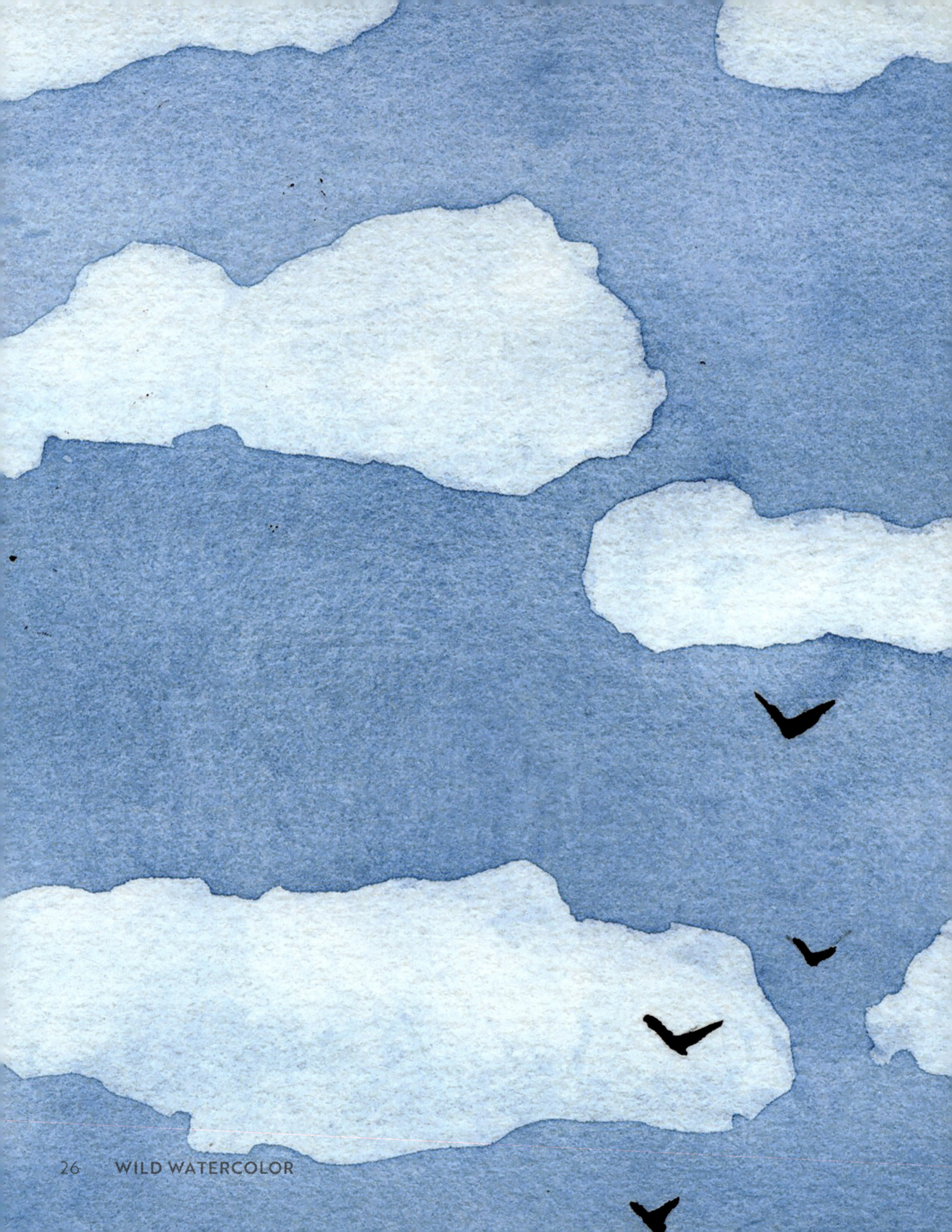

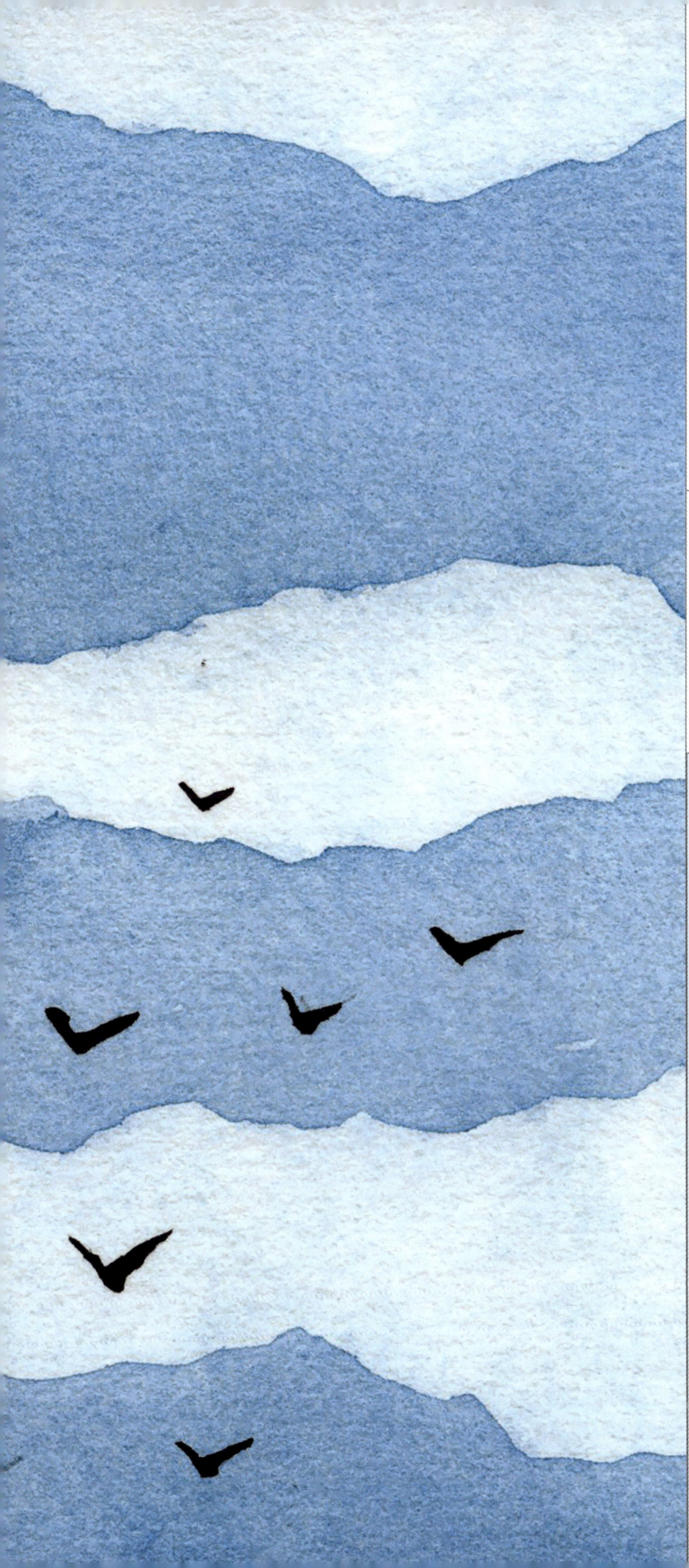

Sky with Clouds

A nonstaining blue watercolor and soft facial tissue are the secrets to creating clouds.

COLORS

 Cerulean Blue

 Payne's Gray

TECHNIQUES

- Flat wash
- Color lifting
- Glazing

MATERIALS

- Watercolor paper, 5" × 7"
- ½" flat wash brush
- Small round watercolor brush
- Facial tissue

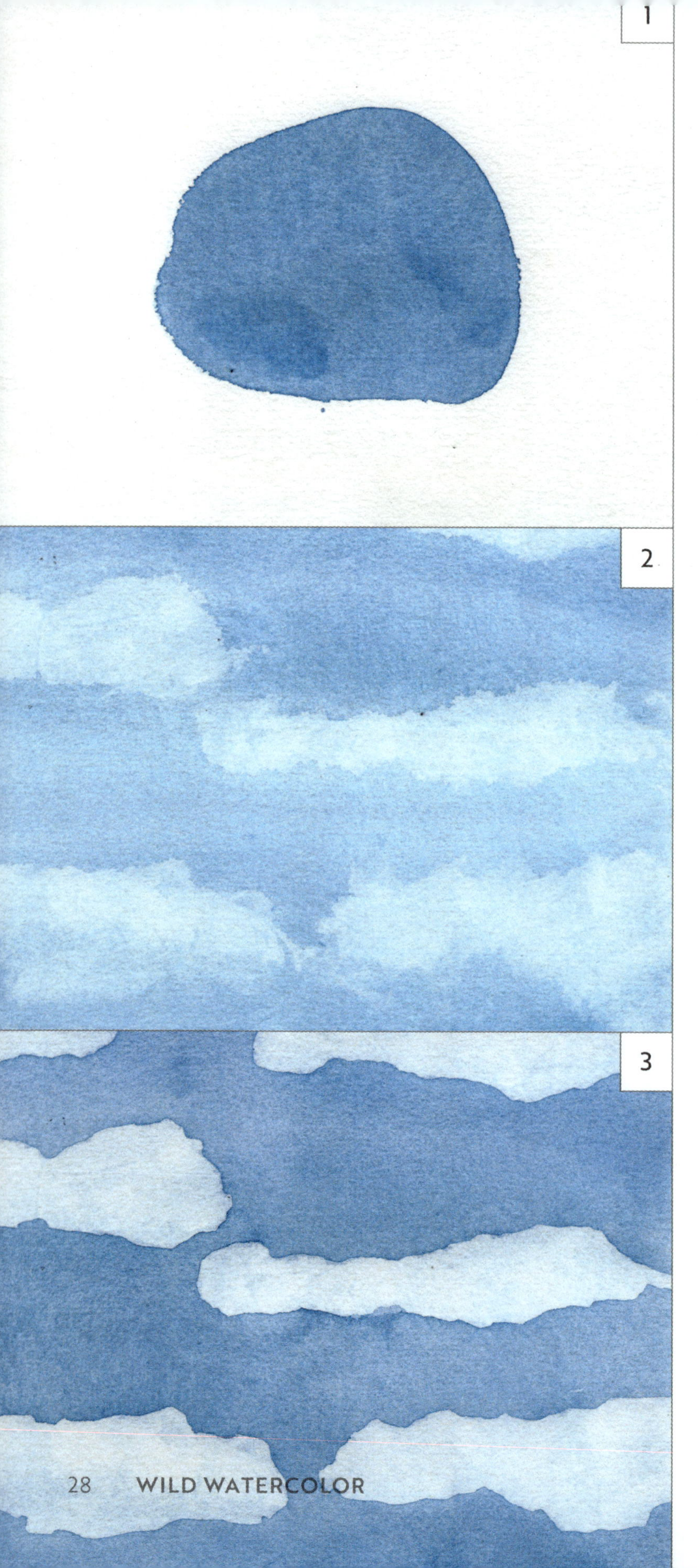

STEP ONE

Mix Cerulean Blue with enough water in your palette to achieve a light to medium value. Cerulean Blue watercolor is easy to lift because it is nonstaining.

STEP TWO

Using a flat brush apply a light saturated wash evenly in a side-to-side motion over the entire surface of the paper, starting at the top until you reach the bottom of the paper. You may need to fill, or "load," your brush with more color for a smooth wash. You want the watercolor to glide on the surface without dripping wet. While the paint is still wet, blot small areas with a crumpled facial tissue to lift the color and make cloud shapes. Let dry.

STEP THREE

Brush on a light layer of the same blue color around the cloud shapes to add contrast. Let dry.

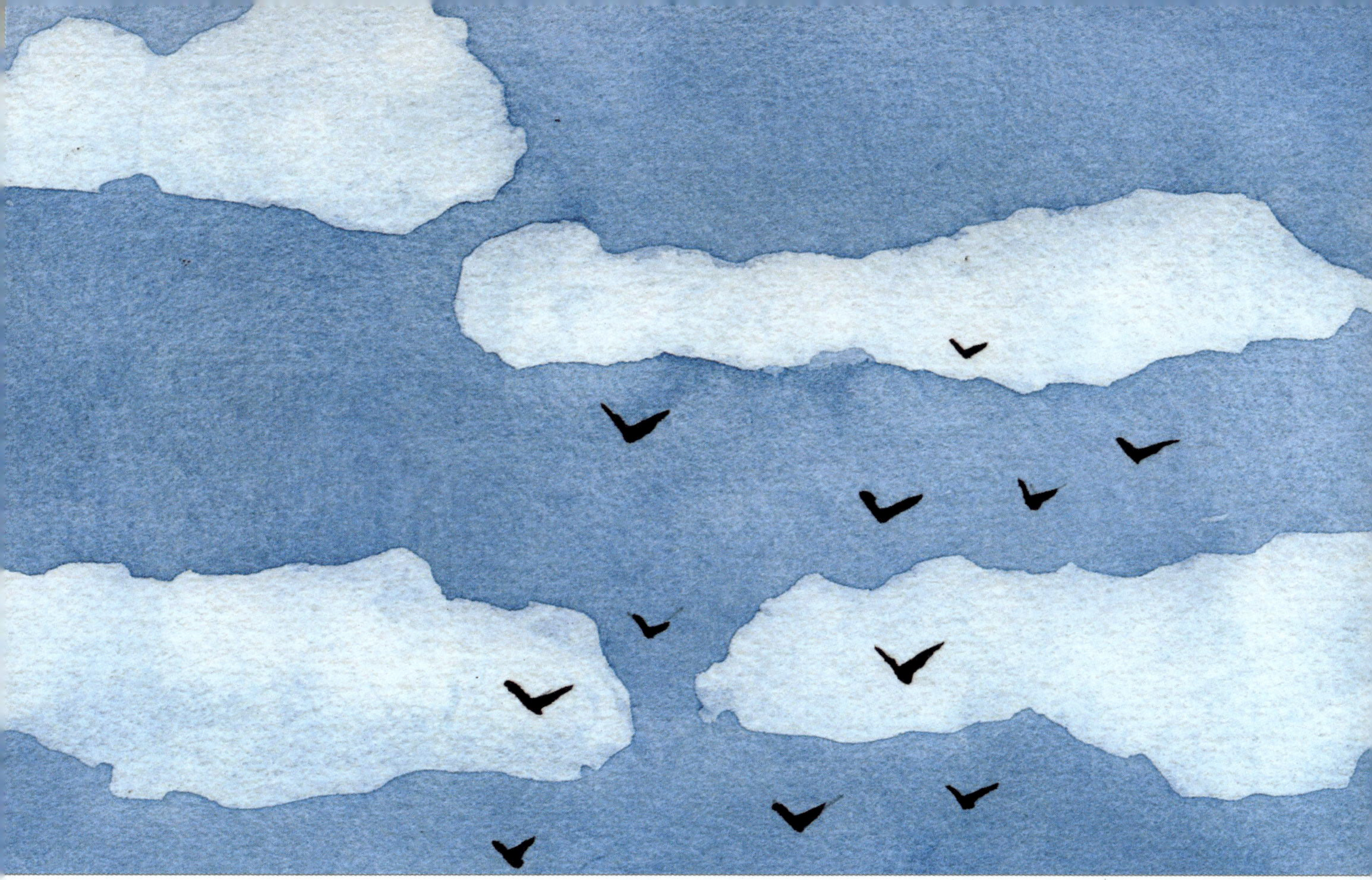

STEP FOUR

Mix a dark value of Payne's Gray watercolor. With a small round brush, paint simple V-shaped birds in the sky. Vary the size and distance of the birds for a more natural look.

Twilight Sky

Have you ever seen the evening sky at dusk, the mountains silhouetted beneath it? A beautiful sight, captured in watercolor.

COLORS

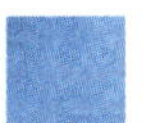 Phthalo Blue

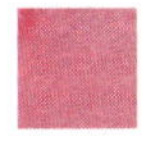 Quinacridone Magenta

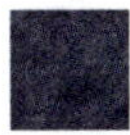 Payne's Gray

TECHNIQUES

- Wet on dry
- Color mixing
- Graded wash

MATERIALS

- Watercolor paper, 3½" × 5"
- 2H lead mechanical pencil
- Medium round watercolor brush
- White ink (optional)
- Facial tissue (optional)

STEP ONE

Mix mostly Phthalo Blue with a little Quinacridone Magenta in your palette to create a saturated cool blue.

STEP TWO

Load a medium round brush with the blue color and apply it at the top of the paper going across from left to right. Add some water to the mix to reduce saturation, then apply it to the paper, going over the first stroke and painting another layer beneath it. Continue adding water to the mix and adding more layers until you have filled the paper. You will see the wash becoming lighter as you add water to the mix. Let dry.

STEP THREE

About 1 inch from the bottom of the paper, sketch a mountain horizon with a mechanical pencil using a light touch.

Place some Payne's Gray in the palette and mix it with a little water for a deep saturated value that reads almost black. Add some of the blue mixture to it for a cooler value.

Paint in the mountain horizon with the almost-black watercolor mix. Let dry.

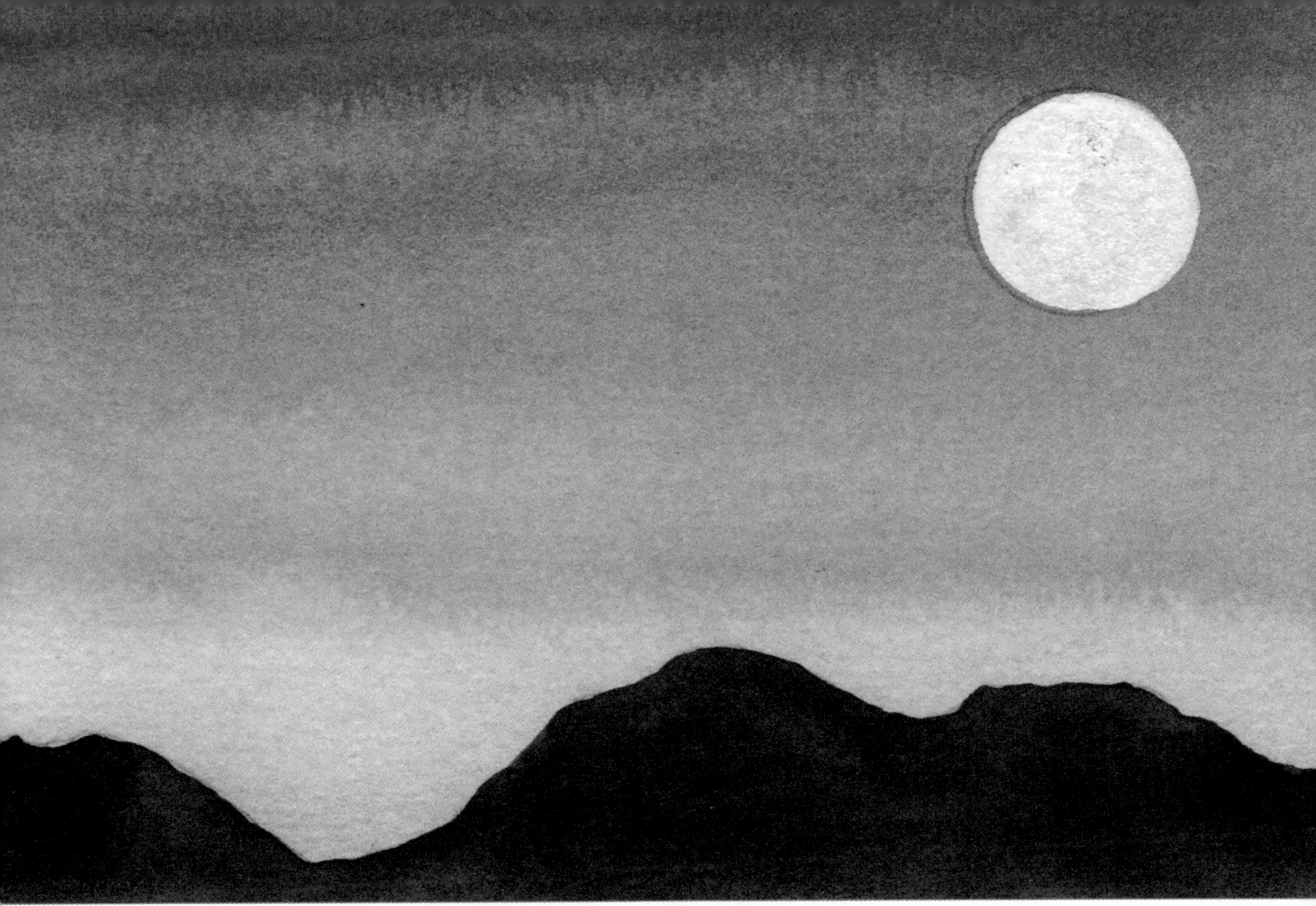

OPTIONAL: Paint a white moon with white ink for a more interesting composition and added contrast. To give texture to the moon, dab a crumpled facial tissue into the damp white ink and blot.

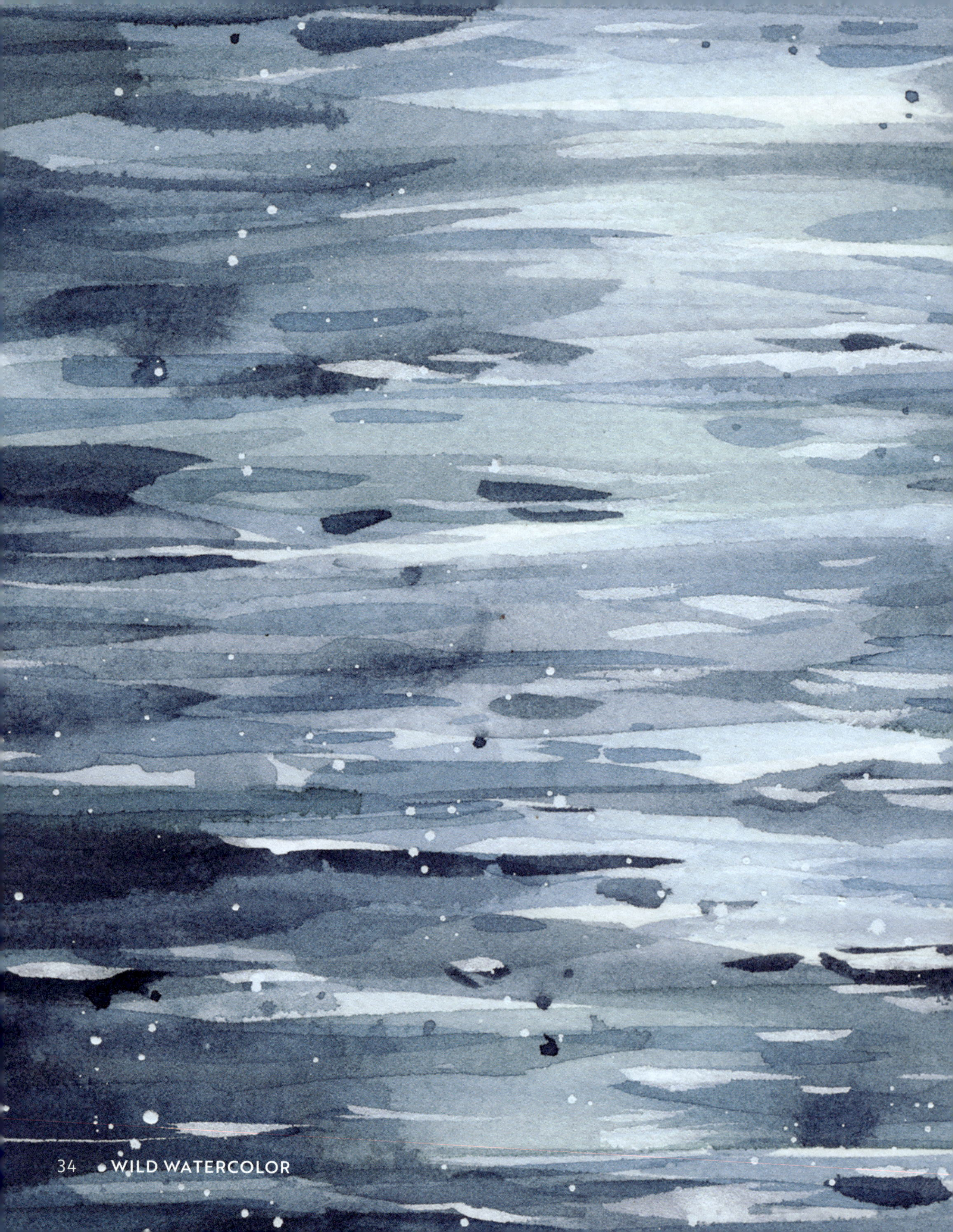

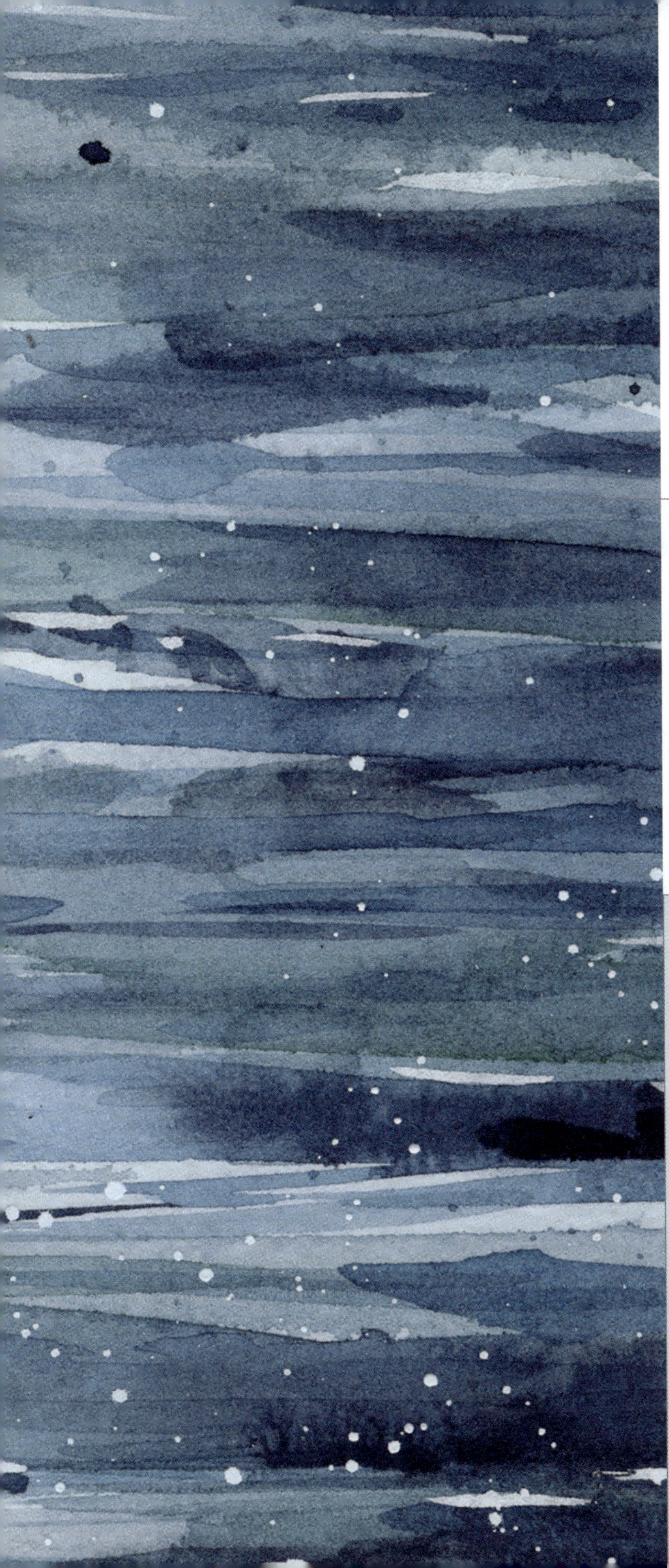

Waterscape

Whether it's the tranquil surface of a lake, the crashing waves of an ocean, or a meandering river, capturing the essence of water requires keen observational skills and a variety of simple watercolor techniques.

COLORS

 Indigo (or a mix of Phthalo Blue, black, and magenta)

 Payne's Gray

 Phthalo Blue (Green Shade)

Viridian

TECHNIQUES

- Wet on dry
- Wet on wet
- Layering
- Splattering

MATERIALS

- Watercolor paper, 5" × 7"
- Masking or washi tape
- Masonite panel
- Medium round watercolor brush
- Small round watercolor brush
- White ink
- Facial tissue

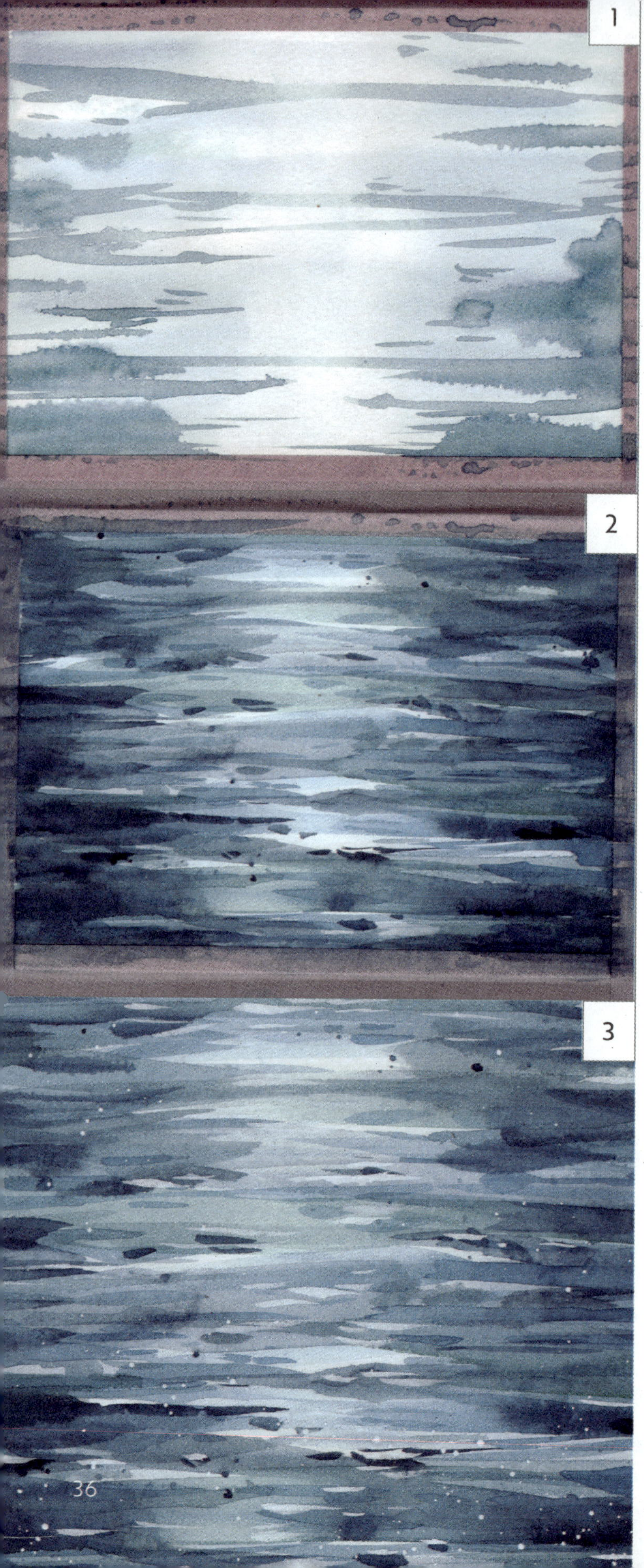

STEP ONE

Attach the paper to a board with masking or washi tape, creating a thin border with the tape on all edges of the paper. Using the medium brush, wet the paper with water until it is shiny but not dripping wet.

Mix together Indigo with a small amount of Phthalo Blue for a light value and load the medium brush with a generous amount of color. Sweep the brush back and forth horizontally on the paper, making strokes of varying sizes across the paper. Lift the brush to make smaller strokes. Blot the center area with a tissue if needed.

Mix a medium-value blue and use the medium brush to make sweeping strokes across the paper to build depth with layers. Let dry.

STEP TWO

Mix a medium-value Indigo with a small amount of Phthalo Blue (Green Shade) and paint varying strokes sweeping back and forth horizontally on the paper. Leave white areas alone and concentrate the color on the left and right edges of the paper.

Keep creating sweeping strokes to deepen the color, leaving the area in the center lighter than the edges.

Add a small amount of Viridian to the blue mixture and make sweeping strokes to blend. Keep building depth and contrast with more layers of paint strokes. Splatter a small amount of Indigo while it's still wet. Let dry.

STEP THREE

Thin white ink with water to a creamy consistency and use a small brush to paint highlights on the water, right above the darker values of blue. Let dry, then carefully remove the masking tape.

Wild Grasses

Wild grasses play a crucial role in many ecosystems, providing food and shelter for various wildlife while sustaining ecosystem health. Learning to paint these grass blades with long, smooth strokes can be both calming and fun.

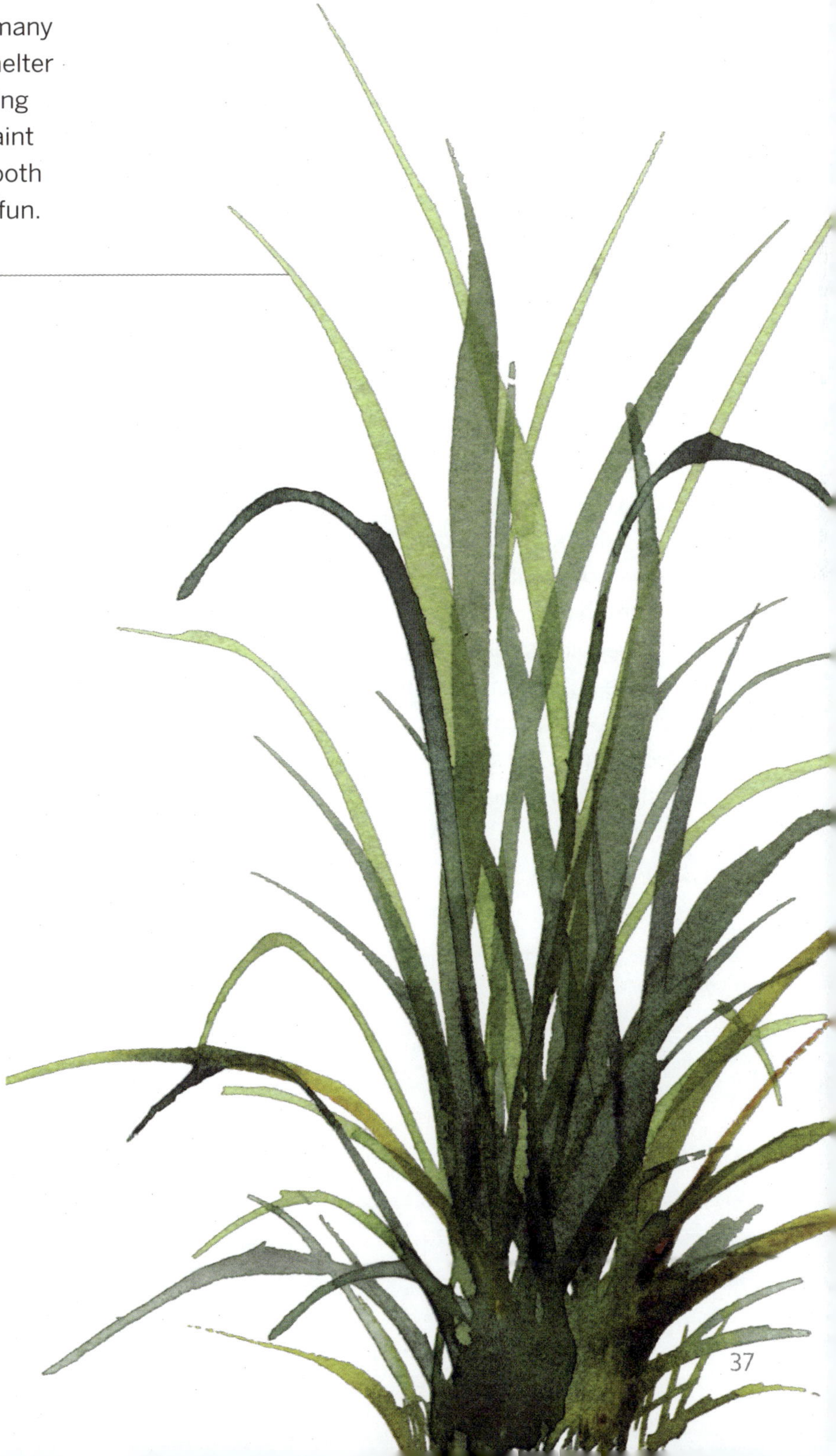

COLORS

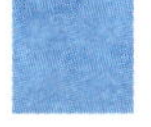 Phthalo Blue

 Hansa Yellow

 Payne's Gray

TECHNIQUES

- Wet on wet

MATERIALS

- Watercolor paper, 5" × 7"
- Fine-line brush
- Medium round watercolor brush with a sharp tip

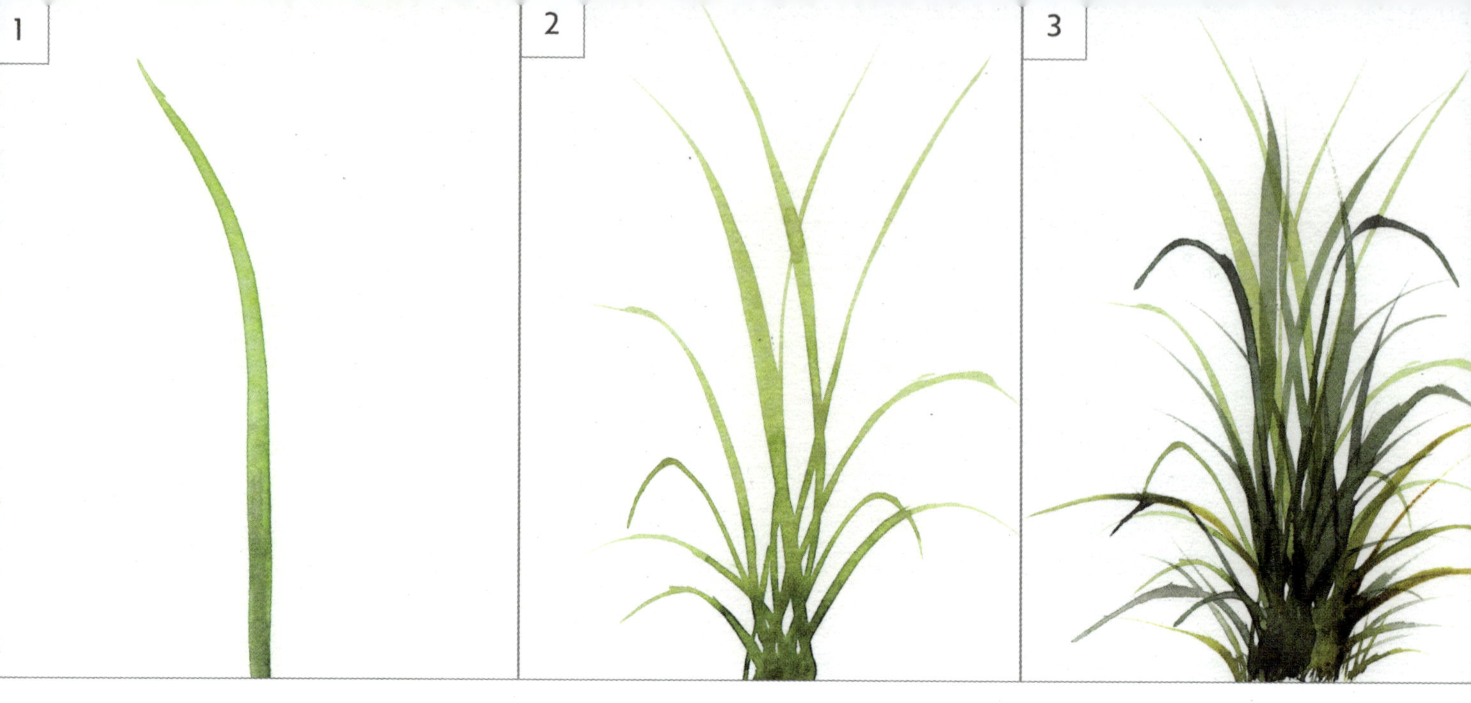

STEP ONE

Combine blue and yellow watercolors in your palette to create a mid-value green and a dark-value green. Load a fine-line brush with the mid-value green paint and paint long, sweeping strokes, starting at the bottom of the paper moving upward in a smooth motion. Curve the stroke slightly as you move upward.

STEP TWO

Paint several grasses of different lengths and curves going in different directions. Let dry.

STEP THREE

Load the fine-line brush with the darker green and paint long, sweeping, curved lines overlapping and crisscrossing the other grasses. Drop some darker green or Payne's Gray at the bottom of the grasses while it's still wet. Mix a little yellow into the lighter green and add a few grasses. Let dry.

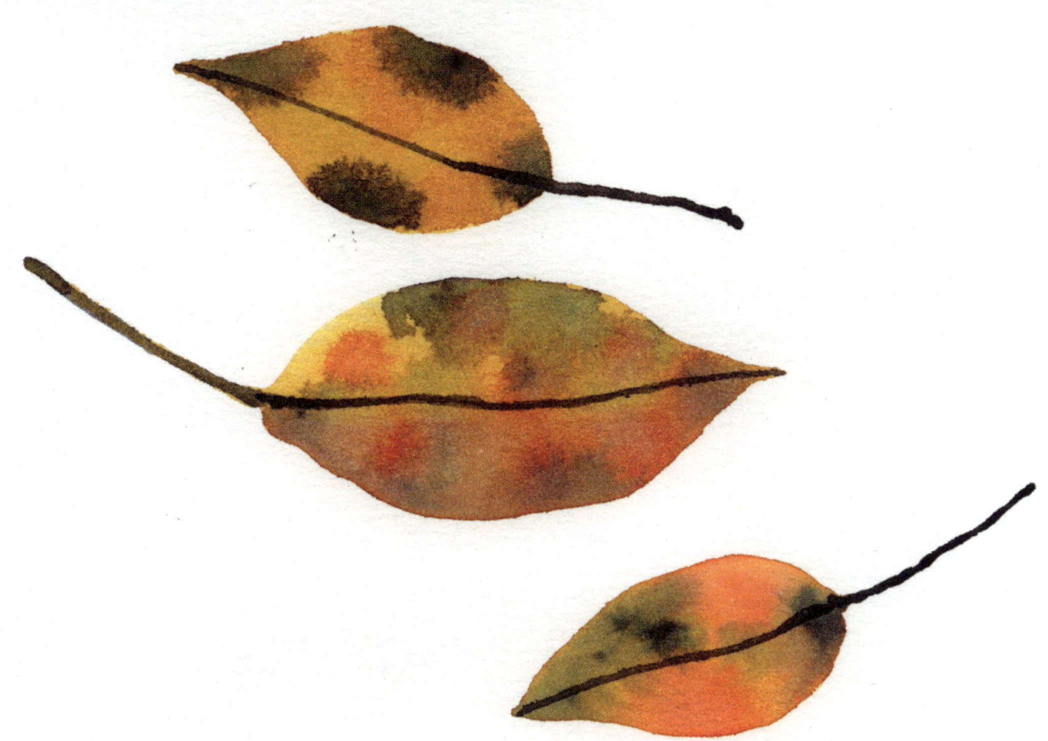

WEEK 5
Fall Leaves

Here we see the vibrant colors of changing
leaves in the fall, preparing us for winter rest.

COLORS

 Quinacridone Magenta

 Quinacridone Gold

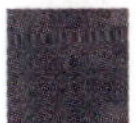 Moonglow (or a mix of Ultramarine Blue
and a tiny amount of Quinacridone Gold)

 Payne's Gray

TECHNIQUES

- Color mixing
- Layering

MATERIALS

- Watercolor paper, 5" × 7"
- 2H lead
  mechanical pencil
- Medium round
  watercolor brush with
  a sharp tip
- Fine-line brush

STEP ONE

Sketch three simple leaf shapes of different sizes and directions on the paper with a mechanical pencil.

STEP TWO

Mix Quinacridone Magenta, Quinacridone Gold, Moonglow, and Payne's Gray into separate puddles in your palette.

Using the medium round brush, paint the leaves with the medium value of Quinacridone Gold. Rinse the brush with clear water and load it with magenta. Apply the magenta with the tip of the brush into small random areas of the leaves while they're still wet. Follow with Moonglow. Observe the colors spreading and mixing inside the leaf shapes. Paint dark stems with Moonglow and let dry.

STEP THREE

Load a fine-line brush with Moonglow and paint a dark midrib through the center of each leaf.

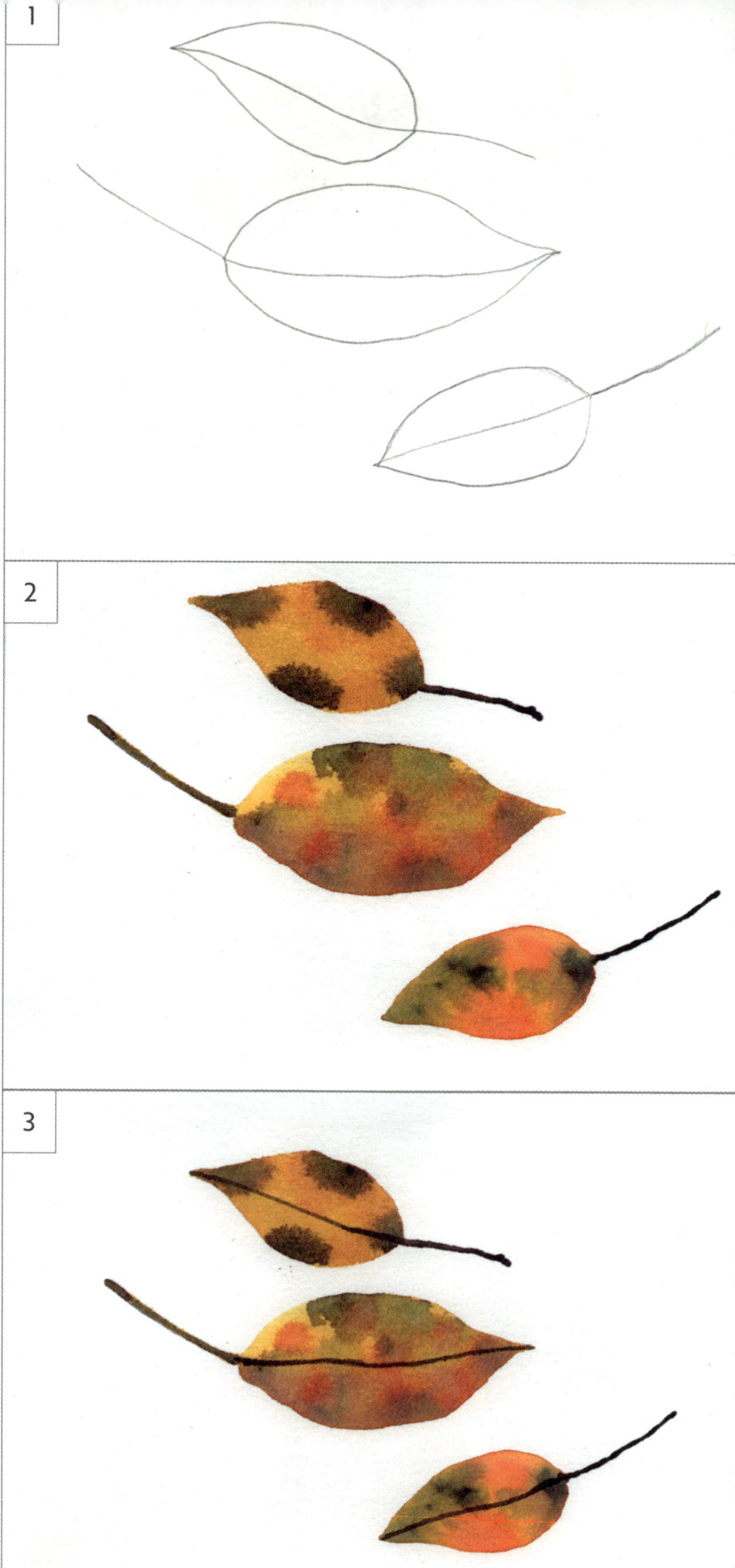

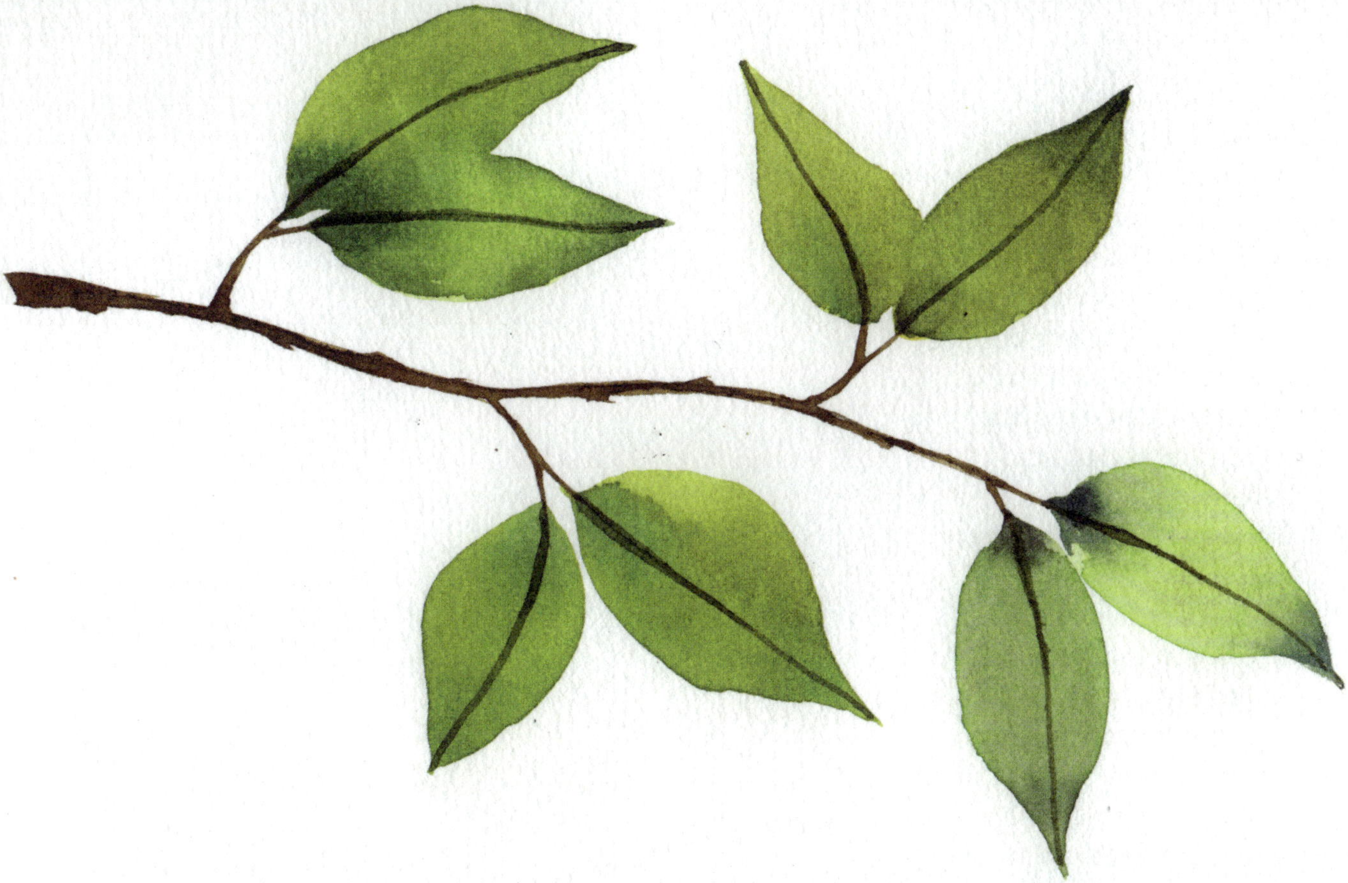

WEEK 6

Spring Leaves on Branches

When spring comes, we witness fresh leaves budding on the branch tips of bare trees, ushering in a new season and warmer weather.

COLORS

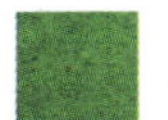 Sap Green

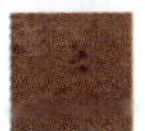 Burnt Umber

 Payne's Gray

 Quinacridone Gold

TECHNIQUES

- Direct color mixing
- Wet on wet
- Layering

MATERIALS

- Watercolor paper, 5" × 7"
- Medium round watercolor brush with a sharp tip
- Fine-line brush

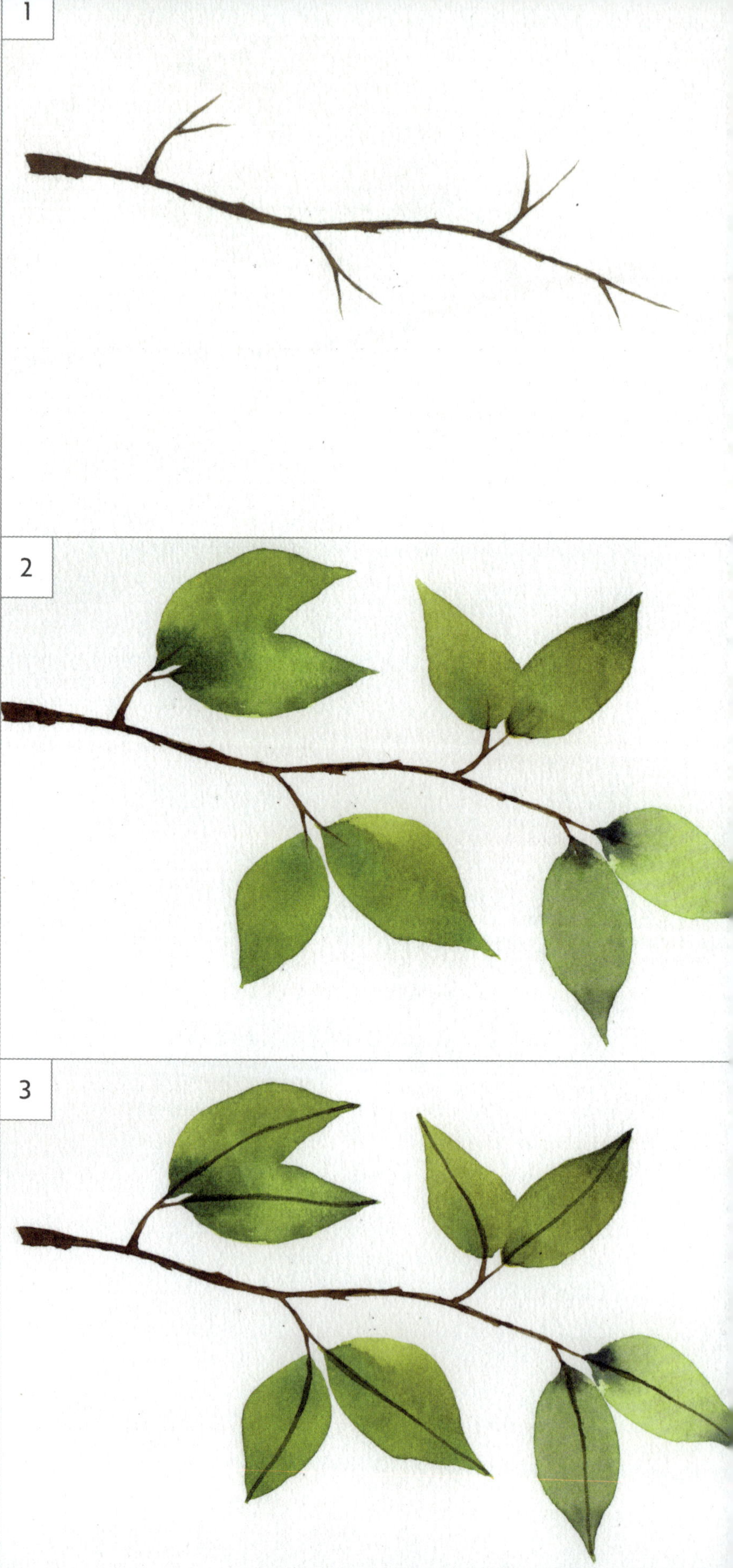

STEP ONE

Mix Burnt Umber and a small amount of Payne's Gray in your palette to create a rich brown color. This will be for the branches. Use a fine-line brush to paint a single branch on the paper. Paint smaller branches going off the single branch. Thicken the main branch if needed with another stroke of color while it's still damp. Let dry.

STEP TWO

Mix yellow, or Quinacridone Gold and Sap Green, with water in your palette to make a bright-green color. Mix another separate small batch of green and add a little Payne's Gray to darken the mix.

Load a round brush with the bright-green watercolor and paint a simple leaf starting below the tip of each branch. To paint the leaf shape, press the belly (underside) of the brush downward to start the stroke and gradually lift upward to create a tip. Drop a little of the dark-green mixture at the base and tip of each leaf while the leaves are still wet. The dark-green mixture will blend into the leaf for a soft gradation effect. Let dry.

STEP THREE

Add a little of the brown color from the branches to the dark-green mixture. Use the fine-line brush to paint a thin midrib line on each of the leaves. Let dry.

Black~Eyed Susan

These vibrant wildflowers grow abundantly in fields and on roadsides in Arizona. They look like a cross between a daisy and a sunflower and are even known to have medicinal qualities.

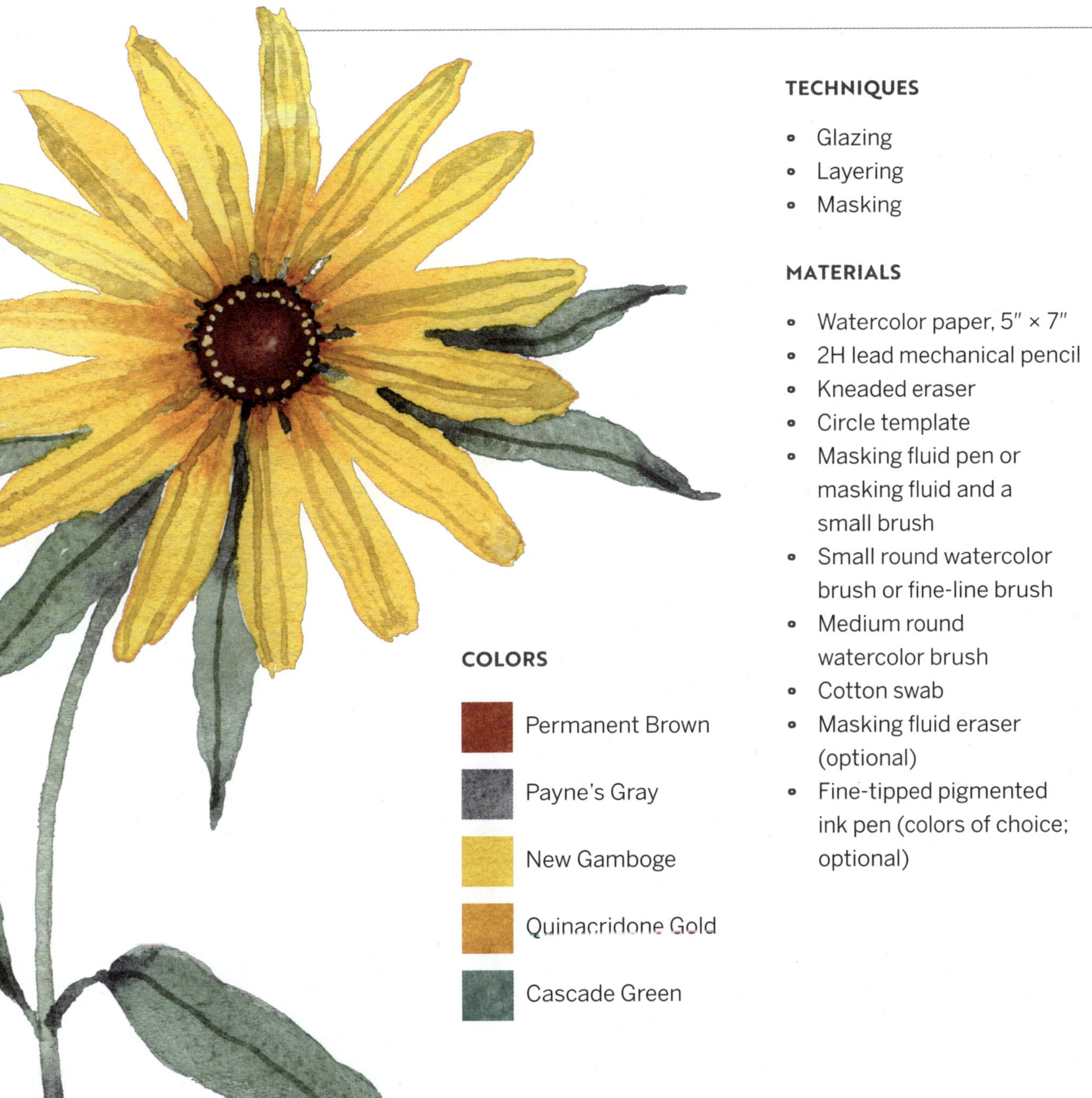

TECHNIQUES

- Glazing
- Layering
- Masking

MATERIALS

- Watercolor paper, 5" × 7"
- 2H lead mechanical pencil
- Kneaded eraser
- Circle template
- Masking fluid pen or masking fluid and a small brush
- Small round watercolor brush or fine-line brush
- Medium round watercolor brush
- Cotton swab
- Masking fluid eraser (optional)
- Fine-tipped pigmented ink pen (colors of choice; optional)

COLORS

- Permanent Brown
- Payne's Gray
- New Gamboge
- Quinacridone Gold
- Cascade Green

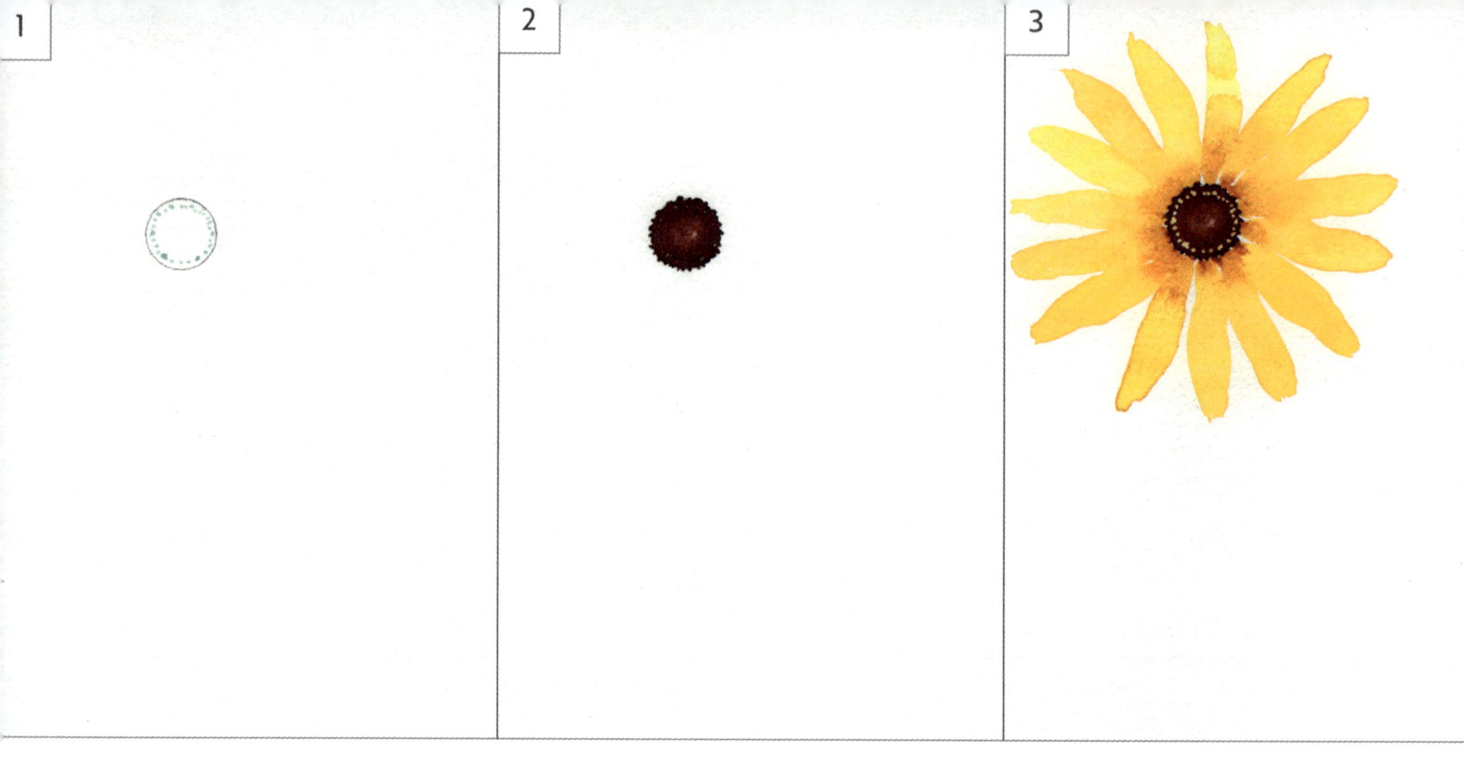

STEP ONE

Sketch a circle slightly off center on the paper with a mechanical pencil using a light touch. I used a circle template, but you can use a small bottle cap or something round measuring about 1¼ inches in diameter. Paint tiny, evenly spaced dots with the masking fluid on the inside of the circle. Let dry.

STEP TWO

Mix a medium to dark value of permanent brown with a little Payne's Gray and use a small brush to paint inside the circle. Blot the inside of the circle with a cotton swab to lighten the center. Carefully remove the masking fluid by rubbing it with your fingers, or use a masking fluid eraser. Let dry.

STEP THREE

Mix a medium to intense value of New Gamboge and add a small amount of Quinacridone Gold. Paint petals close to each other about 1½ inches from the circle and going all the way around it. While each petal is still wet, drop some Quinacridone Gold just outside the circle so it blends into the wet petals. Paint the small dots in the circle with a light-value wash of New Gamboge and let dry.

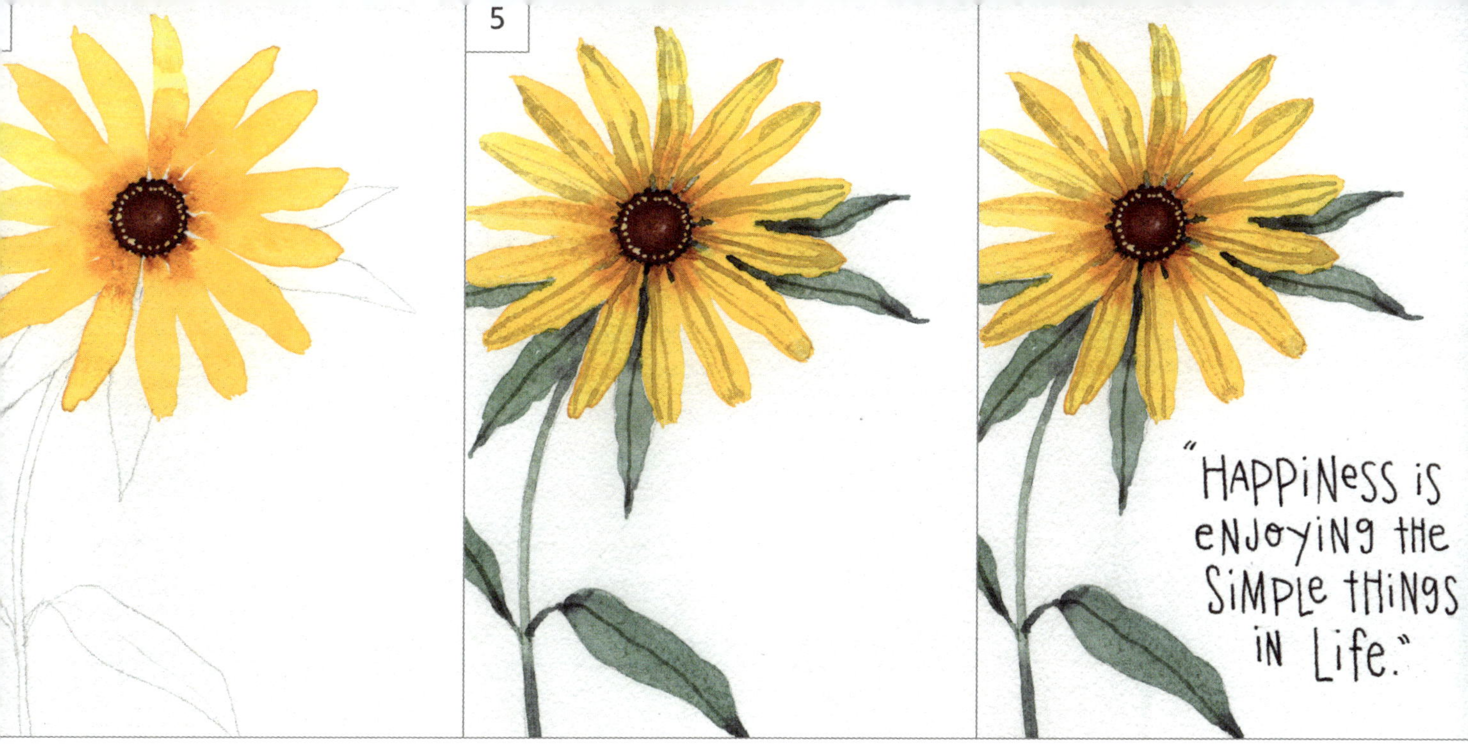

STEP FOUR

Sketch the stem and leaves on the paper with a mechanical pencil. Erase any heavy or extra lines with a kneaded eraser.

STEP FIVE

Mix a light to medium value of Cascade Green and paint the stems and leaves. Drop in a light value of Payne's Gray at the base and tips of the leaves and stem.

Mix a light value of Permanent Brown, Quinacridone Gold, and Payne's Gray and use a fine-line brush to paint details in the petals.

Mix a medium value of Cascade Green and Payne's Gray and paint midrib lines in the leaves. Let dry.

OPTIONAL: Write an inspirational quote or sentiment with pigmented ink in the space next to the flower for a beautiful greeting card. Write the message first with pencil to make sure the letters are placed correctly, then use a fine-tipped pigmented pen to go over the letters. The pencil lines can be erased with a kneaded eraser after the ink has dried.

Wild Tulip

Wild tulips not only add variety to your garden but also provide a valuable source of enrichment for the local insect population. These flowers continue to grow even after they are cut, always bending and stretching toward the light.

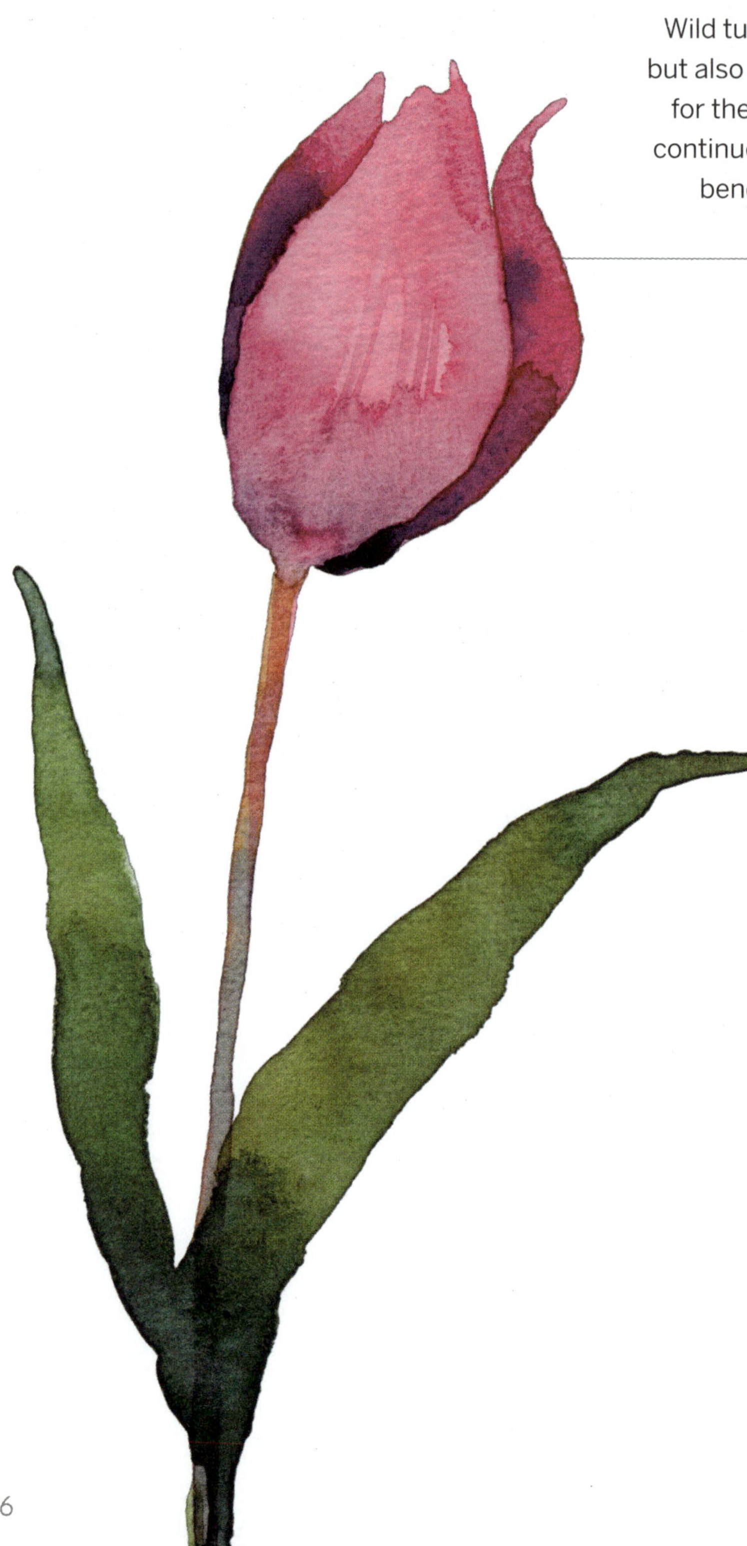

COLORS

- Phthalo Blue (Green Shade)
- Quinacridone Gold
- Quinacridone Magenta
- Payne's Gray

TECHNIQUES

- Color mixing
- Brush control
- Blending

MATERIALS

- Watercolor paper, 5" × 7"
- Medium round watercolor brush with a sharp tip

STEP ONE

Create saturated mixes of Phthalo Blue (Green Shade), Quinacridone Gold, Quinacridone Magenta, and Payne's Gray separately in your palette. Load the brush with a medium value of Quinacridone Magenta.

Paint a petal shape, starting at the base of the petal by pressing down on the brush belly (underside) and lifting it up as you get to the tip of the petal. Drop a medium-value mix of Payne's Gray at the base of the petal.

STEP TWO

While the petal is still wet, paint a stem starting at the base of the petal with a mix of Quinacridone Gold and move down the paper with the tip of the brush. Drop a small amount of Phthalo Blue into the middle and bottom of the stem so the yellow and blue blend into a soft green color. Phthalo Blue is an intense color, so use very little. Let dry.

STEP THREE

Mix up more magenta, using less water for a darker value. Start the second petal at the base of the first petal with the tip of the brush and make a thinner, more saturated petal. Lift and twist the brush until it comes to a point at the top of the petal. Drop in a little Payne's Gray at the base of the petal while it's still wet. Repeat on the other side of the first petal.

STEP FOUR

Mix a blend of Phthalo Blue and Quinacridone Gold and load your brush with a medium-value green. Starting at the base of the stem, create a long leaf shape with the tip of the brush, pressing down and twisting slightly as you go upward until the leaf comes to a point.

Repeat on the other side of the stem, changing the shape and direction of the leaf with your brush. Drop a little Payne's Gray at the base and the tip of the leaf while it's still wet. The colors will blend beautifully on the paper without the help of the brush!

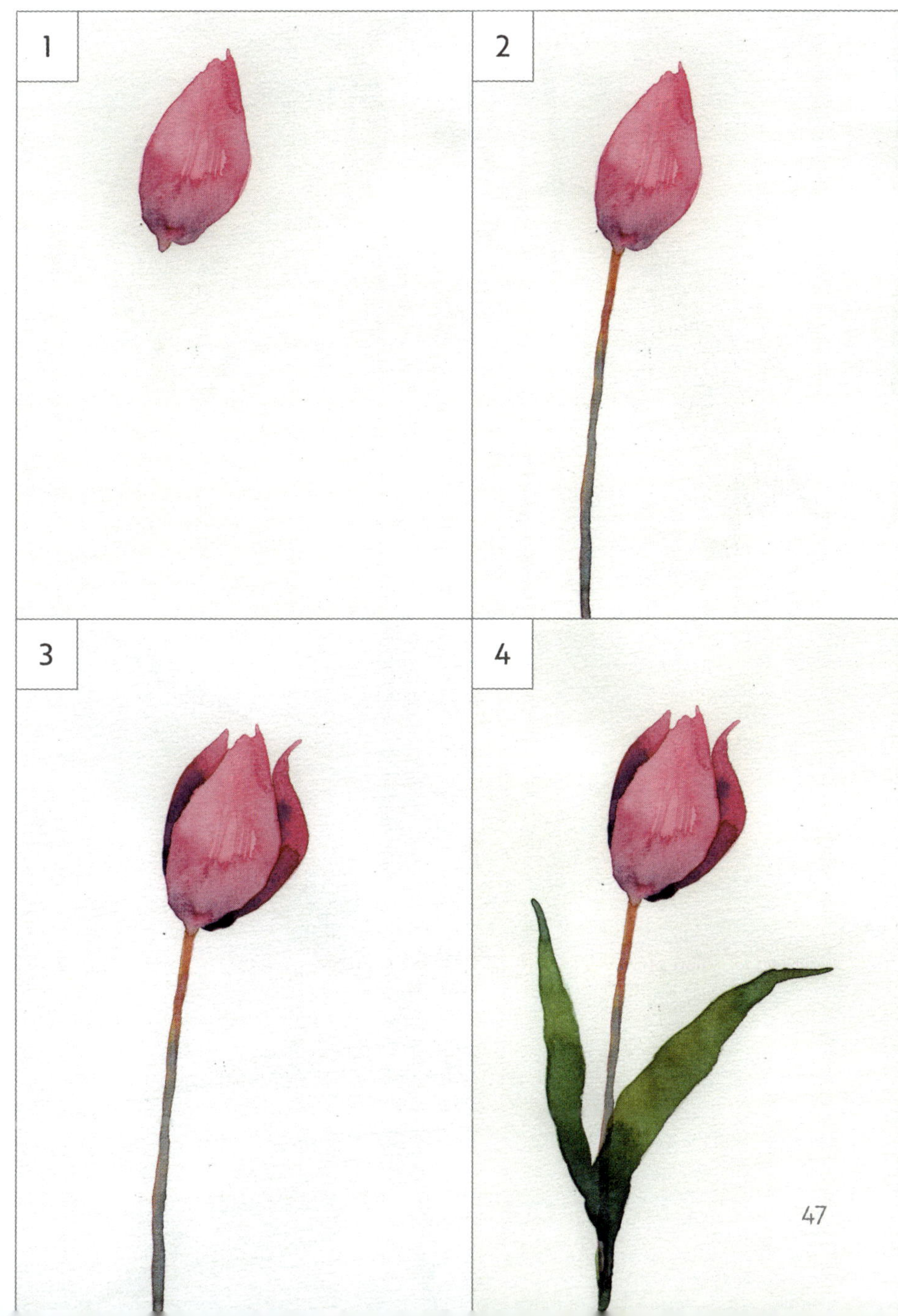

Bellflower

Campanula americana, also known as American bellflower, is a wildflower native to moist, open woods, meadows, streambanks, and shady areas of eastern North America. It can be grown from seed in spring in Arizona and is beautiful in flower arrangements.

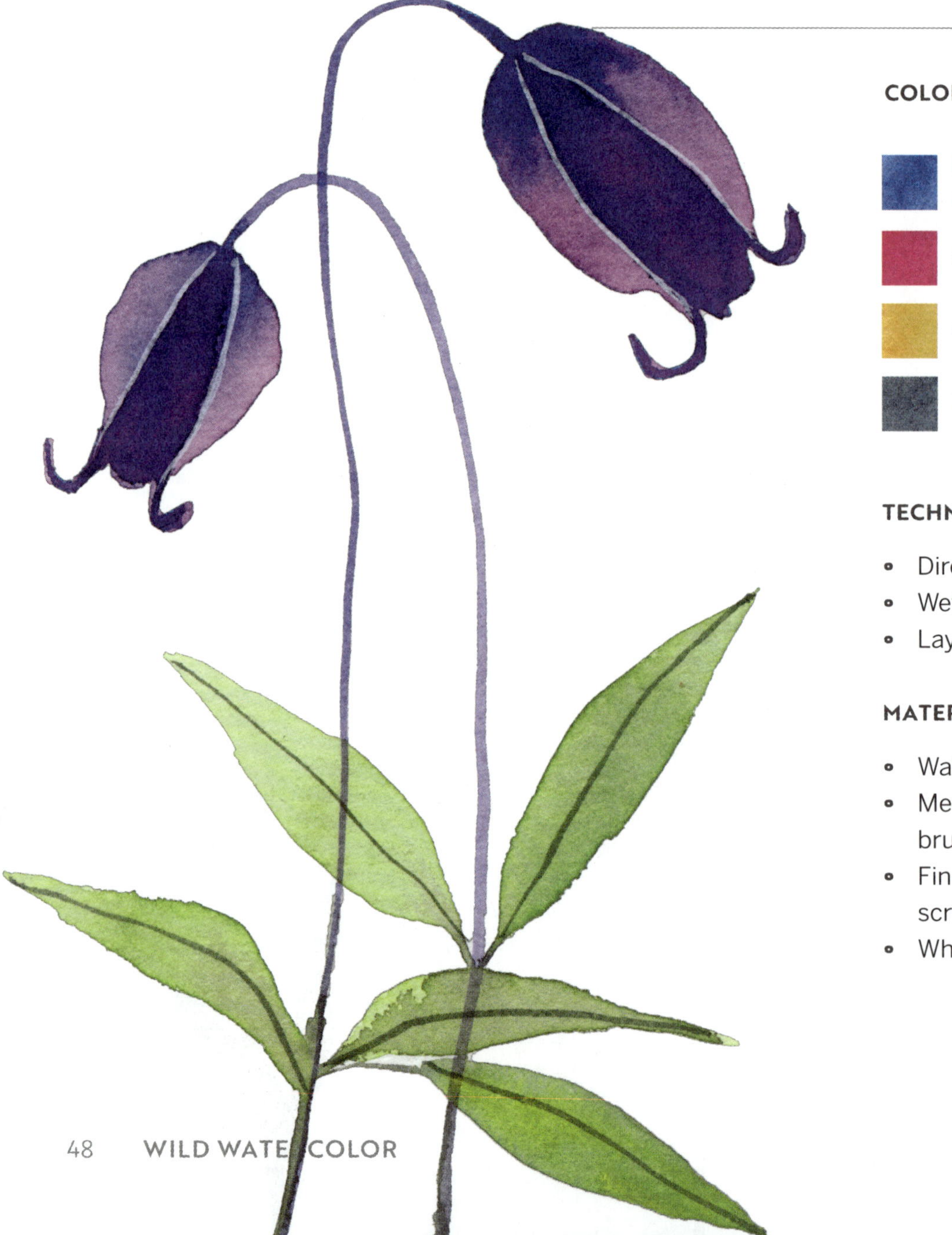

COLORS

- Phthalo Blue (or Ultramarine Blue)
- Quinacridone Magenta
- Quinacridone Gold
- Payne's Gray

TECHNIQUES

- Direct color mixing
- Wet on wet
- Layering

MATERIALS

- Watercolor paper, 5" × 7"
- Medium round watercolor brush with a sharp tip
- Fine-line brush or script brush
- White ink (optional)

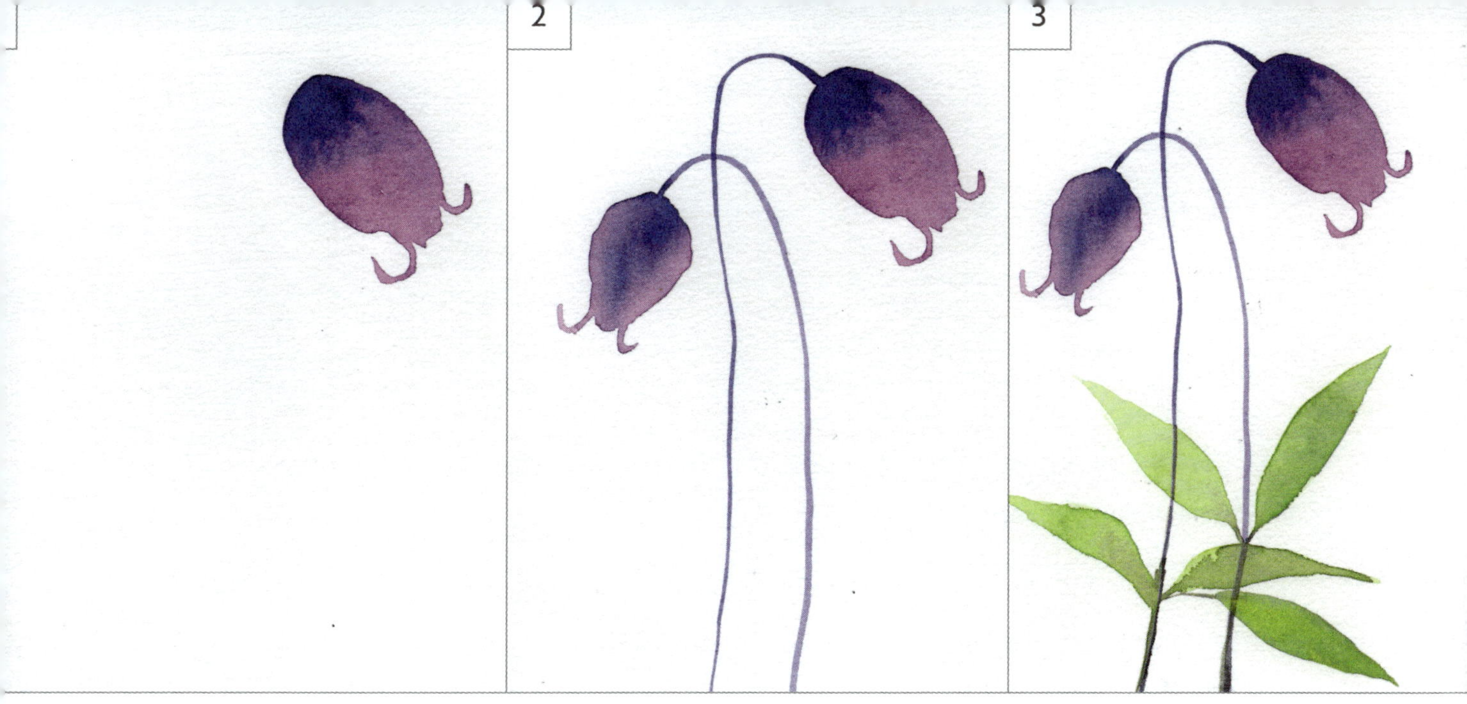

STEP ONE

Create a mix of purple by blending together Phthalo Blue and Quinacridone Magenta. Add water for a dark-value mix. Separately, make a light-value mix of purple, adding more magenta and water.

Load a round brush with the light-value mix and create the bellflower by pressing the belly (underside) of the brush into an oval shape, then lifting and turning the tip upward to make the curved petal. Add another curved petal on the other side.

STEP TWO

Load a fine-line brush with the dark-value mix and create the stem starting from the base of the flower. Paint upward, then curve downward to the base of the stem. Drop some dark-value purple into the base of the flower.

Paint a smaller bellflower and stem going in a different direction. Let dry.

STEP THREE

Create a mid-value green color by combining Phthalo Blue and Quinacridone Gold. Use the fine-line brush to paint a thin branch at the base of the flower stems.

Then, paint small, long leaves using the medium round brush. Drop some of the purple mix into the branch and base of the leaves while it's still wet. Let dry.

Paint details in the flower and leaves with the colors from the existing mixes. Let dry.

OPTIONAL: Create highlights using white ink and a fine-line brush.

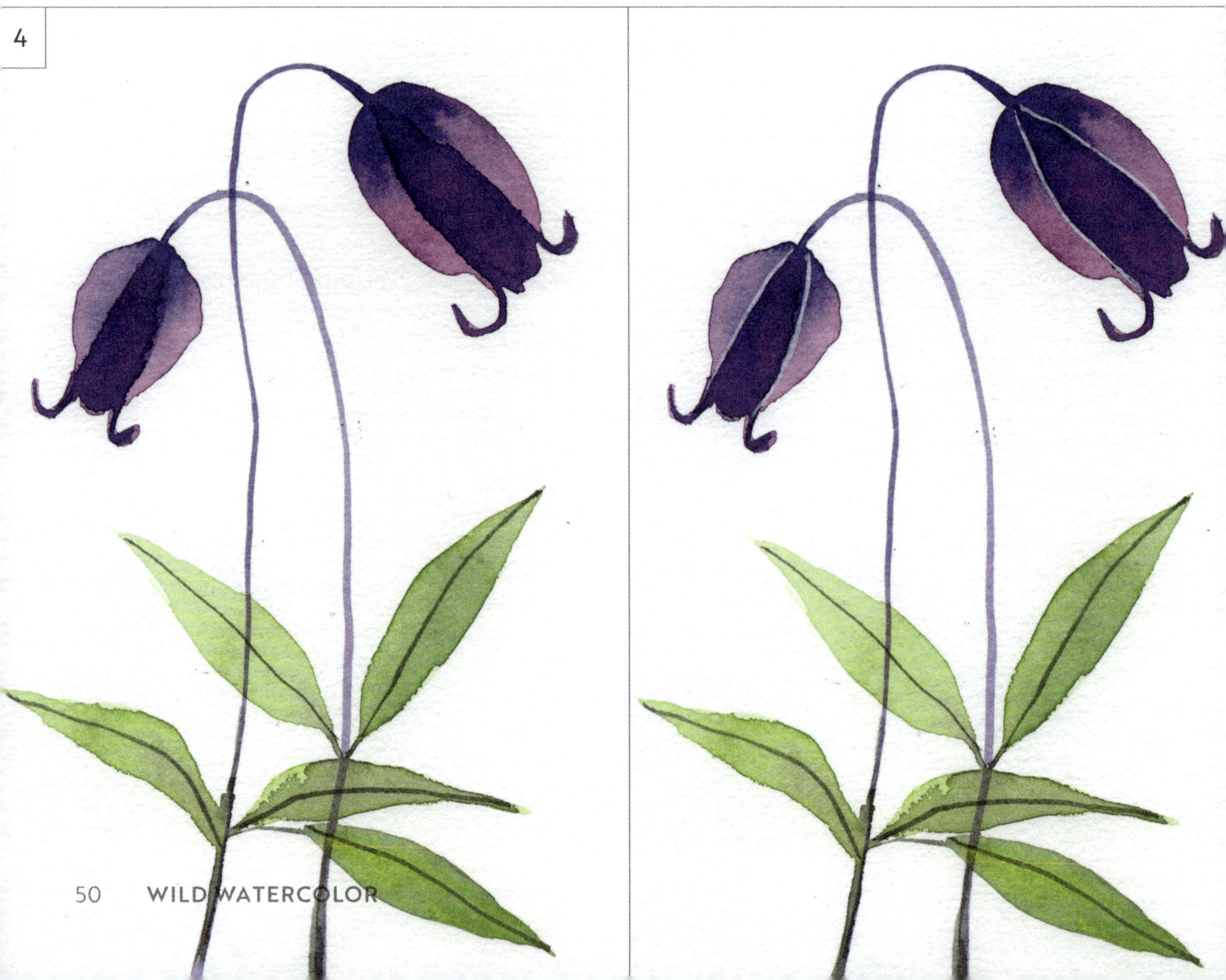

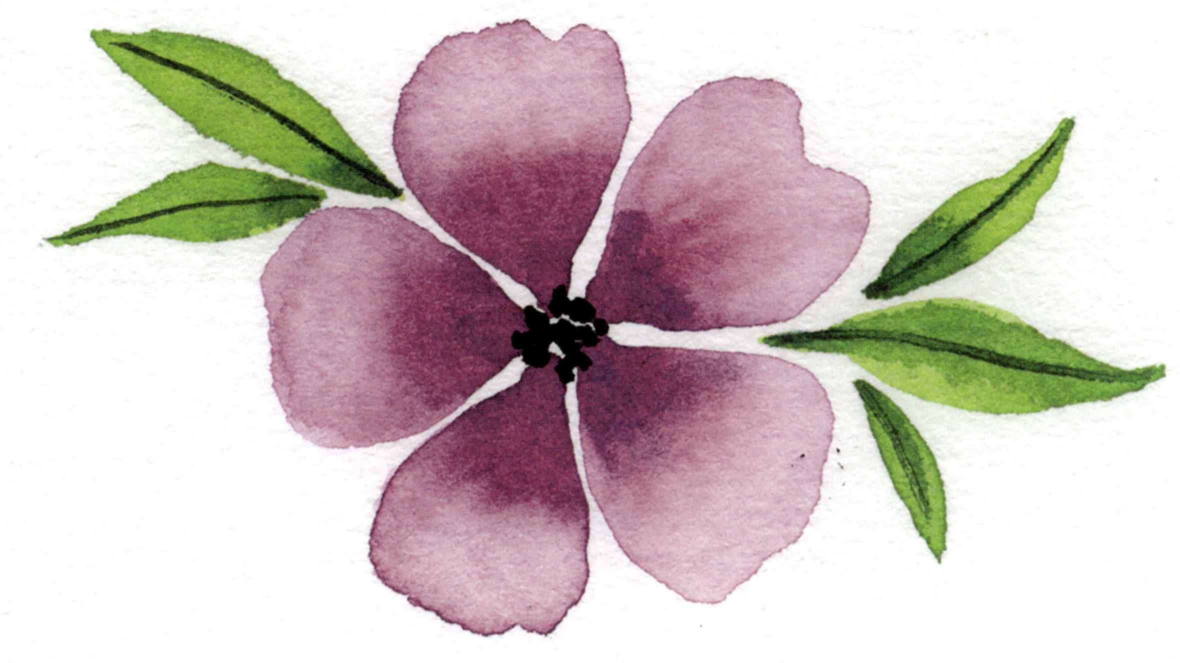

Five-Petal Flower

The daisy is probably the most well-known
five-petal flower, but there are many others,
including the aster, the rose, and the lily.

TECHNIQUES

- Direct color mixing
- Wet on wet
- Layering

MATERIALS

- Watercolor paper, 5″ × 7″
- Medium round
  watercolor brush
- Small round
  watercolor brush
- Fine-line brush

COLORS

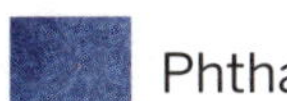 Phthalo Blue (Red Shade)

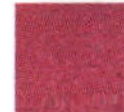 Quinacridone Magenta

 Quinacridone Gold

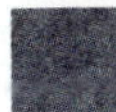 Payne's Gray

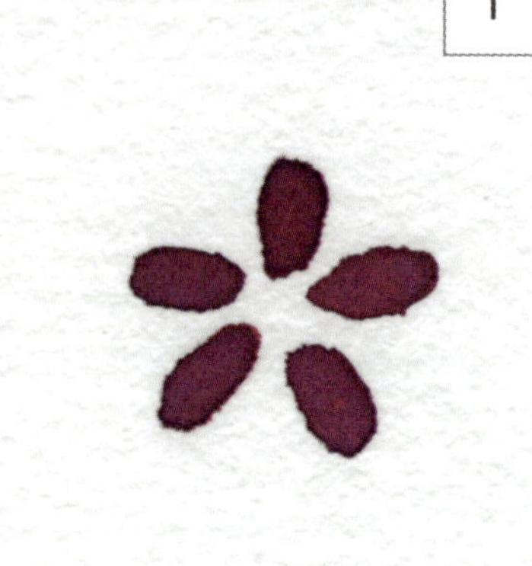

STEP ONE

Mix a concentrated but small amount of magenta in your palette. Then, on your paper, make five small oval shapes with the tip of your round brush, spaced evenly apart.

STEP TWO

Rinse the brush, place the tip into one of the oval shapes, and paint a triangle petal shape from the center going outward. Repeat on all of the oval shapes. It's important to do this while the oval shapes are still wet. This allows the color to blend into the petal from dark to light. Let dry.

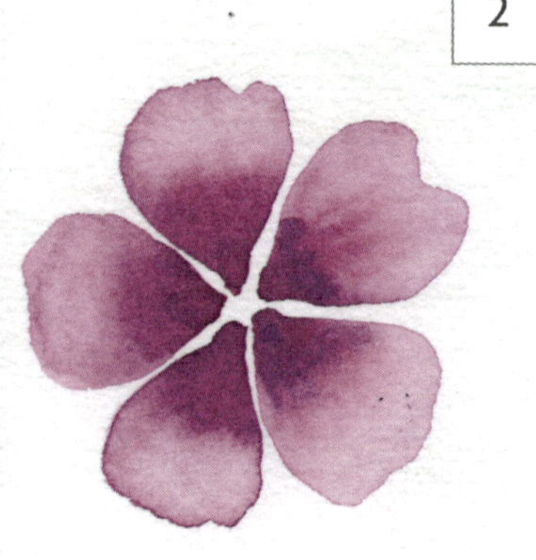

STEP THREE

Pick up some magenta and add a little Payne's Gray to the brush to deepen the color. Paint small dots in the center of the flower with the tip of your brush.

STEP FOUR

Mix together Phthalo Blue and Quinacridone Gold with water to make a light-green color. Use a small round brush to paint a few small leaves around the flower. Let dry.

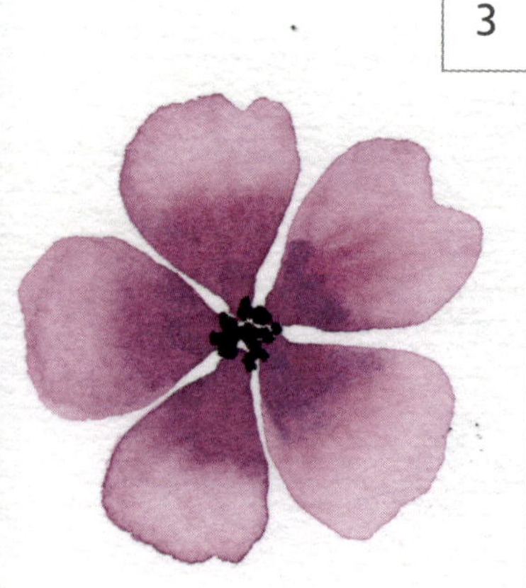

STEP FIVE

Using a fine-line brush, add midrib lines on the leaves with a darker green to finish.

OPTIONAL: Paint several of these flowers on a larger sheet of paper in different sizes, color combinations, and directions. Once dry, cut them out and use as focal points for greeting cards and journals.

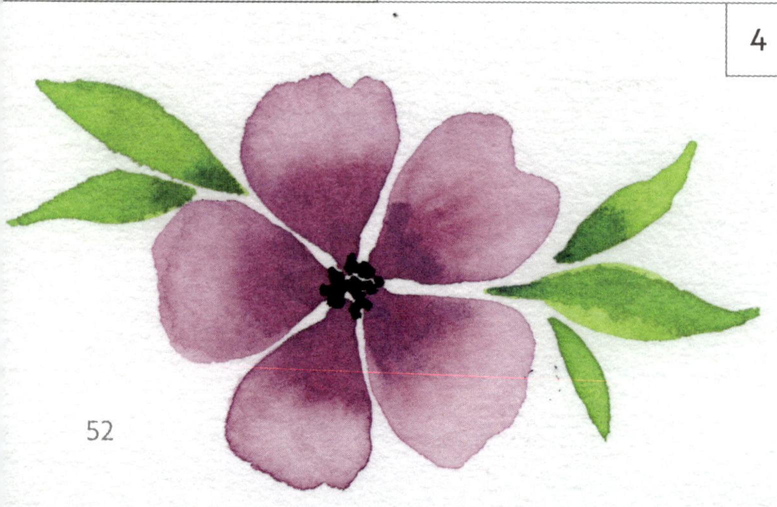

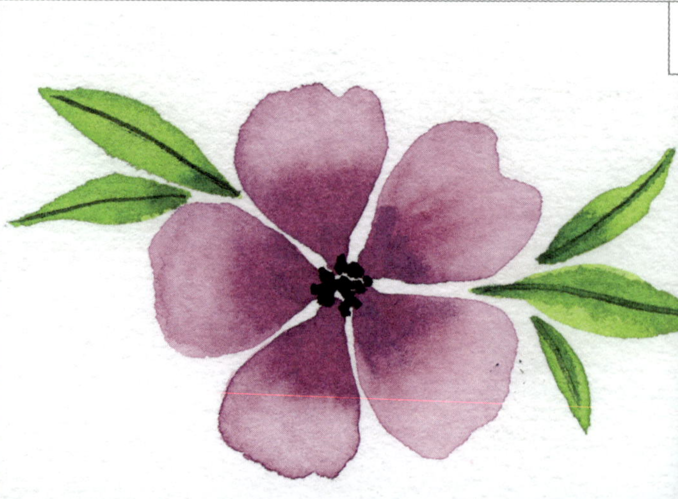

Wild Poppy

The poppy is an annual wildflower with stunning red blossoms. Its seeds can remain inactive for up to 80 years and then suddenly sprout when the soil is disturbed.

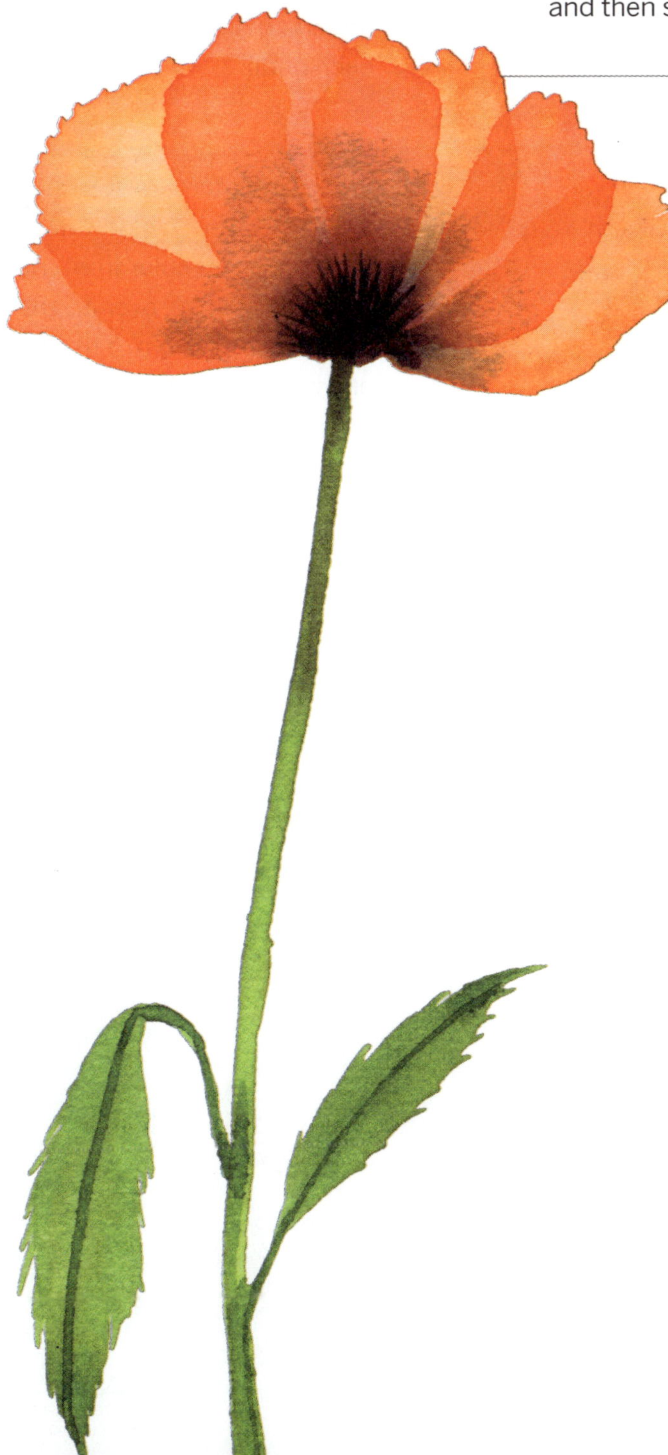

COLORS

 Quinacridone Red

 Hansa Yellow

 Phthalo Blue (Red Shade)

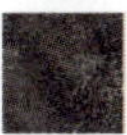 Lunar Black

TECHNIQUES

- Color mixing
- Wet on wet
- Color lifting
- Layering

MATERIALS

- Watercolor paper, 5" × 7"
- Medium round watercolor brush with a sharp tip
- Small round watercolor brush
- Fine-line brush or script brush
- Facial tissue

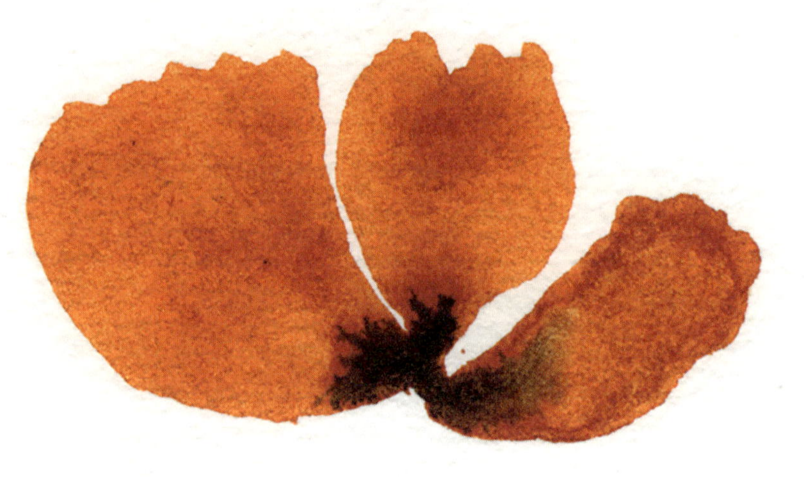

STEP ONE

Mix together red and yellow for a saturated orange color. Using the medium round brush, paint three petals on the paper with an even wash. Then, with the tip of the brush, drop a small amount of black at the base of each petal.

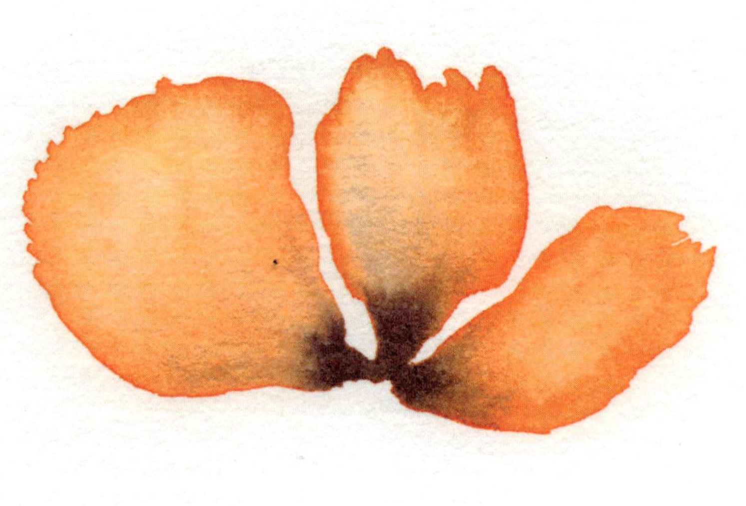

STEP TWO

While the petals are still wet, rinse the brush, blot it with a tissue, then lift color from the petal by brushing over it lightly; clean the brush with a tissue and brush over the petal again. Keep repeating this process, or "lifting" the color, until the insides of the petals look smooth and lighter than the edges. Let dry.

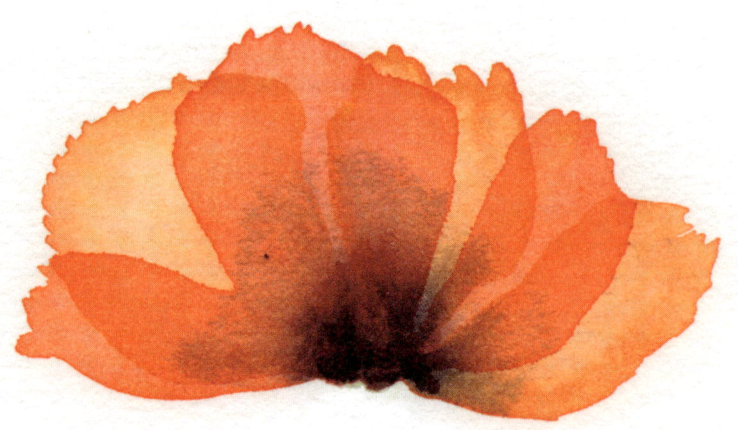

STEP THREE

Paint three more petals overlapping the first three using the same technique as in step 1. Drop some black at the base of the petals while they are still wet.

STEP FOUR

Combine blue and yellow to mix a medium-value light yellow-green color. Load a small round brush or fine-line brush with green and paint a slightly curved stem going downward from the base of the poppy. Drop some of the dark color mix at the top of the stem. Paint leaves with the light-green color.

To make the leaves with jagged edges, with the tip of your brush, make short marks going outward while the leaves are still wet.

STEP FIVE

Use the fine-line brush to paint the midrib lines in the leaves with a darker shade of green. Let dry.

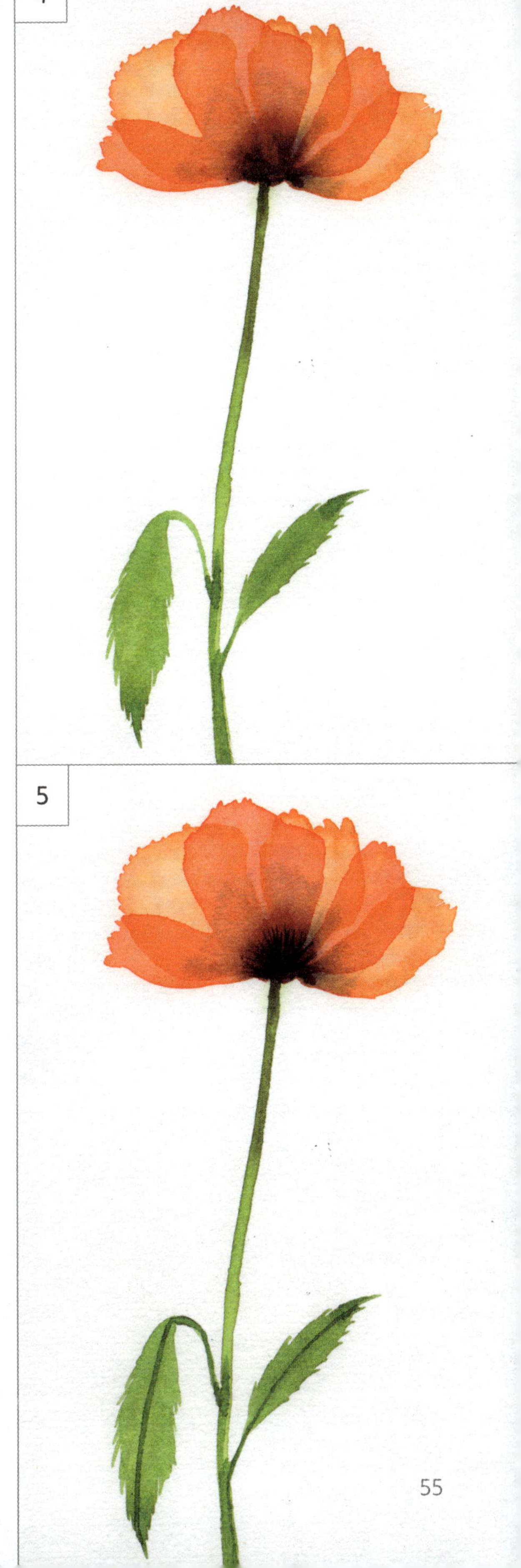

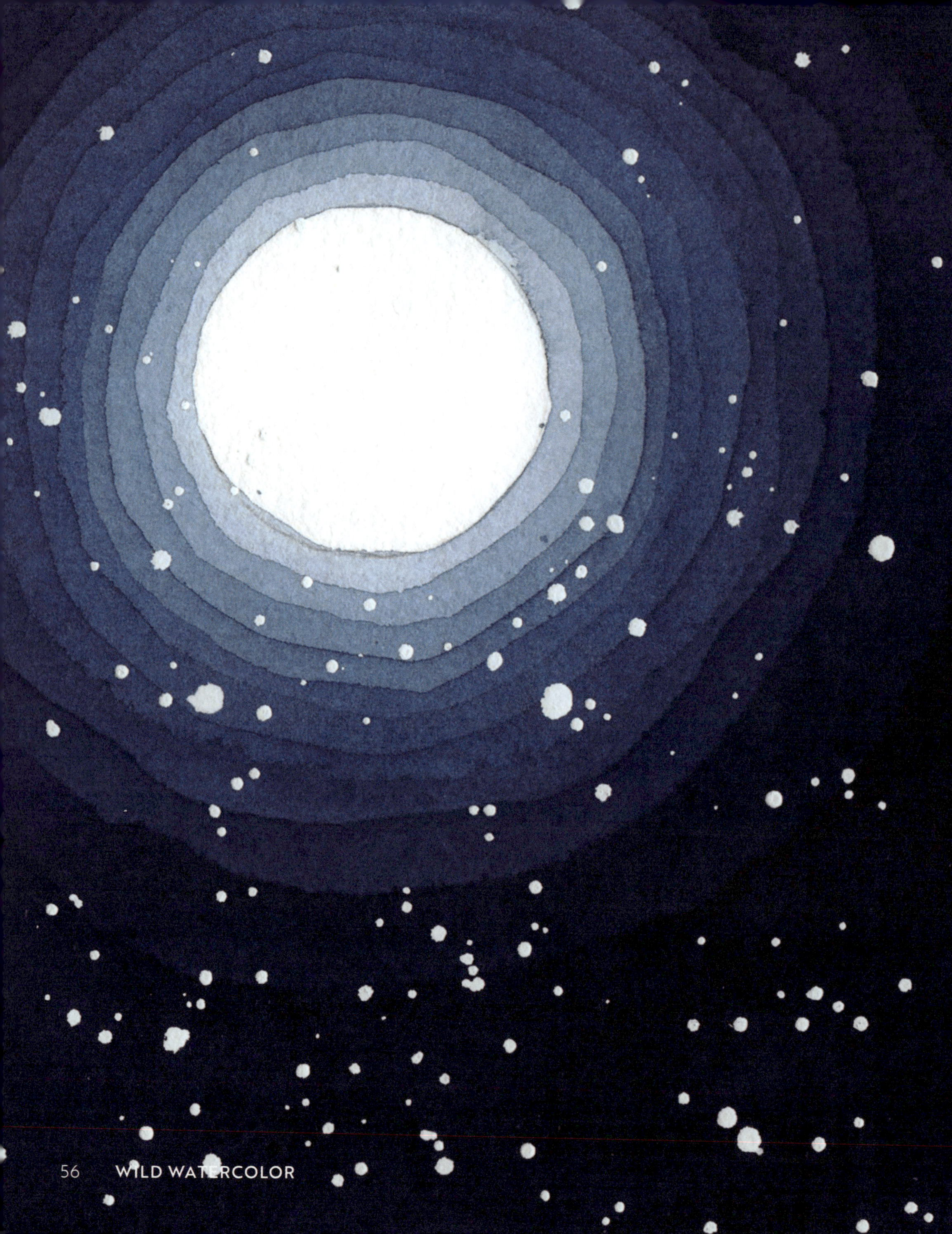

Night Sky, Moon, and Stars

On a cloudless night in the city, the indigo sky is lit by the moon and brilliant stars. Sometimes you can easily see the constellations and even the Milky Way.

COLORS

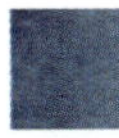 Indigo (or a mix of Phthalo Blue, black, and magenta)

TECHNIQUES

- Glazing
- Layered washes
- Splattering

MATERIALS

- Watercolor paper, 5" × 7"
- 2H lead mechanical pencil
- Small circle template (optional)
- Medium round watercolor brush
- Small round watercolor brush
- Hair dryer (optional)
- White ink

STEP ONE

Sketch a light circle off center on the paper toward the left edge with a mechanical pencil. Your circle should be about 1¼ inches in diameter. Use a template if you like.

STEP TWO

Mix a large amount of medium-value Indigo watercolor (or Phthalo Blue, black, and a little magenta) in your palette. Using a medium brush, paint a light flat wash around the circle going toward the edges of the paper. Let dry completely before continuing with the next step.

STEP THREE

Paint an even flat wash about ⅛ inch away from the last painted edge all around the circle and going to the edges of the paper. Let dry.

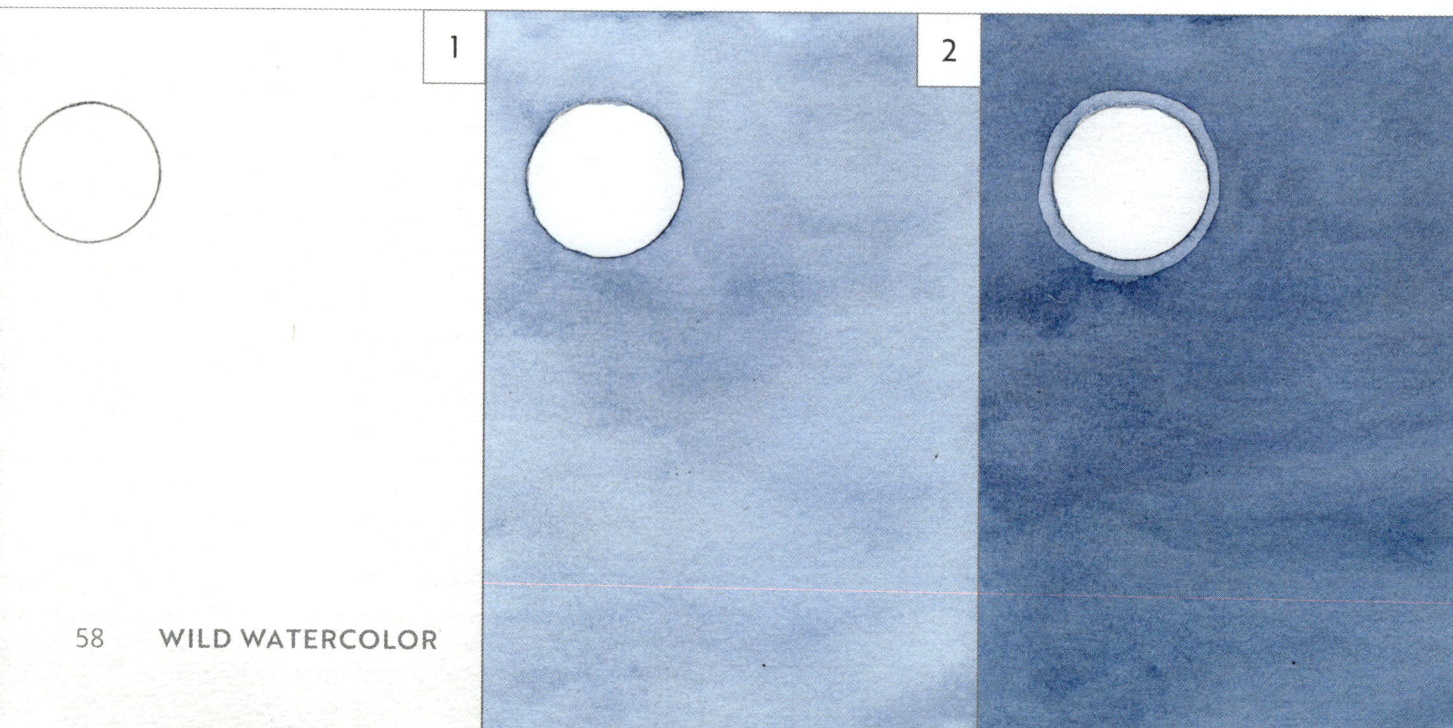

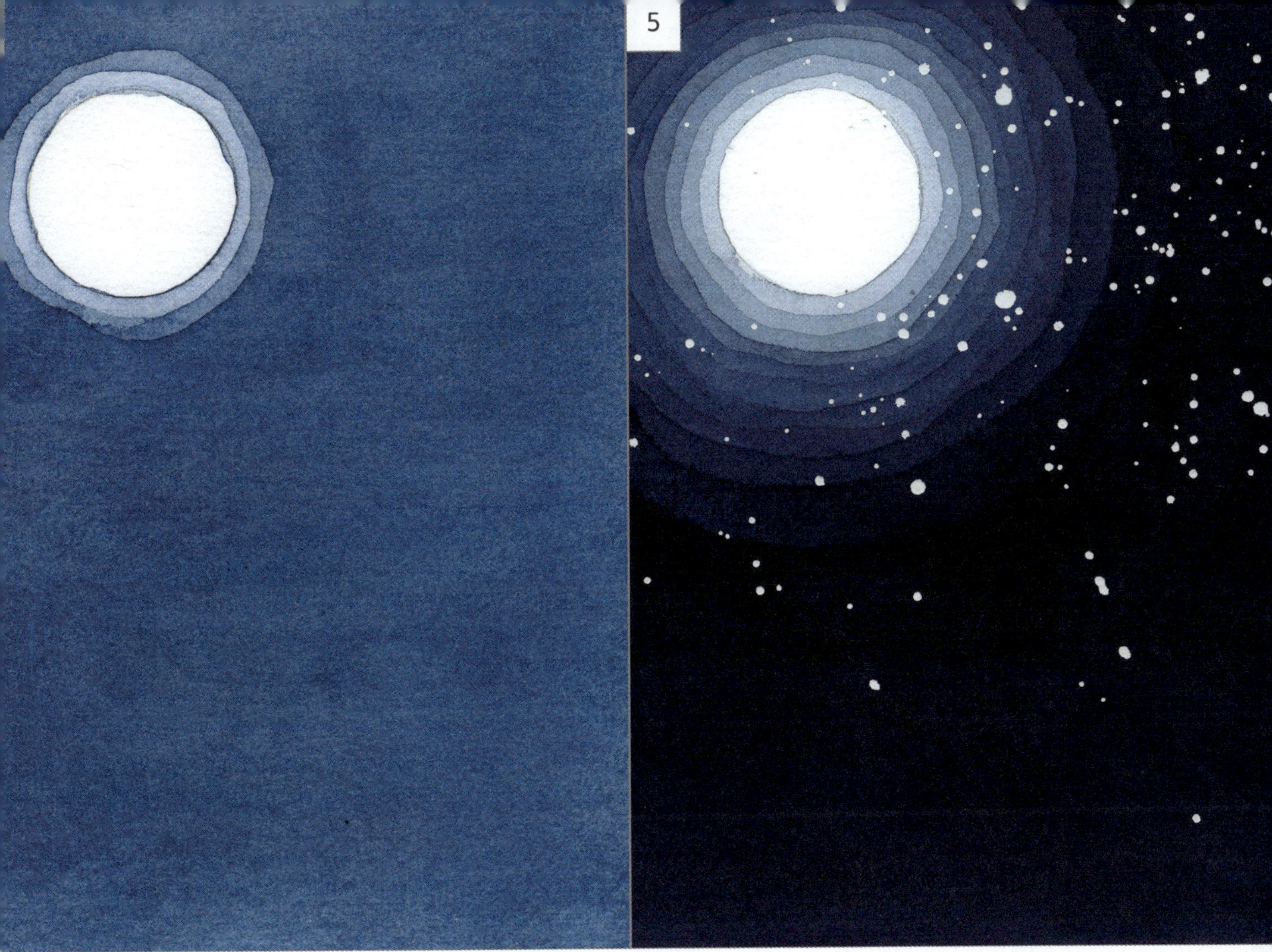

STEP FOUR

Repeat step 3 until the washes around the moon become darker and darker to almost black, and the white of the paper isn't showing through. Dry each layer with a hair dryer to speed up the process, if you like.

STEP FIVE

Load a small brush with opaque white ink and splatter little stars onto the paper—do this by tapping the brush handle lightly with your finger and letting the small paint splatters fall onto the page. Let dry.

Intermediate
WATERCOLOR PROJECTS

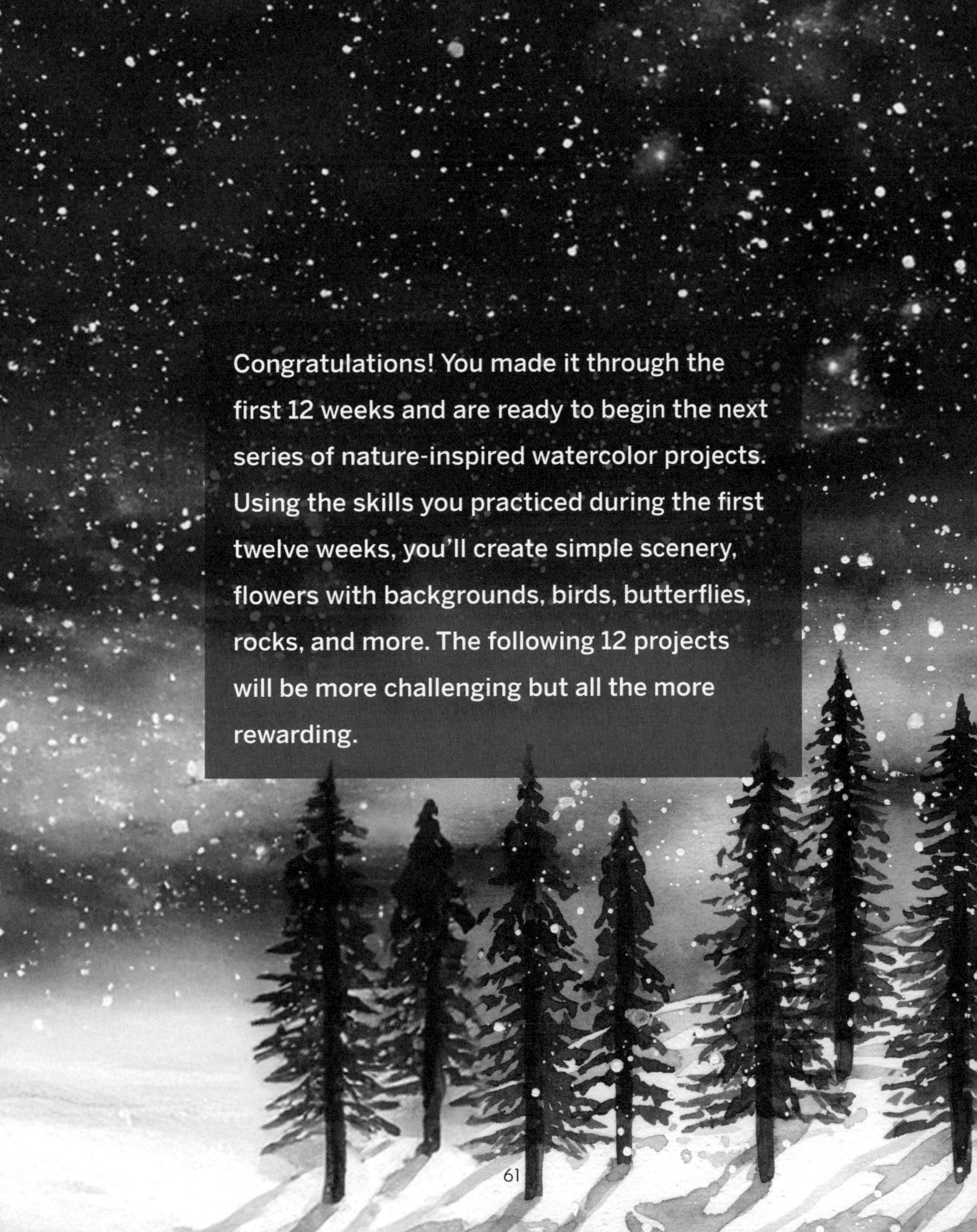

Congratulations! You made it through the first 12 weeks and are ready to begin the next series of nature-inspired watercolor projects. Using the skills you practiced during the first twelve weeks, you'll create simple scenery, flowers with backgrounds, birds, butterflies, rocks, and more. The following 12 projects will be more challenging but all the more rewarding.

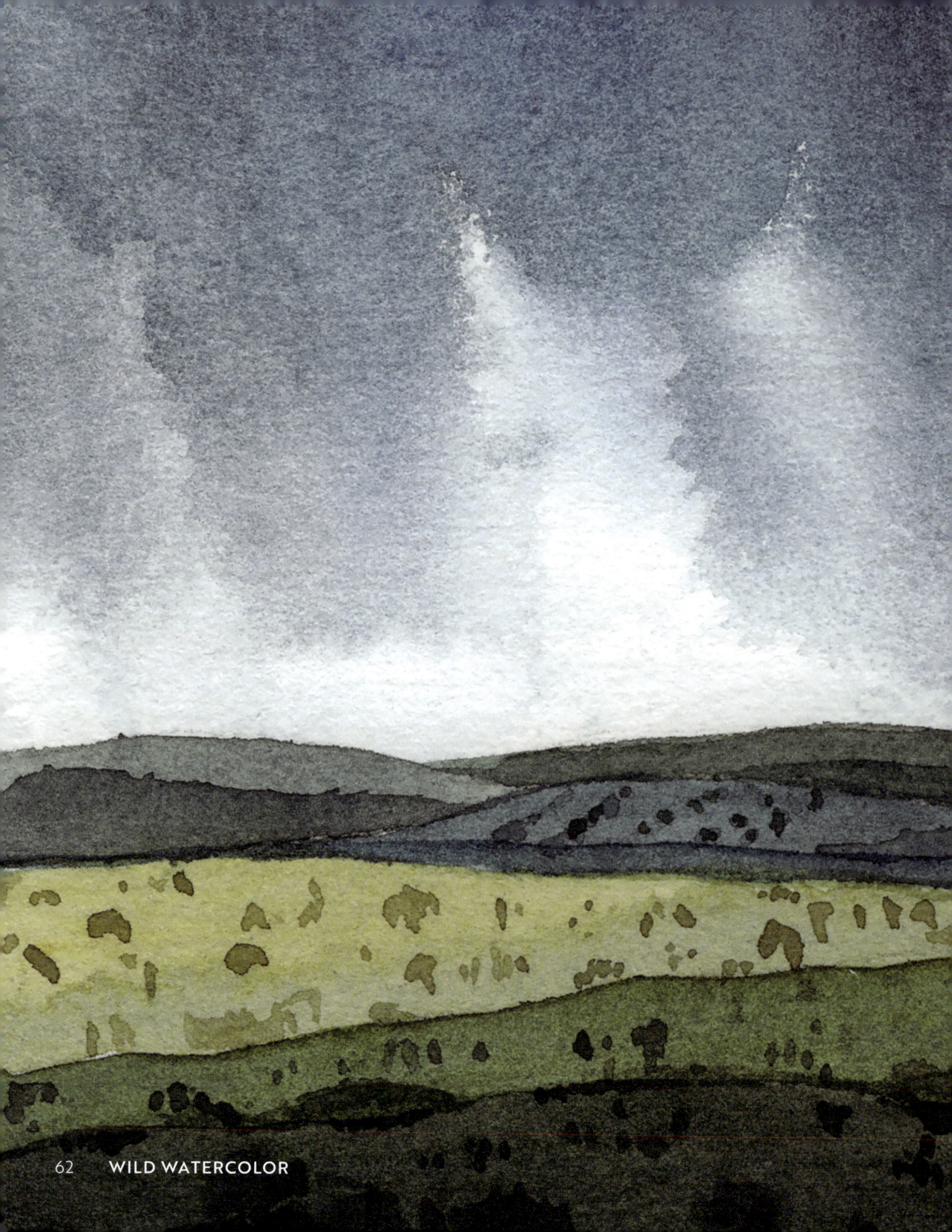

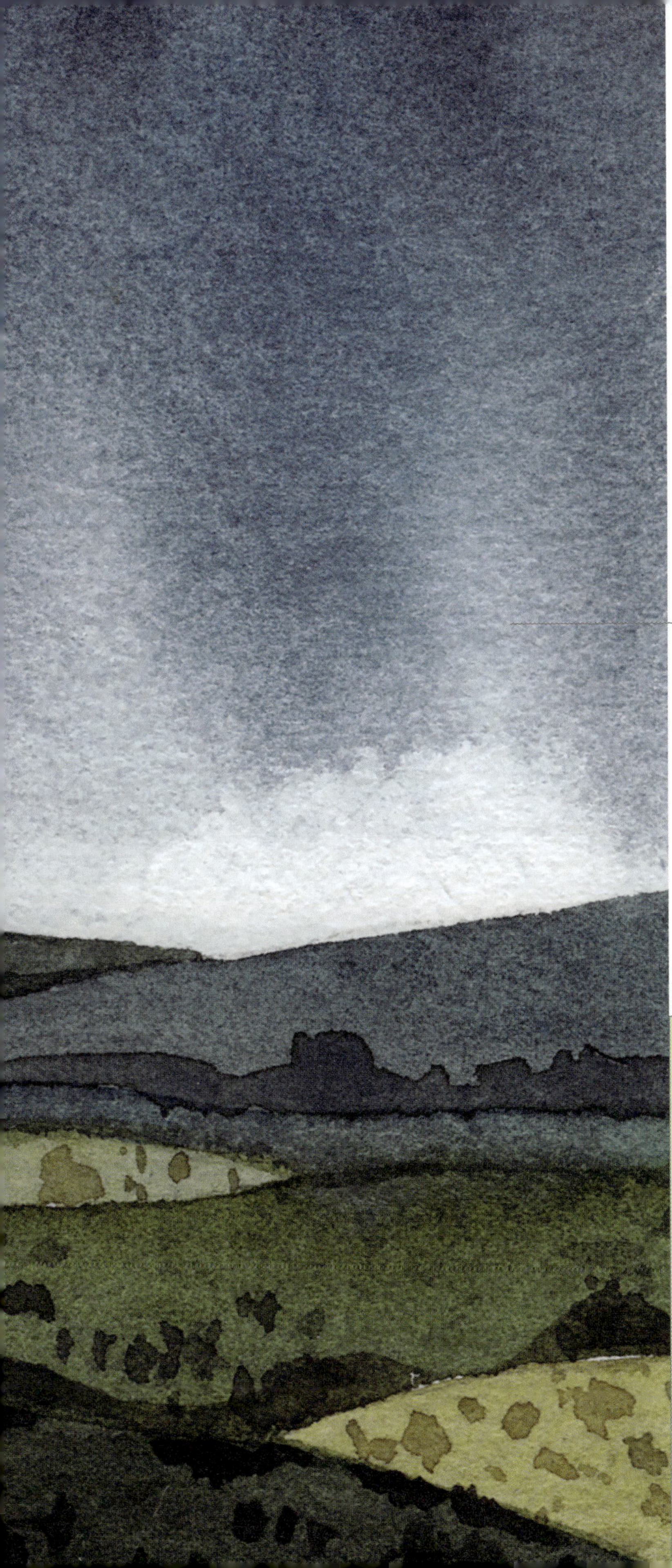

Rolling Hills and Monsoon Sky

Arizona's summer brings the monsoon season, with dramatic thunderstorms and lightning displays that light up the sky. These thunderstorms welcome the cooling of the hot desert landscape.

COLORS

 Payne's Gray

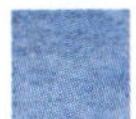 Prussian Blue

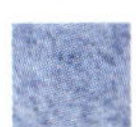 Ultramarine Blue

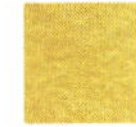 Quinacridone Gold

TECHNIQUES

- Wet on wet
- Color mixing
- Glazing

MATERIALS

- Watercolor paper, 5" × 7"
- Medium round watercolor brush
- Small round watercolor brush
- ½" (minimum) flat wash brush
- 2H lead mechanical pencil
- Fine-mist spray bottle
- Facial tissue

STEP ONE

Create saturated mixes of Payne's Gray, Prussian Blue, and Ultramarine Blue separately in your palette.

Load a medium round brush generously with Payne's Gray and place the tip loaded with color onto the top of the paper. Apply paint randomly and a little apart from each other. Repeat with the two blues.

While the paint is still wet, mist the area below the paint with water to draw the color down the paper. Tip the paper toward you to allow the wet paint to run toward the bottom of the paper. Blot the lower area with a tissue and move the tissue gently upward into the wet areas to blend the colors. Let dry.

STEP TWO

Sketch some rolling hills at the bottom third of the paper with a mechanical pencil.

STEP THREE

Mix a little Quinacridone Gold into the blues already in the palette and use a small round brush to paint each section of the hills a slightly different color. Add more water or Quinacridone Gold to brighten or lighten the wash. Let each hill dry before painting the next. Let dry.

STEP FOUR

Use a small brush to paint details in the hills using a darker value of the colors in your palette. Make small, random dots and blobs by tapping the tip loaded with color to represent low shrubs and trees in the distance. Let dry.

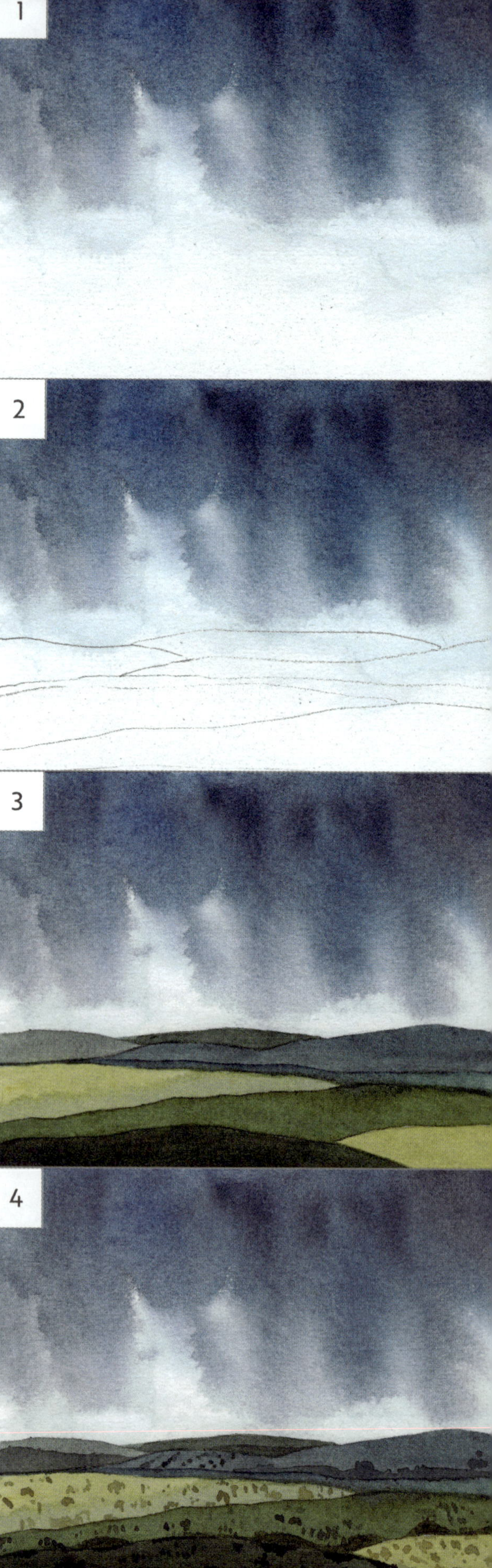

WEEK 14
Stacked Rocks

You may have encountered a carefully arranged stack of rocks while hiking or at the beach. Cairns were initially used as trail markers to guide hikers on the right path, and even to commemorate a person, place, or event. These smooth stacked rocks are meant to evoke a sense of calm.

TECHNIQUES

- Direct color mixing
- Wet on dry
- Sketching

MATERIALS

- Watercolor paper, 5" × 7"
- 2H lead mechanical pencil
- Medium round watercolor brush
- Facial tissue

COLORS

 Ultramarine Blue

 Cerulean Blue

 Raw Umber

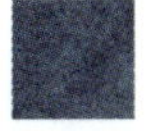 Payne's Gray

 Moonglow

 Lunar Black

STEP ONE

Draw a straight line about 2 inches from the bottom of the paper with a mechanical pencil to create a horizon line. Starting at the horizon line, sketch three to five irregular rock shapes stacked on top of each other, making each rock a little smaller than the last. The pencil lines should be very light.

CONTINUED ➡

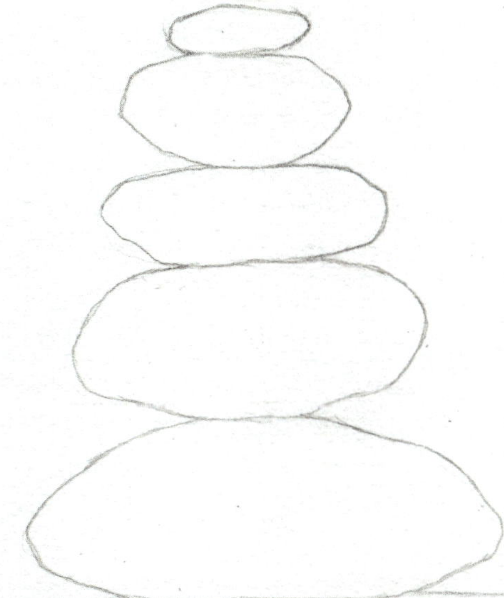

STEP TWO

Mix equal amounts of Cerulean Blue and Ultramarine Blue in your palette to create a medium-value shade of blue.

Use a medium round brush to paint an even wash of blue around the rocks to create a sky. Start at one end of the paper and go quickly around the rock shapes, blending with the brush to avoid dry areas. Blot with a tissue to create clouds. Let dry.

STEP THREE

Mix a light value of Raw Umber and add a tiny bit of Lunar Black to create a pale, granulating sandy color. Paint an even wash in the horizon area below the rocks. Let dry.

STEP FOUR

Mix Lunar Black and a little of the sand color to make a light shade of gray. Paint it on the rocks, leaving a little white at the top left of each rock shape.

While the light gray is still wet, paint a slightly darker value of the gray color at the bottom of each rock and some at the top of each rock (except for the top rock) to create a soft shadow. Let dry.

STEP FIVE

Mix a darker value of Payne's Gray and Lunar Black and paint shadows under the rocks. Keep in mind your light source is above and a bit to the left. Repeat painting shadows with the darker values of gray until the rock shapes have a high contrast.

Finally, paint a light-value glaze of Raw Umber over one of the rocks and add more shadows using Moonglow.

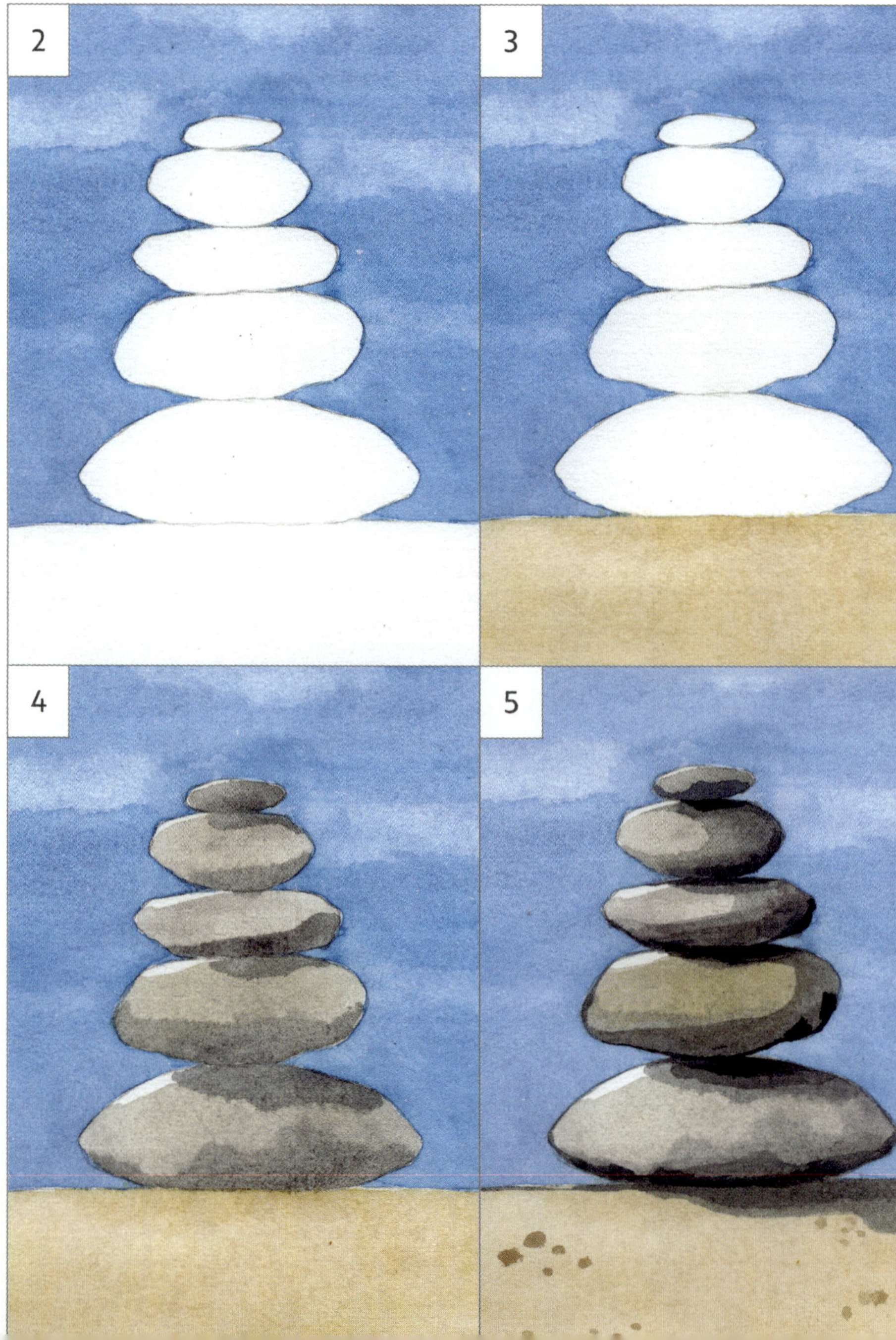

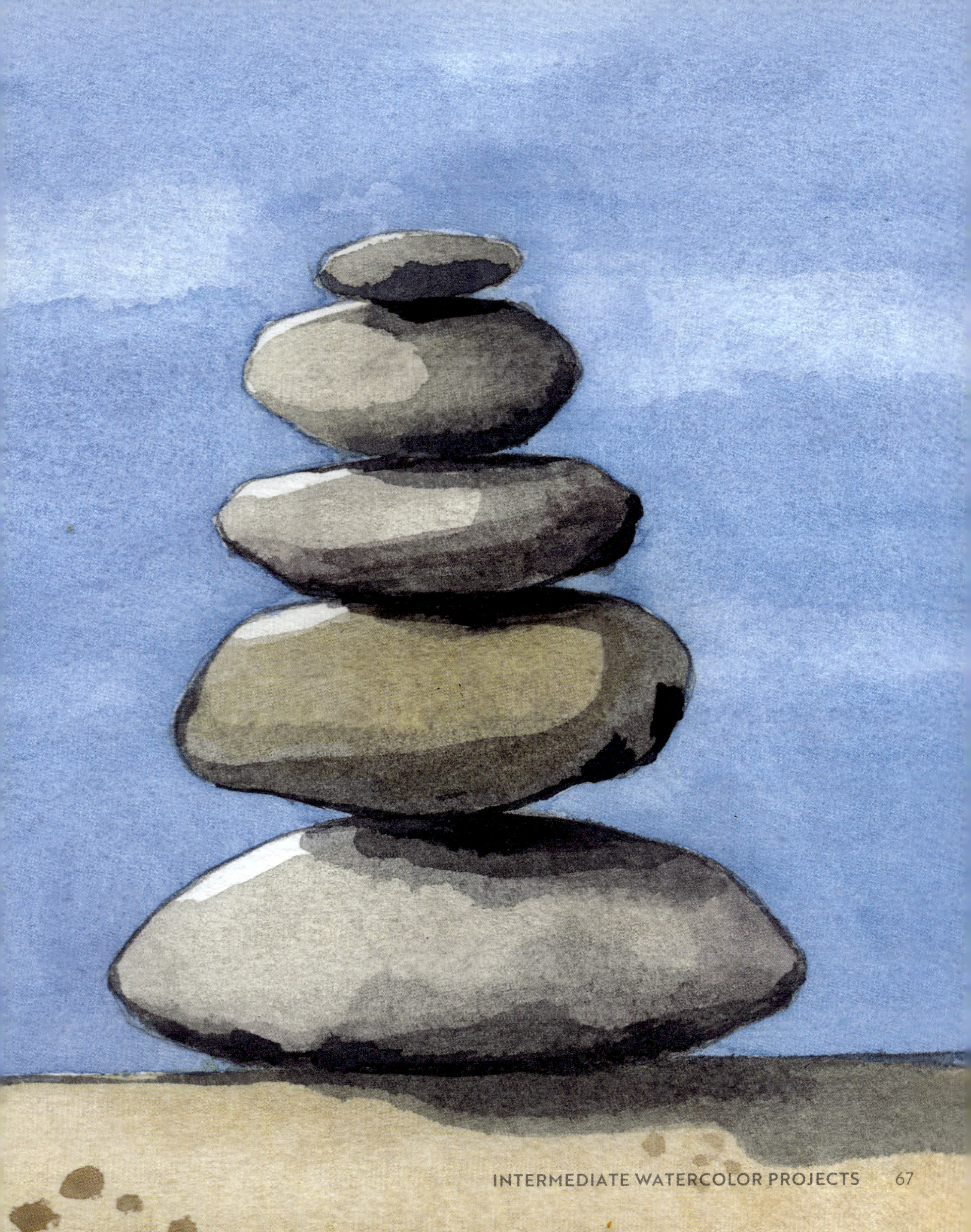

Bird on a Branch

In nature you will find many species of birds in a variety of shapes and colors. The bluebird is particularly wonderful to paint because of its brightly colored chest and blue-gray body.

COLORS

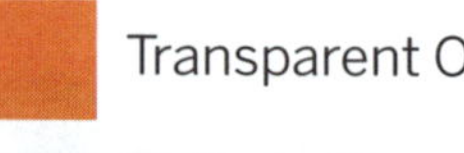 Transparent Orange

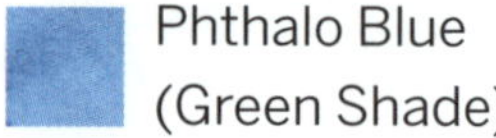 Phthalo Blue (Green Shade)

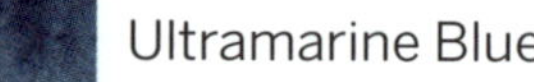 Ultramarine Blue

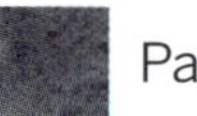 Payne's Gray

 Sap Green

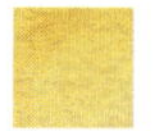 Quinacridone Gold

TECHNIQUES

- Wet on wet
- Direct color mixing
- Layering
- Sketching

MATERIALS

- Watercolor paper, 5" × 7"
- 2H lead mechanical pencil
- Medium round watercolor brush
- Fine-line brush
- Fine-tipped pigmented pen (black)
- Masking fluid (optional)
- Masking fluid eraser (optional)
- White ink

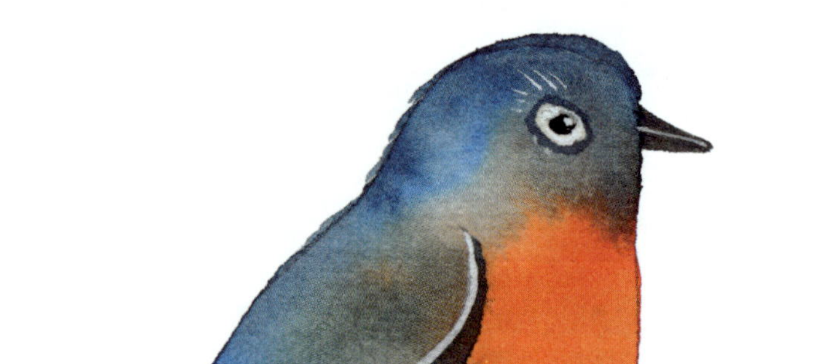

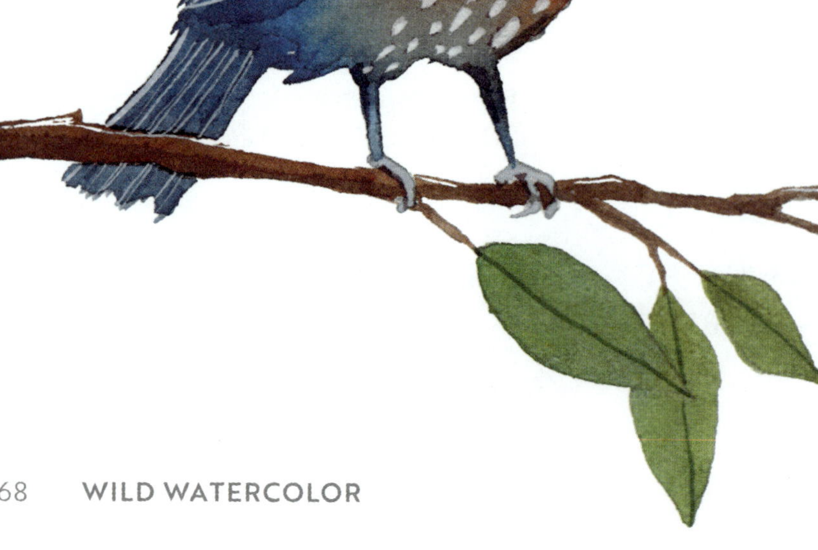

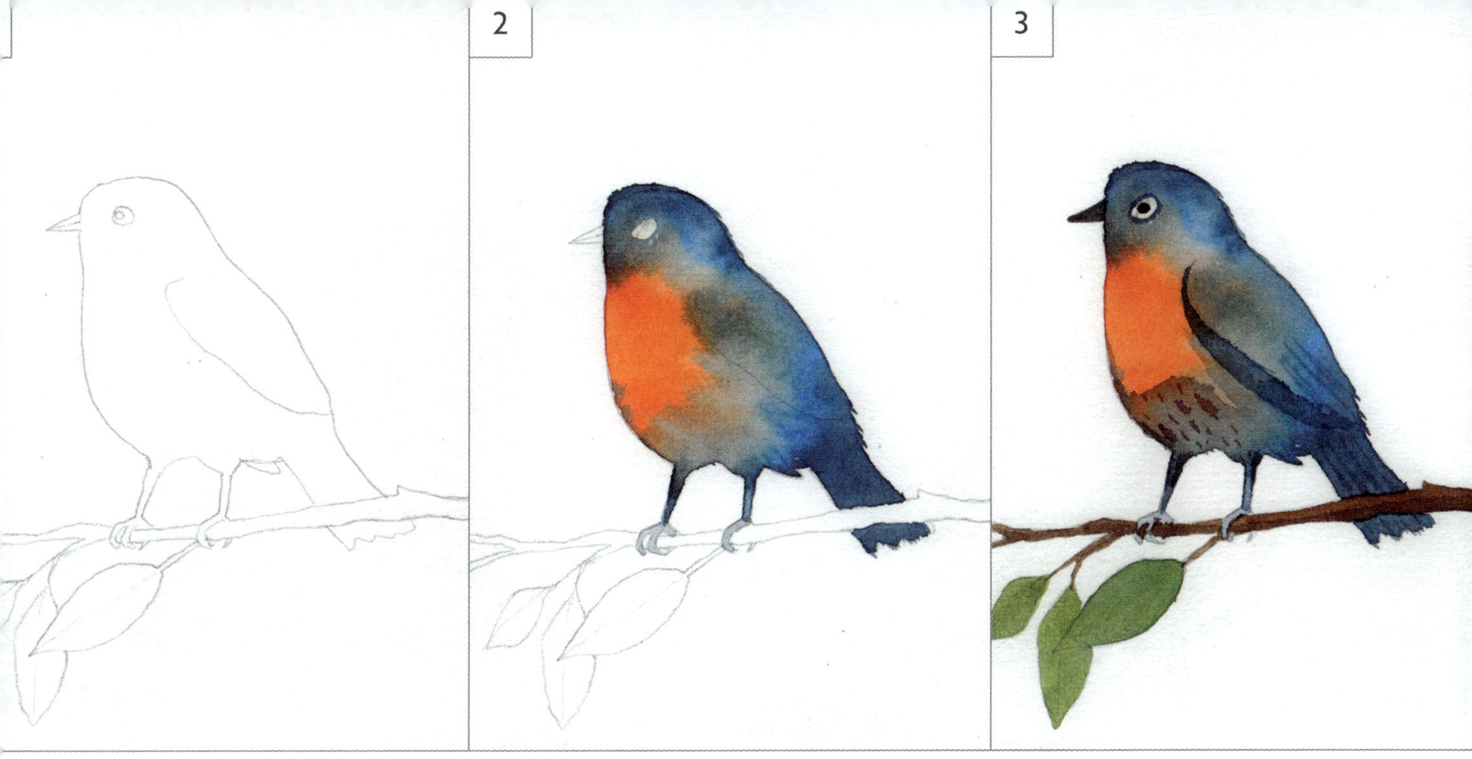

STEP ONE

Sketch the bird, branch, and leaves on the paper with a mechanical pencil using a light touch.

STEP TWO

Use a medium round brush to wet the inside of the bird's body with clear water, being careful not to wet the eye area. With the medium brush, drop Transparent Orange into the area below the beak and in the belly area. Drop Phthalo Blue into the top of the head, the wing, and the area below the wing. Drop Payne's Gray into the top edge of the body, wing, legs, and tail area. Let the colors blend for a smooth, blended wash. Let dry.

STEP THREE

Paint details on the wing and the tail using a mix of Phthalo Blue and Ultramarine Blue or Payne's Gray. Mix a little Transparent Orange and paint small marks in the belly area.

With a black pen, draw a round dot in the white area to make the eye.

Mix Transparent Orange with Payne's Gray and paint the branch with a medium-value brown.

Paint the leaves with Sap Green. Drop in a little Quinacridone Gold at the top while the leaves are still wet for a soft blend of yellow and green. Let dry.

OPTIONAL: Mask the eye area with masking fluid before painting. Remove the masking fluid after this step by rubbing it with your fingers, or use a masking fluid eraser.

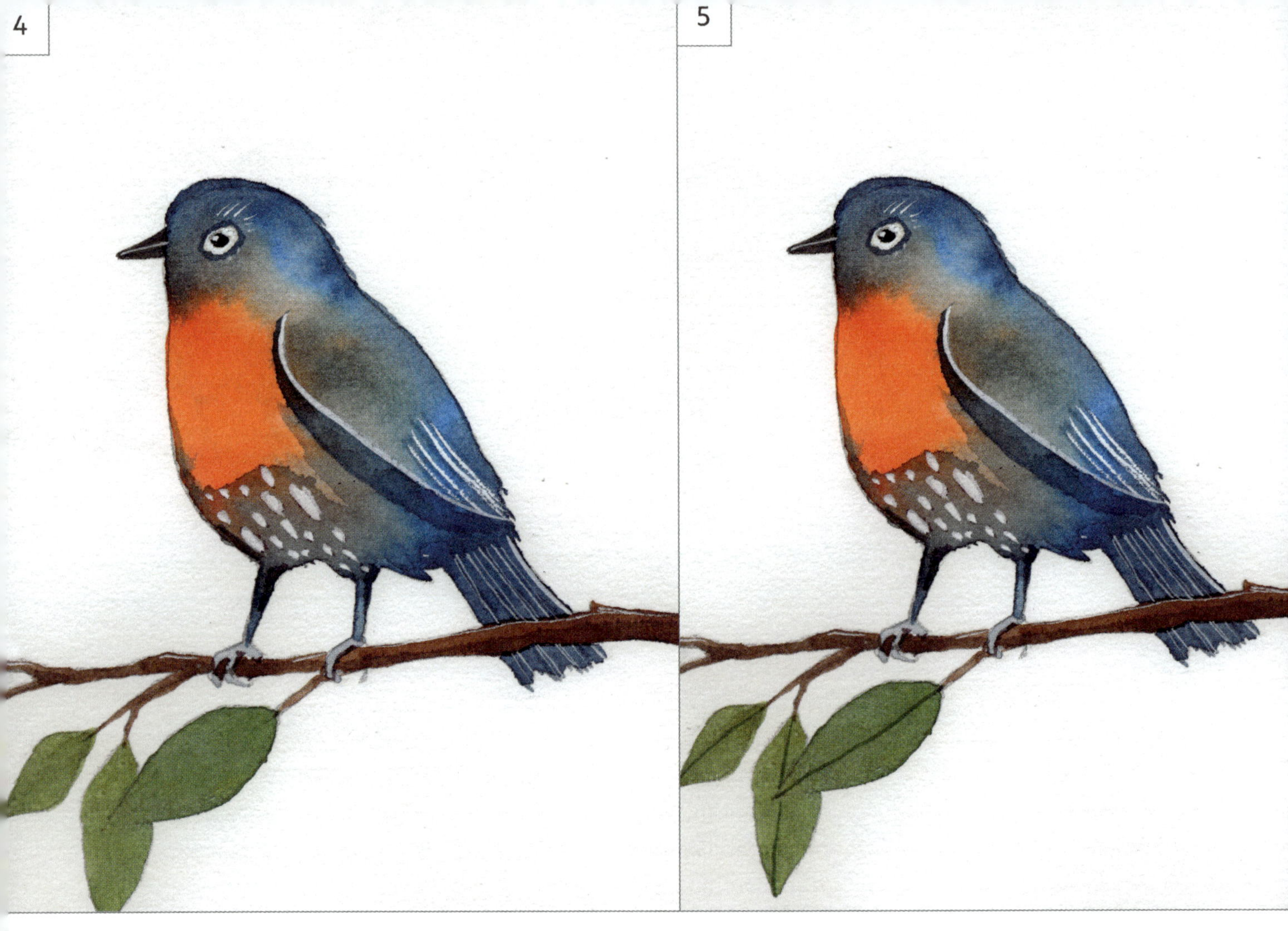

STEP FOUR

Mix a little water with white ink and paint highlights on the wing and around the eye and the tail. Paint a highlight on the branch.

STEP FIVE

Using the fine-line brush, paint the midribs on the leaves with a darker shade of the green mixture. Add more details if necessary.

NOTE: I painted light highlights over the marks on the belly because the previous marks had bled, which was an undesired effect. The highlights essentially covered up the boo-boo!

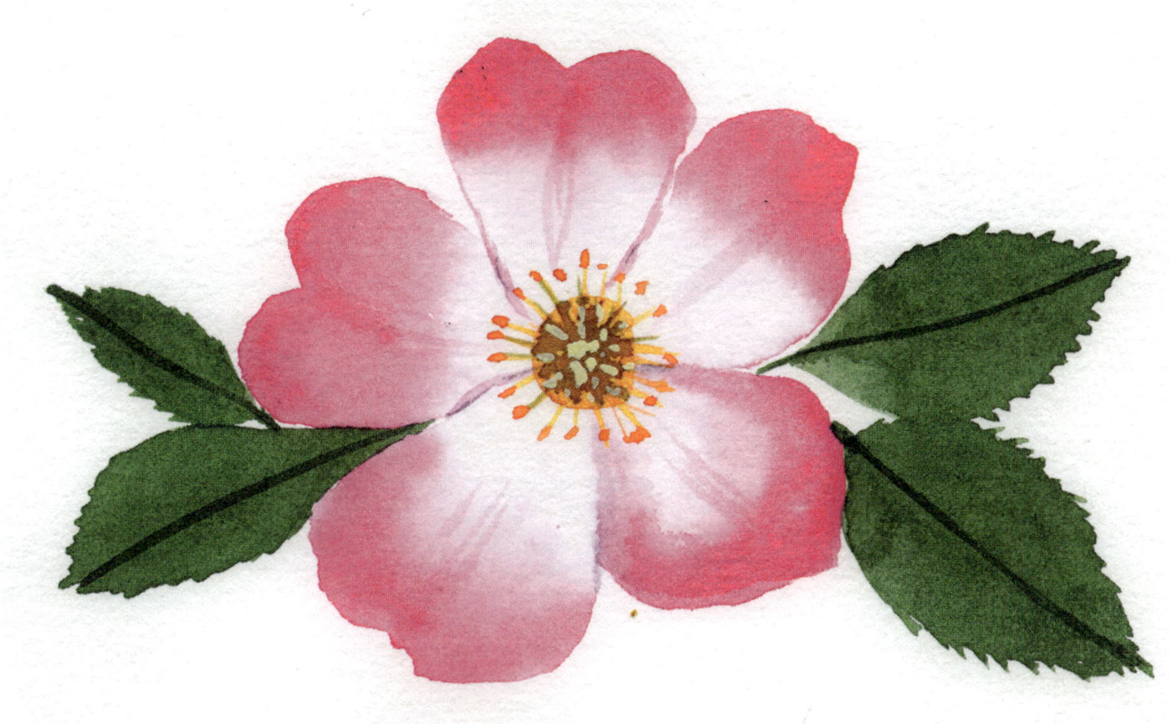

WEEK 16
Wild Rose

The wild rose, with five delicate petals, is fragrant, hardy, and looks much different from its cultivated counterpart.

COLORS

 Quinacridone Magenta

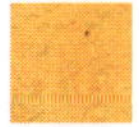 Quinacridone Gold

 Sap Green

 Payne's Gray

TECHNIQUES

- Direct color mixing
- Wet on wet
- Layering

MATERIALS

- Watercolor paper, 5″ × 7″
- Medium round watercolor brush with a sharp tip
- Fine-line brush or script brush
- Opaque white ink
- Facial tissue

STEP ONE

With clear water only, paint five heart-shaped petals with a medium round brush. Then, drop Quinacridone Magenta at the outer tips of the petals. Blot extra moisture or color with a dry brush or tissue in the center of the flower. Let dry.

STEP TWO

Create a yellow mixture for the center of the flower by combining Quinacridone Gold with a small amount of the magenta mix. Use a fine-line brush to paint a small circle in the center of the flower and to make small, fine marks going outward from the center. Dot the ends of the fine marks to create the pistils. Add a little magenta in the center to darken.

STEP THREE

Mix together Sap Green and a little Payne's Gray to make a medium-value green for the leaves. Paint the leaf shapes and make jagged edges with the tip of the brush while still wet. Let dry.

STEP FOUR

Add a little Payne's Gray to the green mixture and use a fine-line brush to paint midrib lines on the leaves. Mix a little yellow with opaque white ink and paint highlights in the center of the flower to finish.

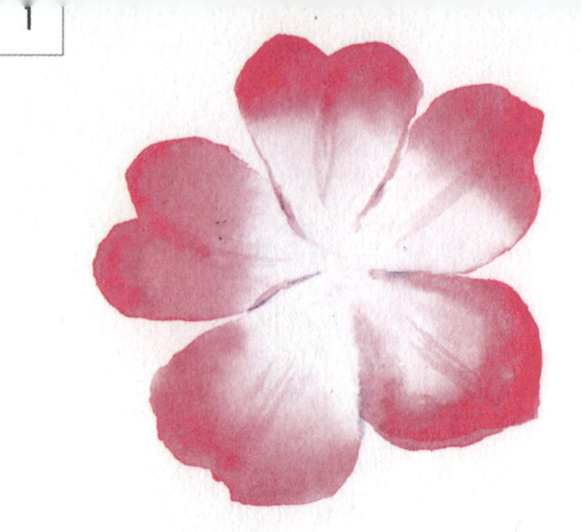

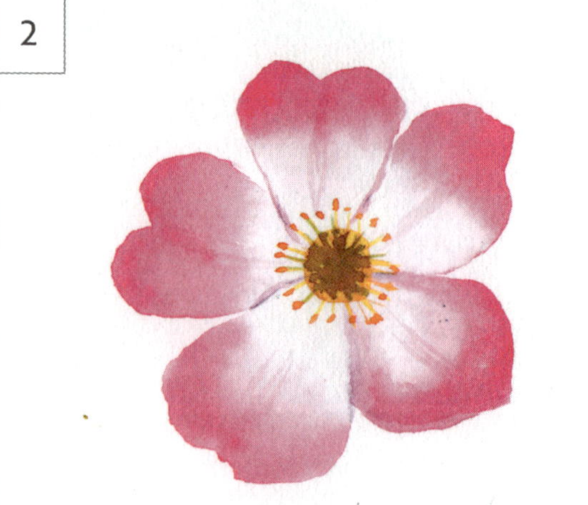

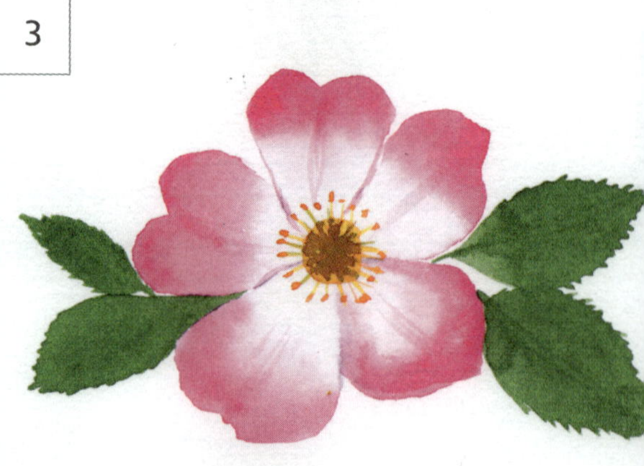

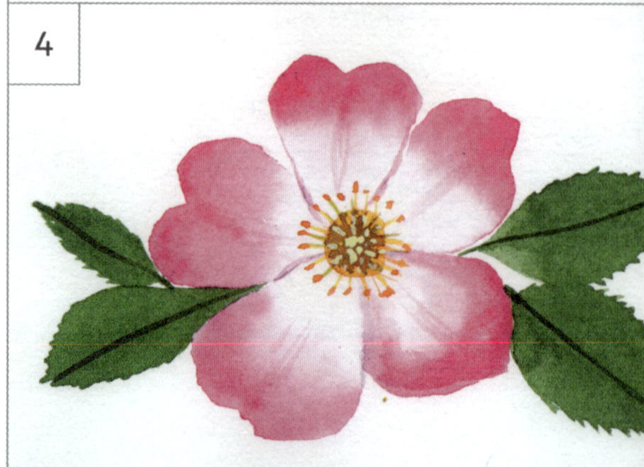

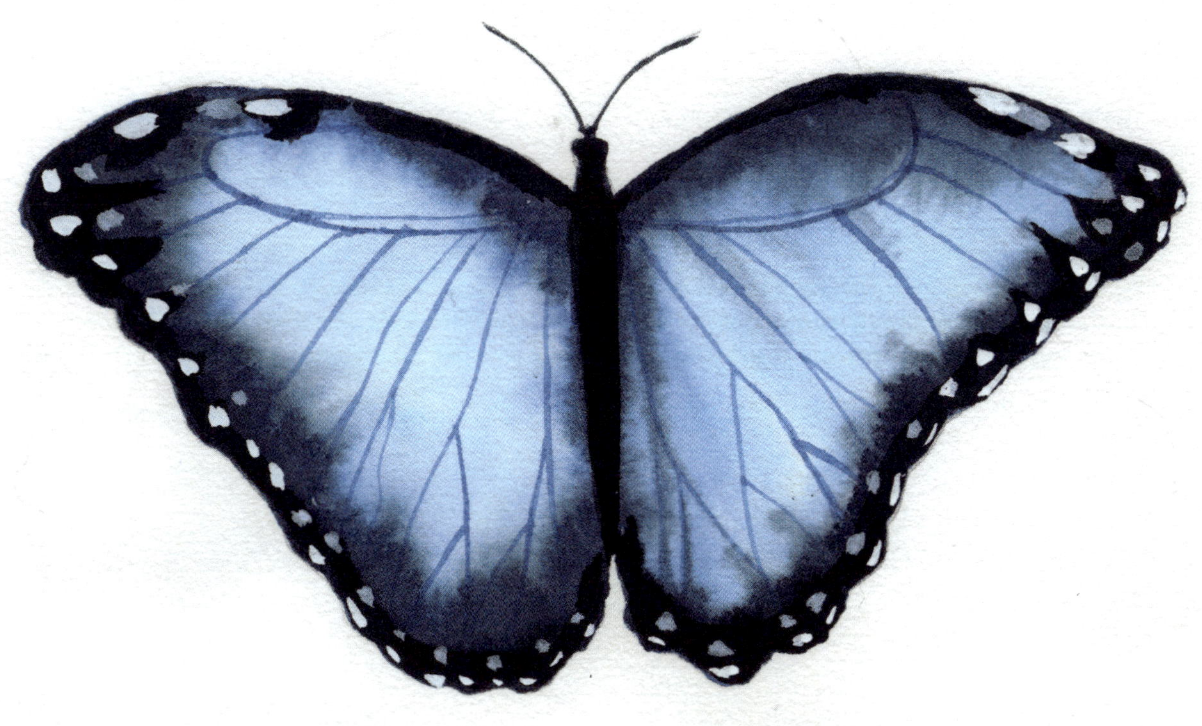

Blue Butterfly

Butterflies are always a perfect subject for watercolor because of their magnificent wings and vibrant colorways. I love watching the blues spread over the butterfly's wing in this project, a striking example of the wet-on-wet technique.

COLORS

 Ultramarine Blue

 Phthalo Blue (Red Shade)

 Indigo (or a mix of Phthalo Blue, black, and magenta)

 Payne's Gray

TECHNIQUES

- Wet on wet
- Layering
- Sketching

MATERIALS

- Watercolor paper, 5" × 7"
- 2H lead mechanical pencil
- Kneaded eraser
- Medium round watercolor brush
- Small round watercolor brush
- Fine-line brush
- White ink (optional)

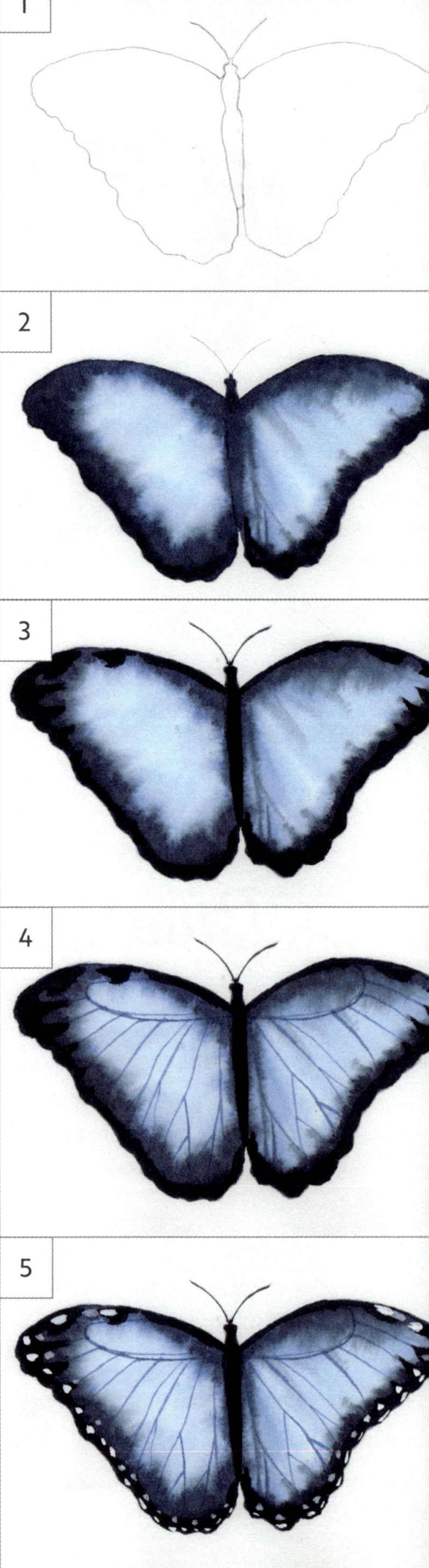

STEP ONE

Sketch the butterfly on the paper with a mechanical pencil using a light touch. Erase any extra lines with a kneaded eraser if needed.

STEP TWO

Load your medium round brush with water and wet the entire wing and body on one side of the butterfly. The wet area should be shimmering but not dripping wet.

Mix a medium value of Ultramarine Blue with Phthalo Blue (Red Shade). Drop the blue mixture along the edges of the wing and body. Watch the color spread into the wing.

While still wet, mix a dark value of Indigo and drop the darker color along the edges. Clean your brush and blot with a towel to remove extra water. Soften the inside of the wings by brushing in the direction of the wing veins. Repeat on the other side of the butterfly. Let dry.

STEP THREE

Load the brush with Payne's Gray and paint a rough edge around the wings to darken them. Use a fine-line brush to paint the body and the antennae. Let dry

STEP FOUR

Create a mix of medium-value blue. Load a fine-line brush and paint the veins on the wings. Let dry.

STEP FIVE

Load a small brush with white ink and paint spots around the wing edges staying within the vein lines. Add a little blue to the white and add more spots to finish. Erase any visible pencil lines with a kneaded eraser.

Fallen Feather

Feathers can exhibit vibrant colors and patterns or subtle, blended hues. Painting fallen feathers in watercolor allows for endless creativity! Don't be afraid to try this project again a little later, using different colors.

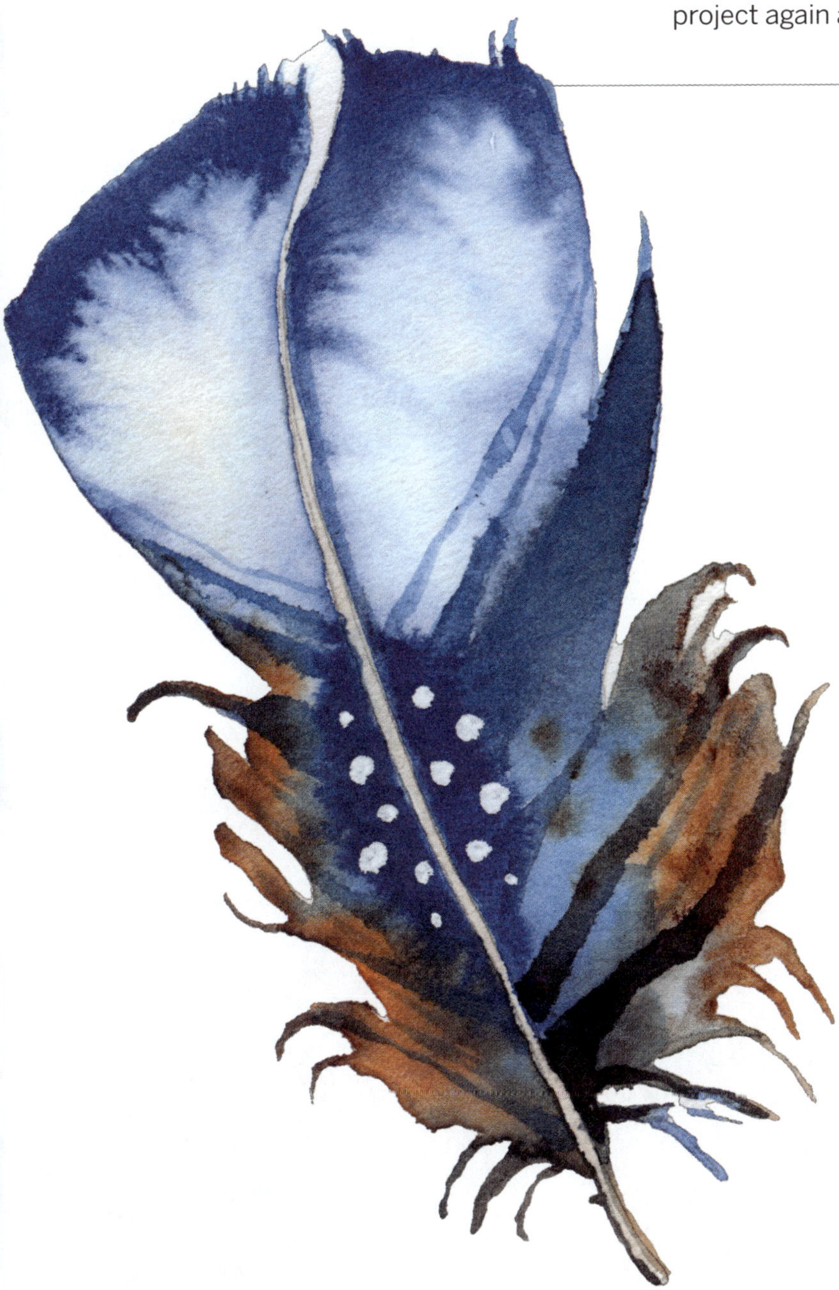

COLORS

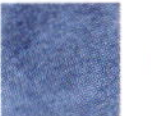 Phthalo Blue (Red Shade)

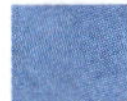 Phthalo Blue (Green Shade)

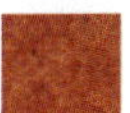 Burnt Umber

 Transparent Orange

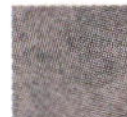 Moonglow

TECHNIQUES

- Wet on wet
- Layering
- Sketching

MATERIALS

- Watercolor paper, 5" × 7"
- 2H lead mechanical pencil
- Kneaded eraser
- Medium round watercolor brush
- Small round watercolor brush
- White ink

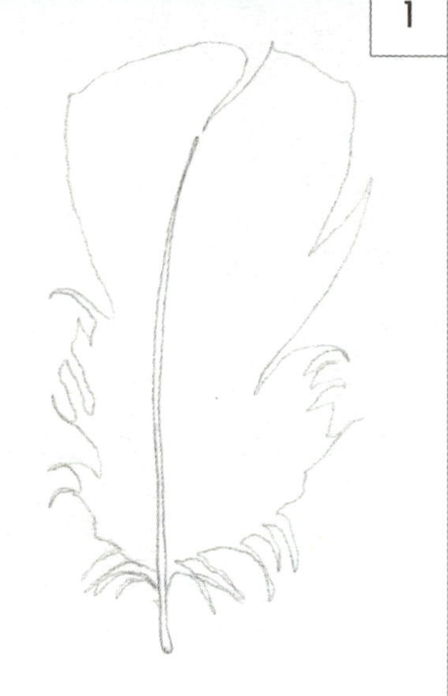

STEP ONE

Sketch a feather shape on the paper with a mechanical pencil using a light touch.

STEP TWO

Using a medium round brush, wet one side of the feather with clear water only. The area should be shiny but not dripping wet. Drop Phthalo Blue (Red Shade) into the outer edges of the top half of the feather. Drop Burnt Umber and Transparent Orange at the edges of the bottom half of the feather. Let the colors blend and dry without brushing them.

While everything is still wet, drop a mix of Phthalo Blue (Red and Green Shades) into the bottom third of the feather in the center rib area. Let it blend and dry without brushing.

STEP THREE

Repeat step 2 on the other side of the feather. Let dry.

STEP FOUR

Using the same colors, paint some detail in the feather on both sides concentrating mostly at the bottom of the feather.

With a smaller brush, bring out the tips of the feathers using a mix of blue at the top of the feather. Paint the center rib with a light wash of Burnt Umber and let dry.

STEP FIVE

With white ink, paint small, odd-shaped circles in the darkest area of the feather for contrast. Add details in the feather as needed. Erase any visible pencil lines with a kneaded eraser.

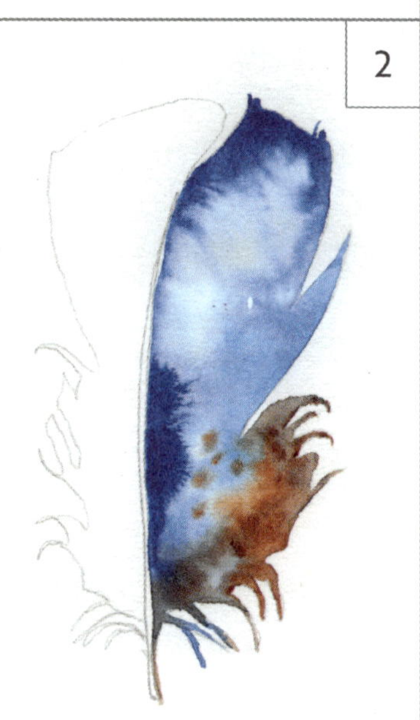

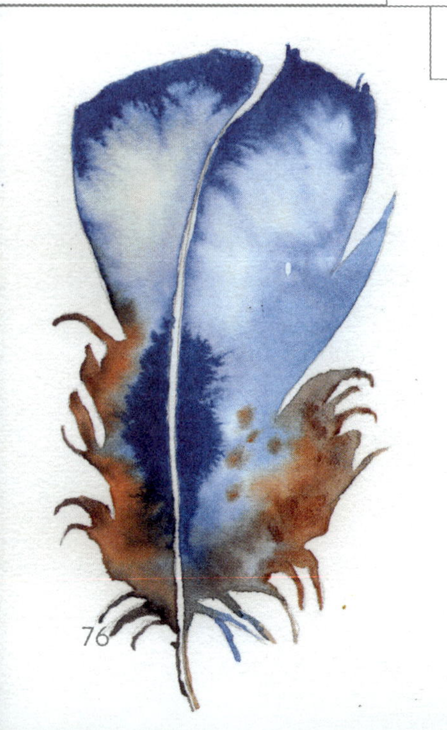

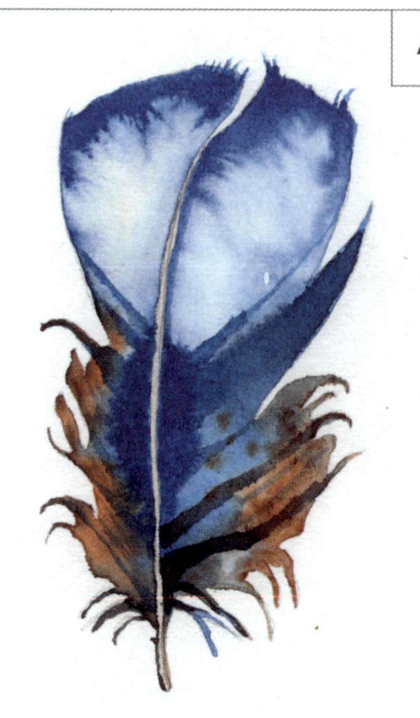

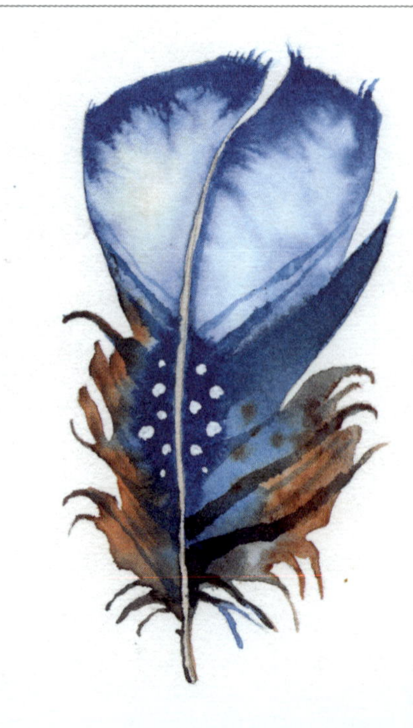

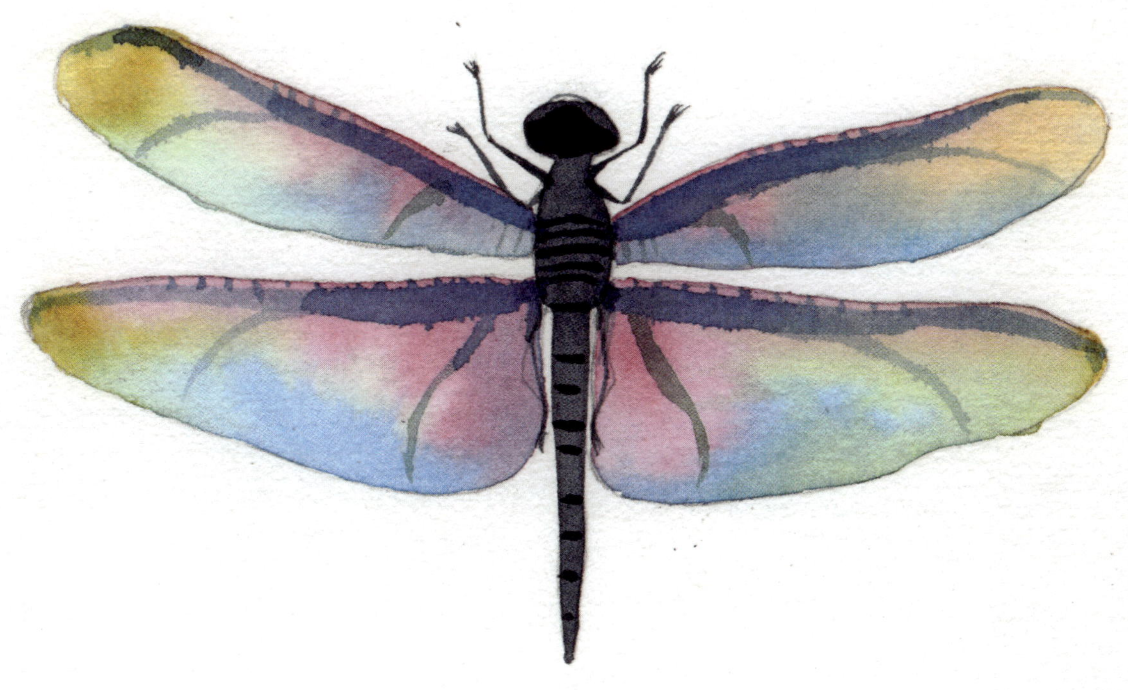

WEEK 19

Dragonfly

Who doesn't love the translucent quality of the dragonfly's wing? For a fun twist, try painting several dragonflies and cutting them out after they dry. Dragonflies make great focal points for journals and greeting cards.

COLORS

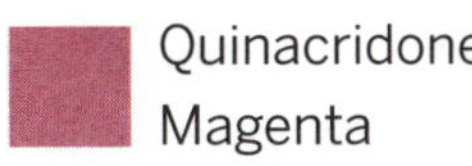 Quinacridone Magenta

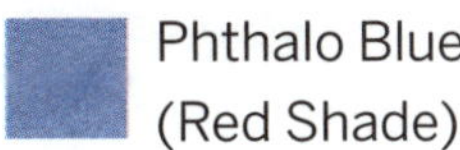 Phthalo Blue (Red Shade)

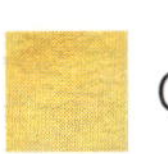 Quinacridone Gold

 Payne's Gray

TECHNIQUES

- Wet on wet
- Layering
- Sketching

MATERIALS

- Watercolor paper, 5" × 7"
- 2H lead mechanical pencil
- Kneaded eraser
- Medium round watercolor brush
- Small round watercolor brush
- Fine-line brush

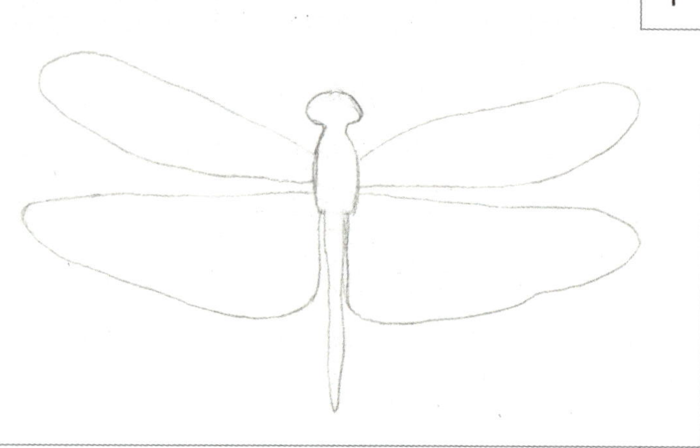

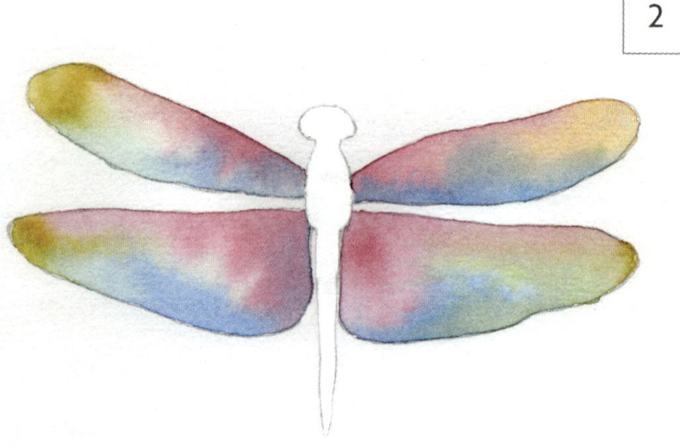

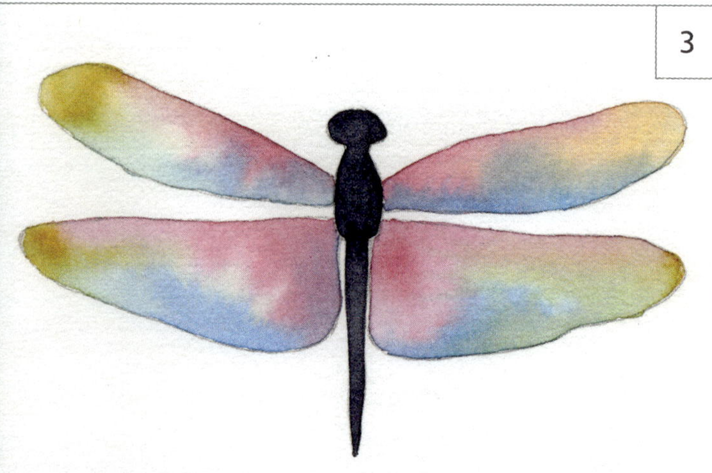

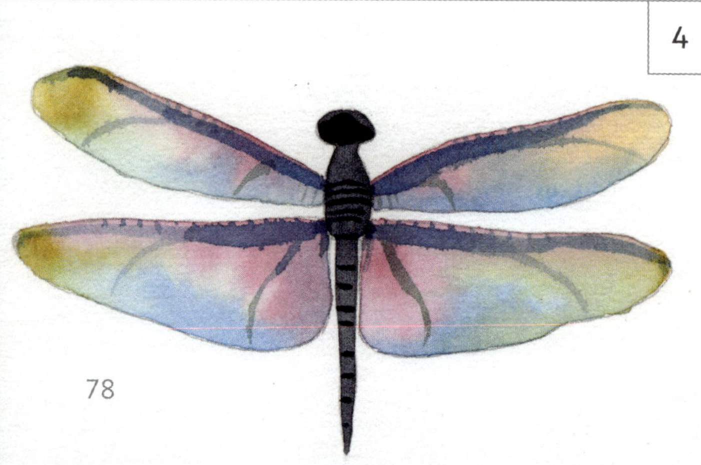

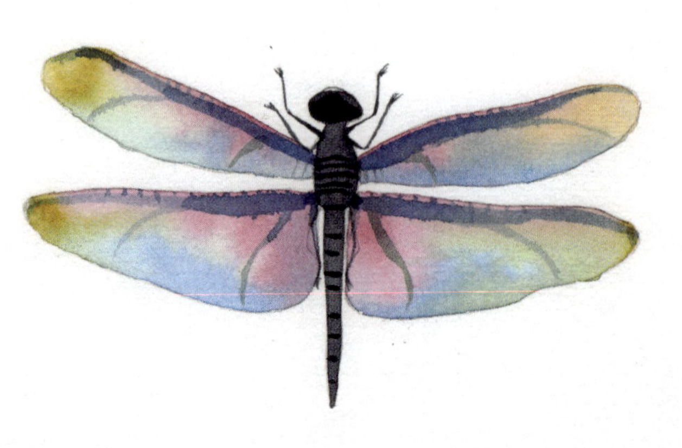

STEP ONE

Sketch the dragonfly wings and body on the paper with a mechanical pencil. Erase any extra lines to keep the drawing clean and simple.

STEP TWO

Use a medium round brush loaded with clean water to wet the wings. The wing area should be shiny but not dripping wet or puddly.

Drop in a medium value of Quinacridone Magenta at the center and top of each wing. While the wings are still wet, drop in a medium value of Phthalo Blue (Red Shade) at the bottom edge of each wing, stopping about halfway to the end of each wing. Finally, drop in a medium value of Quinacridone Gold at the tip of each wing. Watch the colors spread on their own. Let dry.

STEP THREE

Load a small round brush with a medium value of Payne's Gray and paint the insect's body. Let dry.

STEP FOUR

Mix Phthalo Blue (Red Shade) with a small amount of Payne's Gray for a medium value. Use the small round brush to paint details on the wings. Use Payne's Gray to paint details on the head and the body. Let dry.

STEP FIVE

Sketch antennae and legs with a pencil, then paint them with a fine-line brush using Payne's Gray. Erase any visible pencil lines.

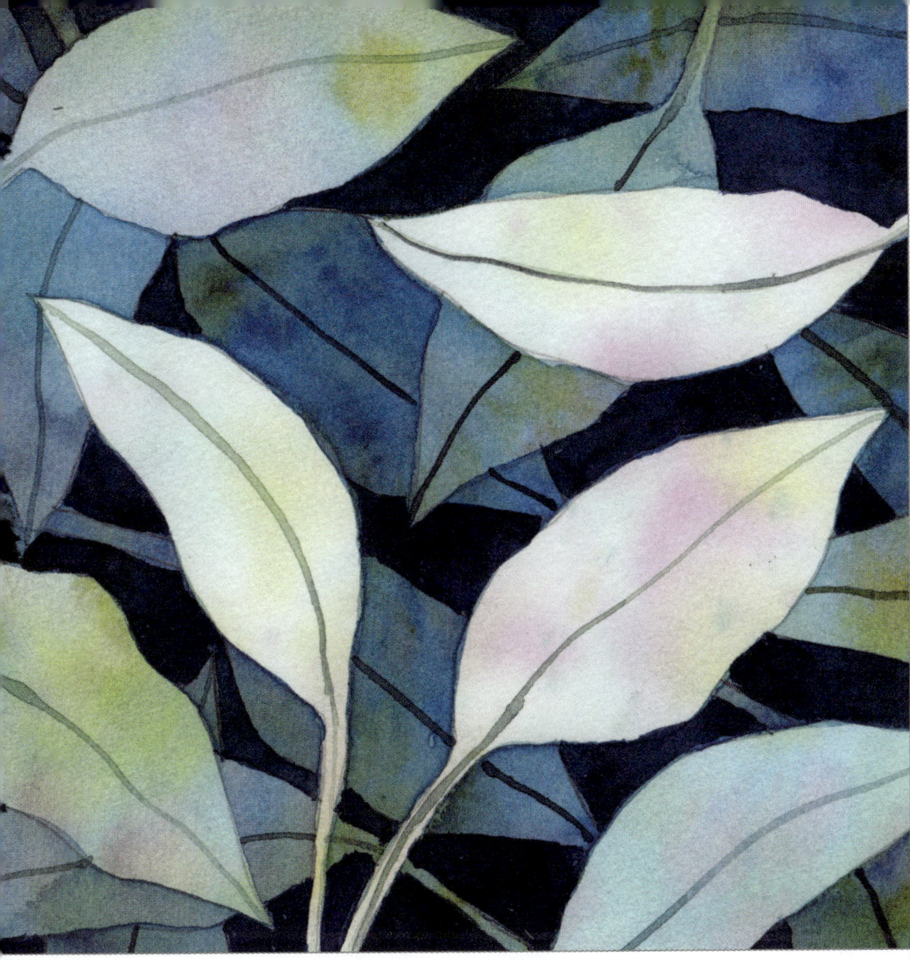

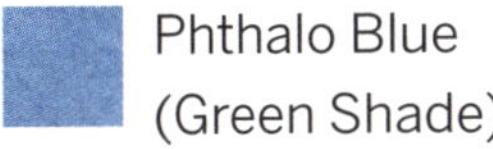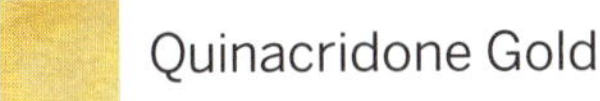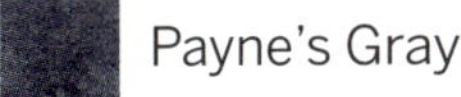

TECHNIQUES

- Wet on wet
- Glazing
- Layering
- Color mixing
- Sketching

MATERIALS

- Watercolor paper, 6" × 6"
- Masking or washi tape
- Masonite panel
- Medium round
  watercolor brush
- Small round
  watercolor brush
- Fine-line brush
- 2H lead
  mechanical pencil

WEEK 20

Negative Painted Leaves

Negative painting is a fun yet effective technique for creating depth and contrast by building layers of values. It is very rewarding once you understand and practice the steps. Leaves are the perfect subject for practicing negative painting— try both warm and cool color combinations.

STEP ONE

Attach the paper to a board using masking or washi tape, creating about a ¼-inch border with the tape on all edges of the paper.

Use a medium round brush to wet the paper with clear water, then brush a very light value of Phthalo Blue (Green Shade) evenly on the paper. It should be just a tint of blue with mostly water.

Drop very light values of Quinacridone Magenta and Quinacridone Gold onto the surface and blend them together for a very pale variegated wash. This will be your lightest value for the painting. Let dry.

STEP TWO

Sketch three leaf shapes with stems on the paper with a mechanical pencil, being careful that the leaves do not overlap.

Paint around the leaf shapes with a light-value Phthalo Blue (Green Shade) and drop light values of Quinacridone Magenta and Quinacridone Gold in random areas of the wash. Let dry.

> **OPTIONAL:** Sketch the leaf shapes on another piece of watercolor paper and cut out the shapes with scissors to create a template. Use the template to trace the leaf shapes onto your watercolor.

STEP THREE

With your pencil, sketch three more leaves on the paper in different directions. Do not overlap the leaf shapes just yet. Paint a light-value variegated wash going around the leaf shapes and stems with the same colors as in the previous steps. Be careful to paint only the areas *around* the leaf shapes and not inside the leaves. Let dry.

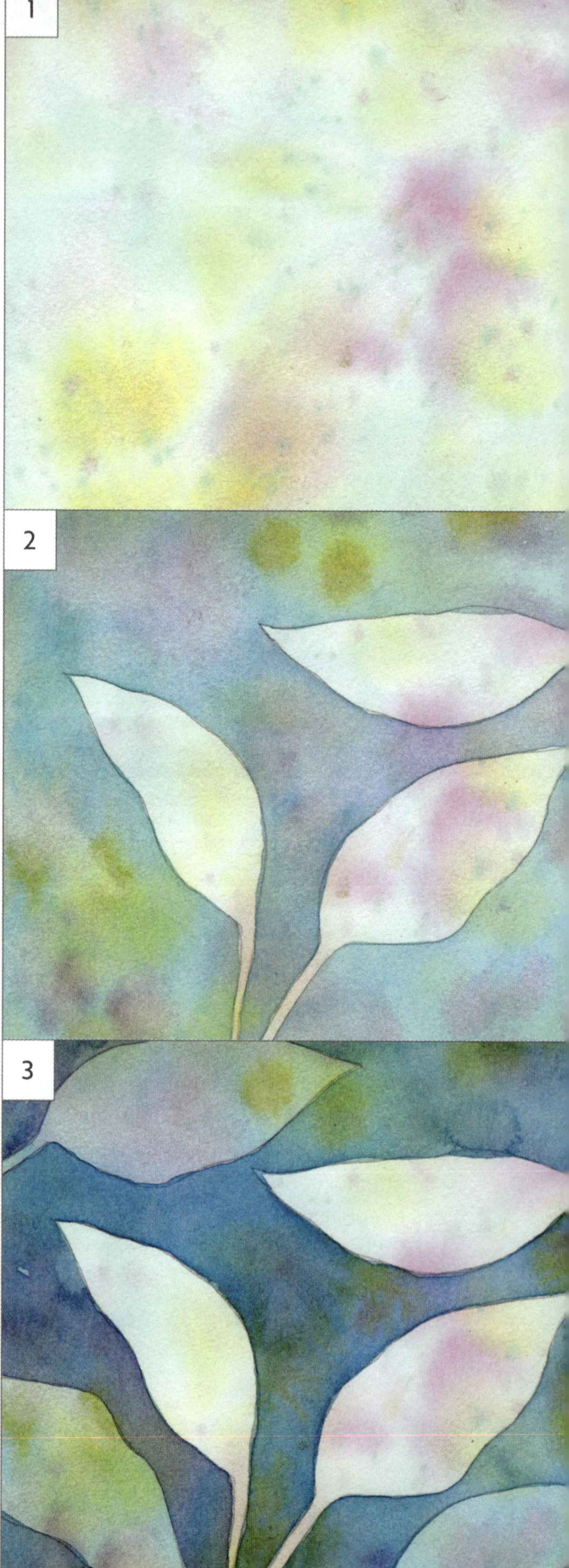

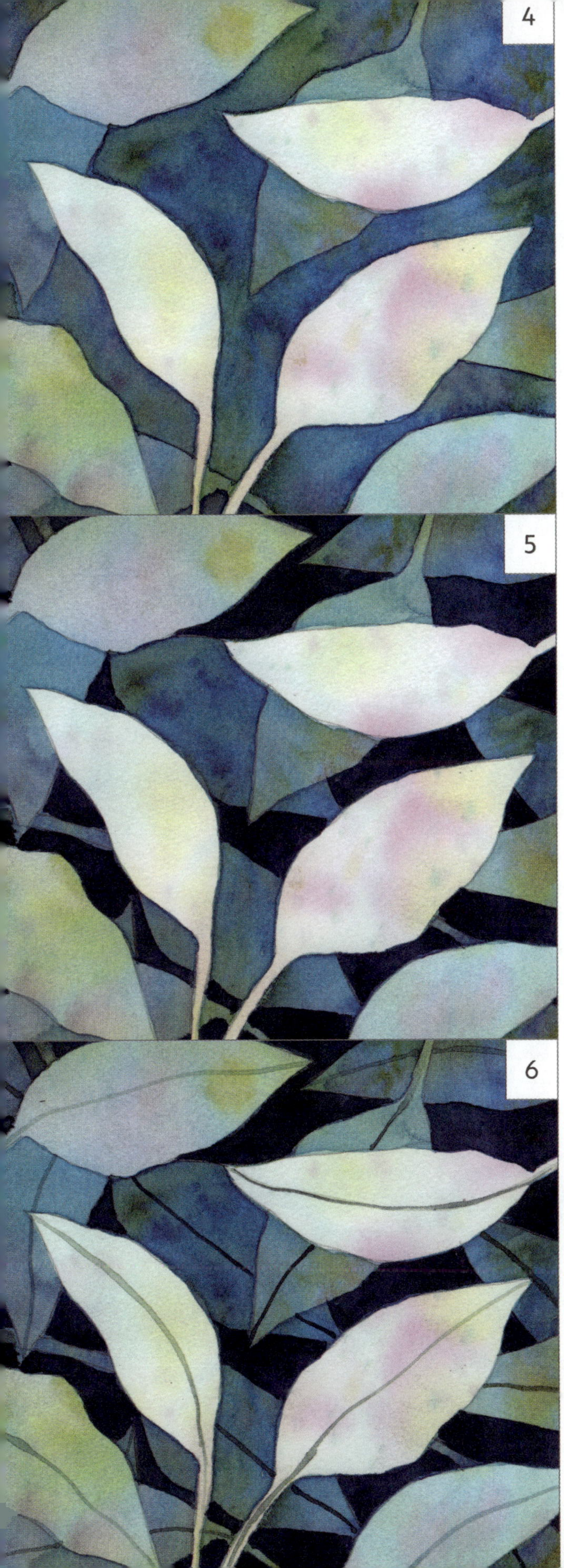

STEP FOUR

Sketch another group of leaves going in different directions. When overlapping a leaf, draw *behind* it so it looks like it's laying underneath the upper leaf. Paint a medium-value wash of Phthalo Blue (Green Shade) in the spaces around all the leaf shapes and drop a little Quinacridone Magenta and Quinacridone Gold in random areas while the wash is still damp so the colors blend.

You might notice that some colors "push" other colors out whereas others don't have any movement at all. This is what makes watercolor so fascinating! Each layer will show more depth and contrast as you proceed with this technique.

STEP FIVE

Sketch more leaves going in different directions, overlapping them by drawing *under* the previous leaves at this point in the process.

Mix a little Payne's Gray with Phthalo Blue (Green Shade) for a dark-value wash and use a smaller round brush to paint around all the leaf shapes. Let dry.

STEP SIX

Use a fine-line brush and light to medium values of Phthalo Blue (Green Shade), Quinacridone Gold, and Payne's Gray to paint midribs in the center of the leaves. Let dry, then carefully remove the masking tape.

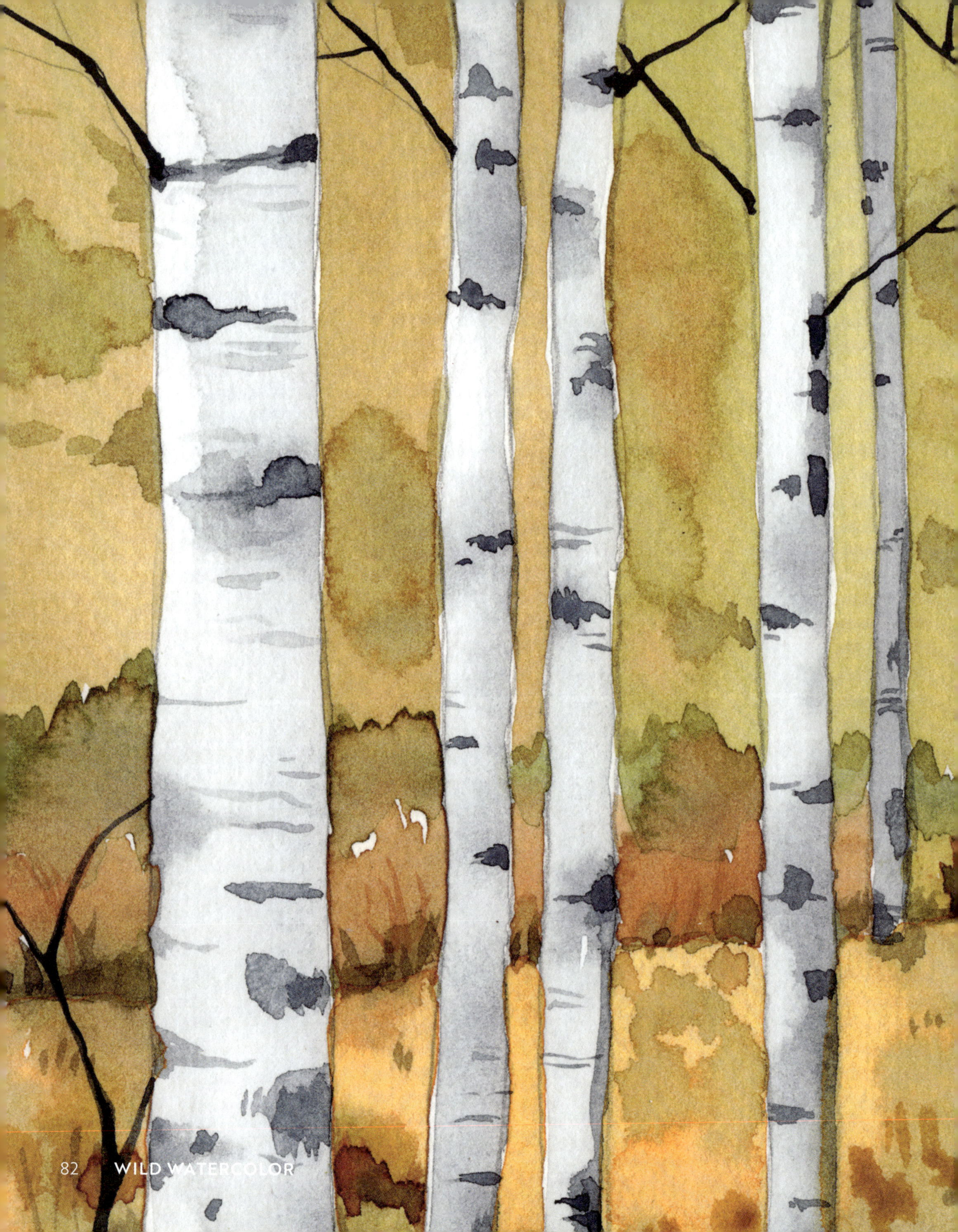

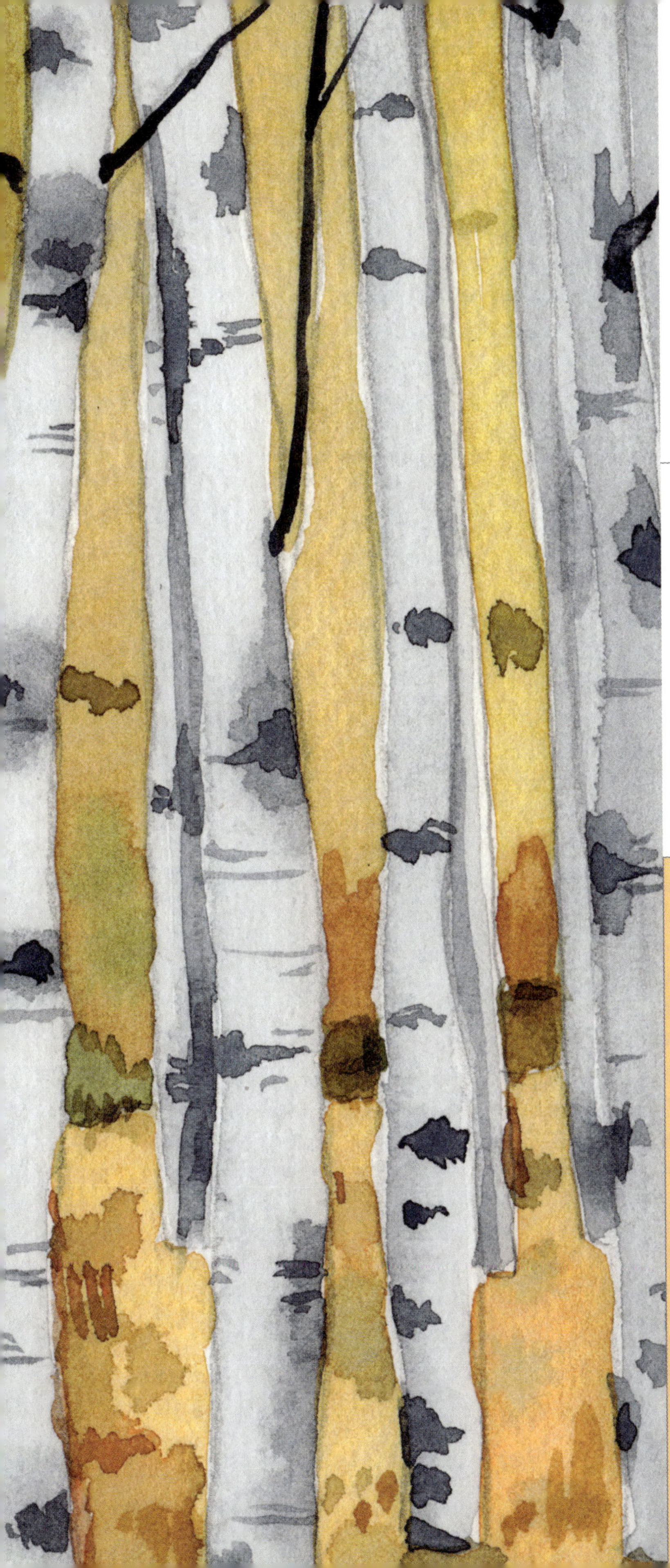

Aspen Forest

The vibrant yellow and rustling leaves of Aspen trees in the fall are strikingly beautiful and serene. Capturing the essence of the trees in watercolor requires only a little simplification.

COLORS

 Quinacridone Gold

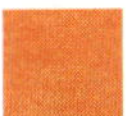 Transparent Orange

 Payne's Gray

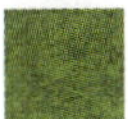 Sap Green

TECHNIQUES

- Wet on dry
- Wet on wet
- Layering
- Color mixing

MATERIALS

- Watercolor paper, 6" × 9"
- 2H lead mechanical pencil
- Medium round watercolor brush
- Small round watercolor brush
- Fine-line brush

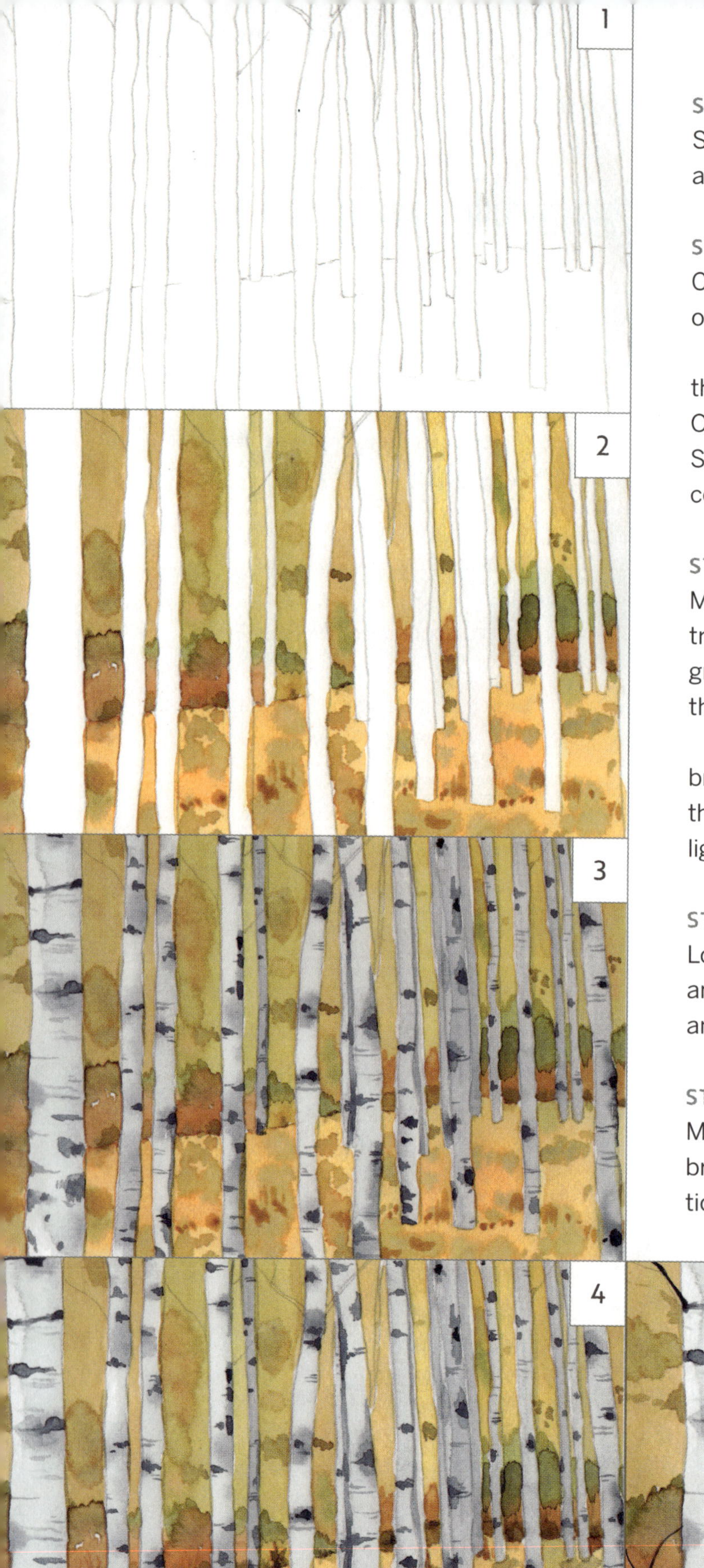

STEP ONE

Sketch tree shapes and a horizon line on the paper with a mechanical pencil using a light touch.

STEP TWO

Create a mix of medium value Quinacridone Gold and of Transparent Orange in your palette.

Paint the foreground and the background around the trees with the gold color. Drop a little Transparent Orange into the areas just painted. Then, drop in a little Sap Green to add texture and variation in color. Let the colors blend together and dry.

STEP THREE

Mix a very light value of Payne's Gray and paint the trees, leaving white on the left side of the closest foreground trees. Paint the light wash of Payne's Gray on the background trees.

Mix a dark value of Payne's Gray and use a fine-line brush to paint dark marks and thin horizontal lines on the bark of the trees. Paint more lines and marks with a lighter-value Payne's Gray. Let dry.

STEP FOUR

Load the fine-line brush with the mix of gold, orange, and green and paint fine lines to represent branches and trunks in the areas just painted in step 3. Let dry.

STEP FIVE

Mix a dark value of Payne's Gray and use the fine-line brush to paint thin branches going in different directions focusing on the top of the trees. Let dry.

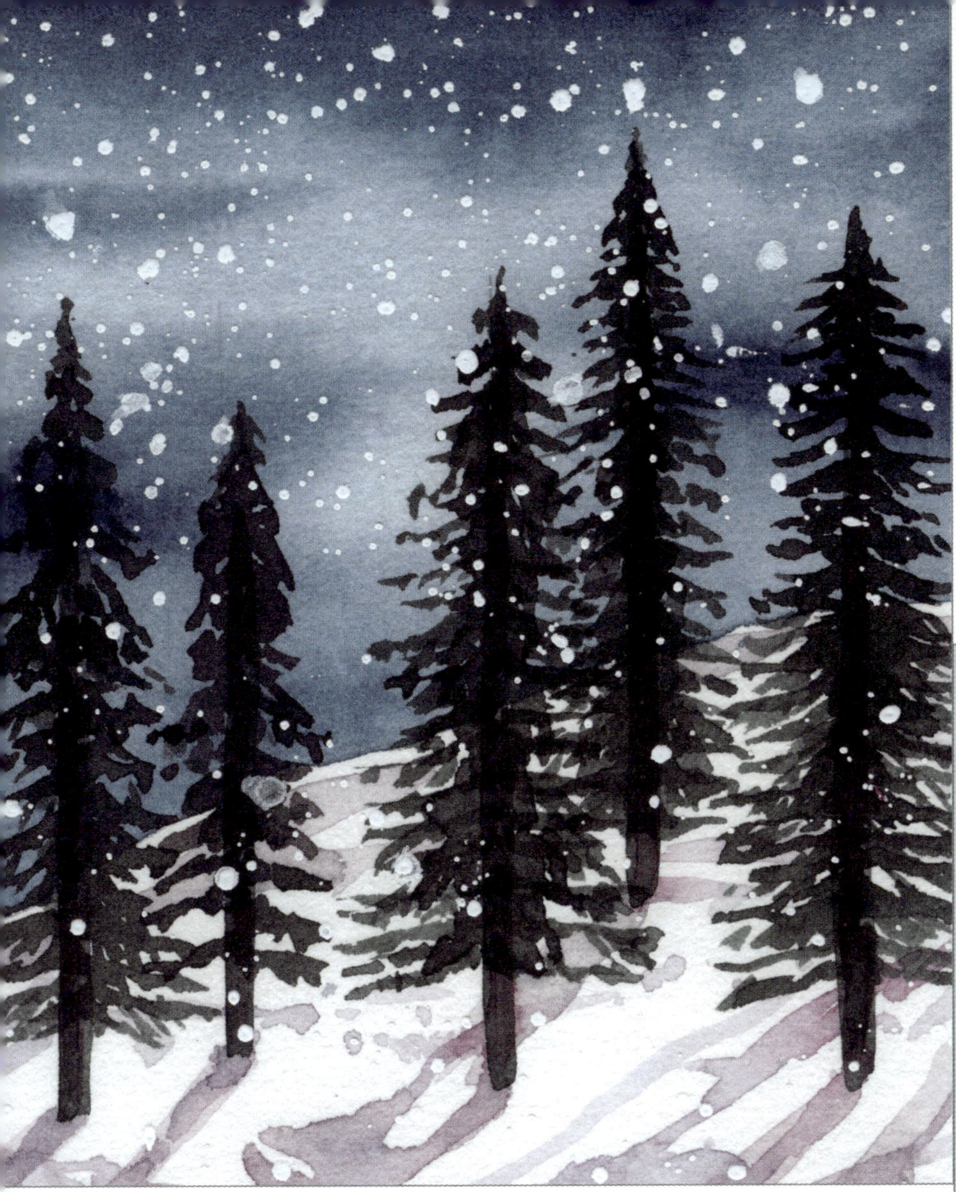

COLORS

 Payne's Gray

 Perylene Green

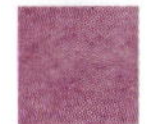 Quinacridone Violet

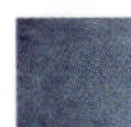 Indigo (or a mix of Phthalo Blue, black, and magenta)

TECHNIQUES

- Wet on wet
- Splattering
- Layering
- Graded wash

MATERIALS

- Watercolor paper, 5" × 7"
- Masking or washi tape
- Masonite panel
- 2H lead mechanical pencil
- Large round watercolor brush
- Medium round watercolor brush
- Small round watercolor brush
- White ink
- Facial tissue

WEEK 22

Pine Trees on Snowy Hill

Paint a dramatic winter wonderland using a few simple but effective techniques. This would be a good project to frame and give as a gift for the holiday season—one can almost hear the snow falling gently on the pine trees.

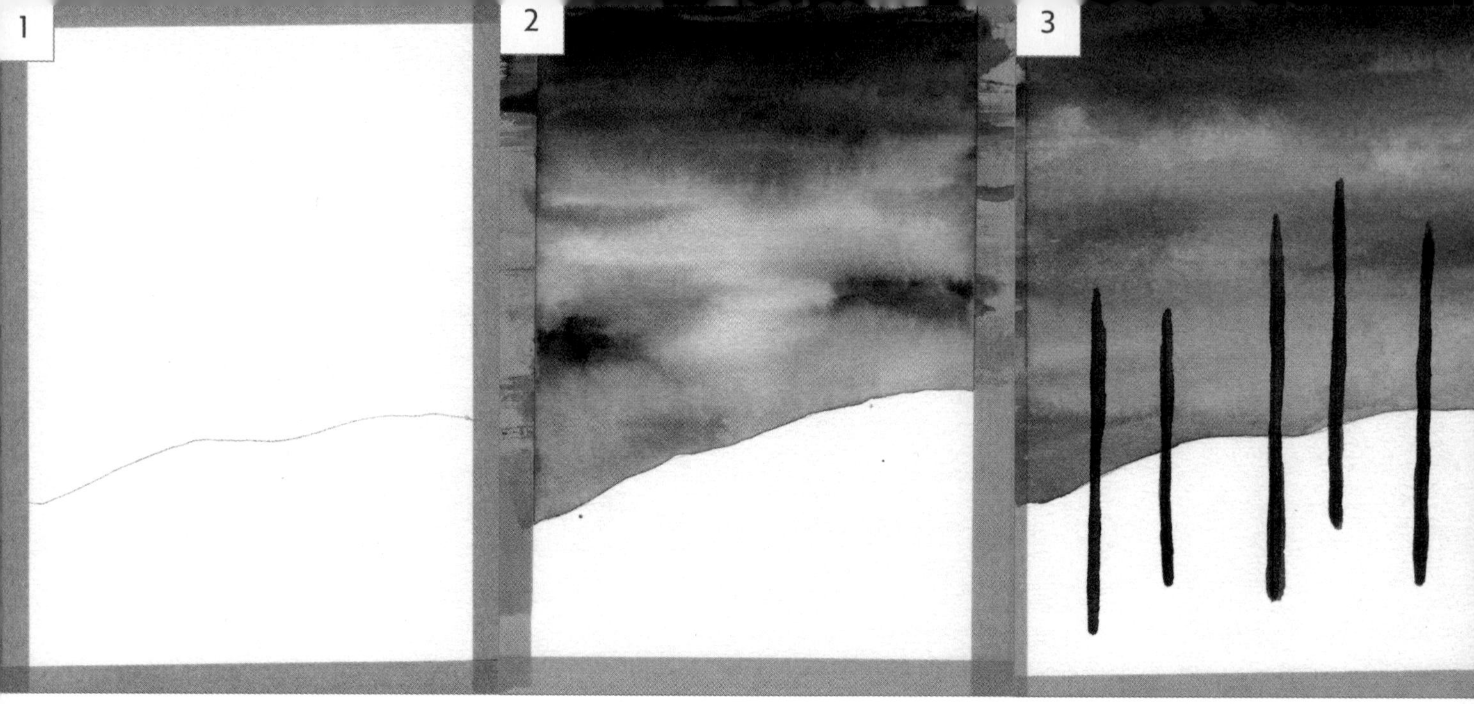

STEP ONE

Attach the paper to a board with masking or washi tape, creating a ½-inch border with the tape on all edges of the paper. Sketch a horizon line about one-third up from the bottom of the paper with a mechanical pencil, going upward to represent a hill.

STEP TWO

Use a medium brush to wet the top section of the paper all the way to the pencil line with clear water. The paper should be shiny but not dripping wet. Load the brush with a medium to dark value of Indigo and brush it on the paper, starting from the top and moving downward to the pencil line. Lift the board to let the color run down the paper.

Load the brush with a dark value of Payne's Gray and drop color at the top of the paper near the tape line.

Clean the brush and drag it across the paper to blend areas creating an atmospheric effect. Blot areas with tissue to lighten if needed. Let dry.

STEP THREE

Mix a dark value of Perylene Green, Quinacridone Violet, and Payne's Gray and use a small round brush to paint several pine tree trunks going upward on the white area. Space them apart at different distances and vary the heights.

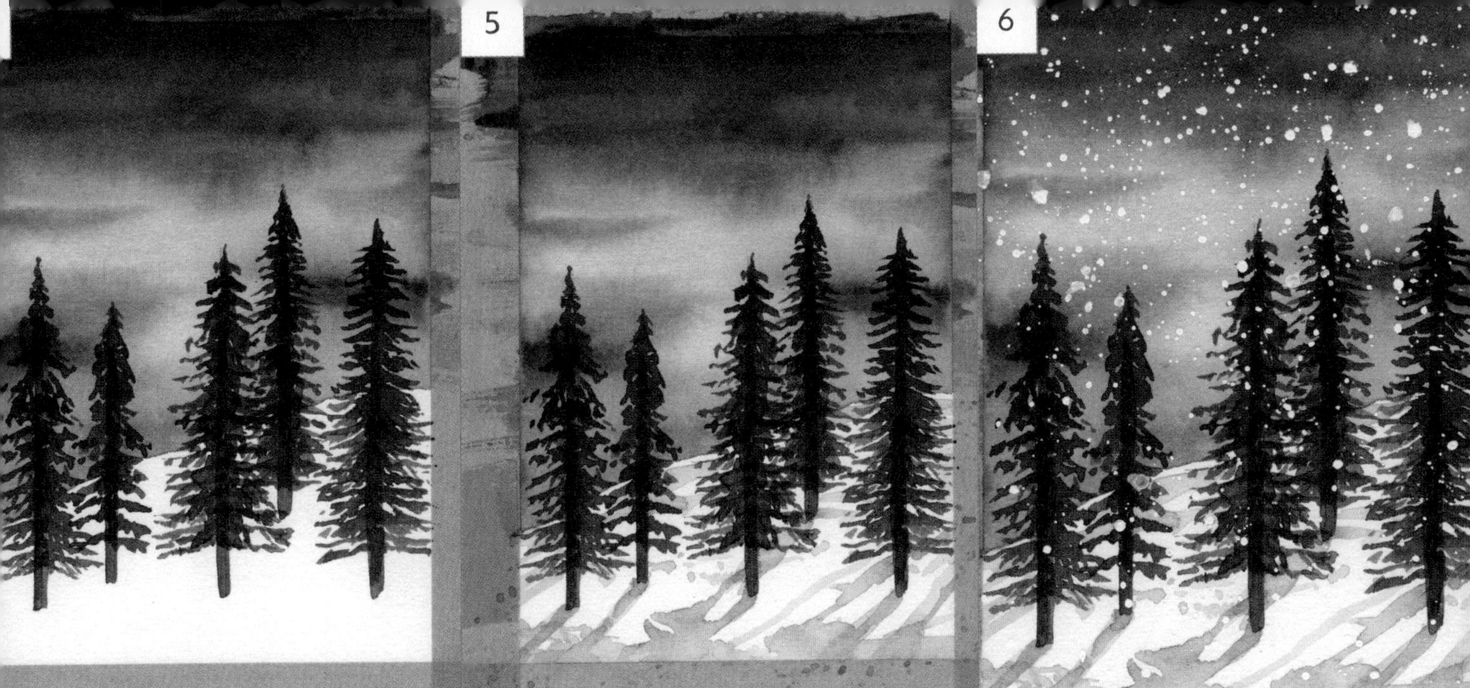

STEP FOUR

Paint the branches with the same mixture by making small squiggly lines back and forth at an angle, getting larger as you go down the trunk. Let dry.

STEP FIVE

Mix a light value of Quinacridone Violet and Payne's Gray and use a medium round brush to paint shadows below the tree trunks. Paint more shadows along the horizon making sure you leave plenty of white areas on the hill. Let dry.

STEP SIX

Add a little water to white ink to make a thick, creamy mix. Load a medium to large round brush with the white paint and make small splatters on the painting by tapping the end of the brush. Change the brush direction and splatter the white until you reach the desired snowy effect. Let dry. Carefully remove the masking tape to reveal your winter wonderland!

NOTE: If the tape tears the paper or paint has seeped underneath, just trim the edges with scissors or a paper cutter, then tape or glue the painting onto a new 5 × 7-inch sheet of watercolor paper or mixed media paper.

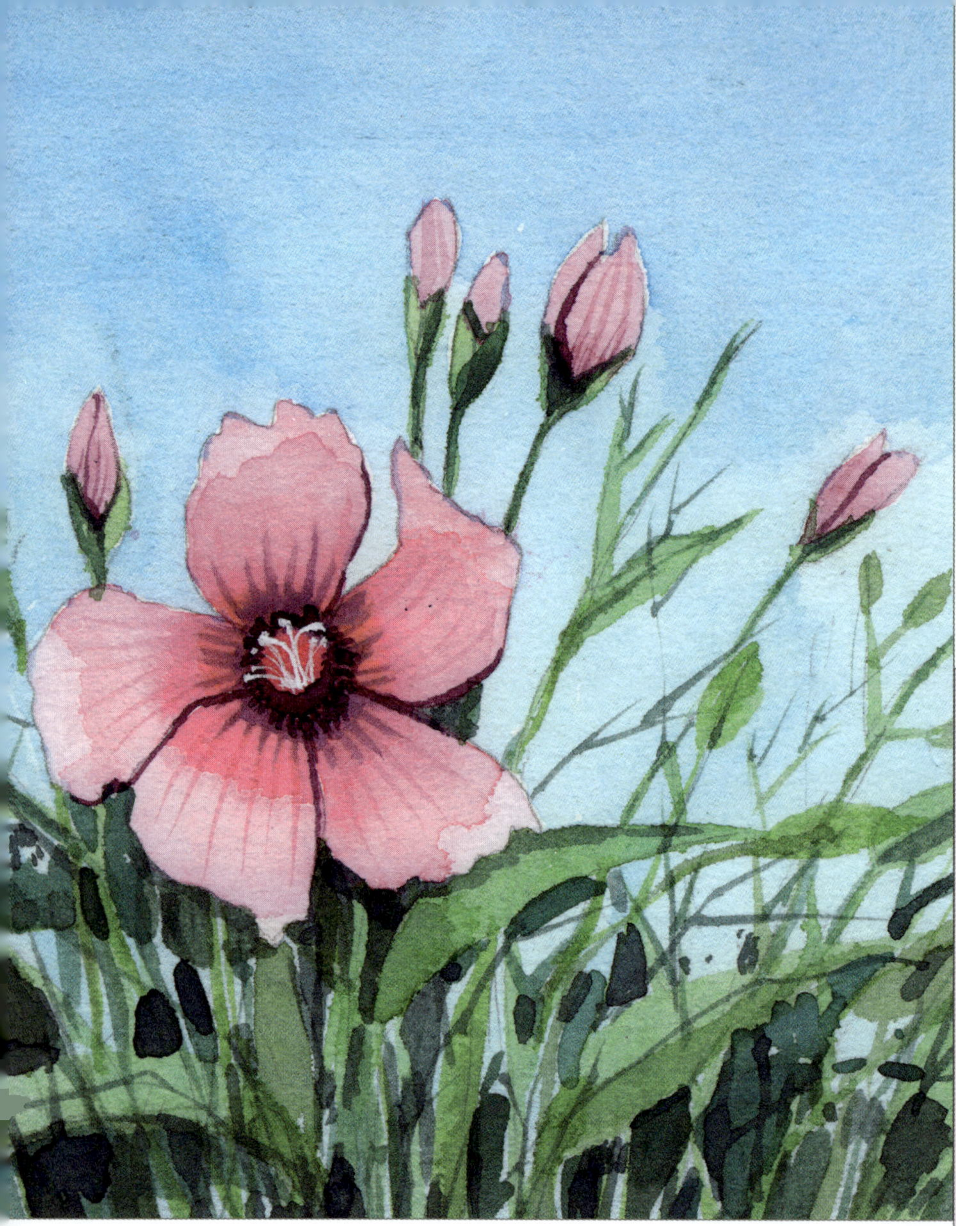

WEEK 23
Dianthus

The dianthus is a delicate, fragrant flower, also known as the sweet William. It grows in the wild but is also a great flower to plant in a garden and even to grow indoors.

COLORS

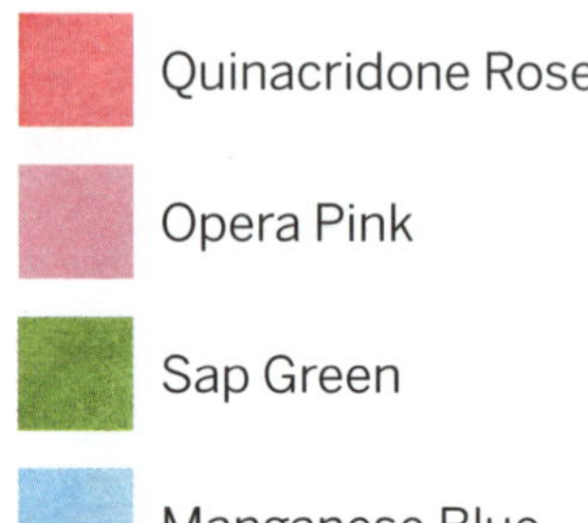

- Quinacridone Rose
- Opera Pink
- Sap Green
- Manganese Blue
- Payne's Gray

TECHNIQUES

- Wet on dry
- Layering
- Sketching

MATERIALS

- Watercolor paper, 4½″ × 6″
- 2H lead mechanical pencil
- Large round watercolor brush
- Medium round watercolor brush
- Small round watercolor brush
- Fine-line brush
- White ink
- Facial tissue

STEP ONE

Sketch the flower, buds, and leaves on the paper with a mechanical pencil using a very light touch.

STEP TWO

Mix a light value of Quinacridone Rose and Opera Pink and use a medium brush to paint a light wash on each petal. Blot the tips with tissue if needed.

Drop a saturated mix of Opera Pink on the inside edge of the petals in the center area until the pink spreads outward toward the edge of each petal. Blot extra moisture with a dry brush if needed.

While the petals are still damp, drop a mixture of Opera Pink mixed with a small amount of Payne's Gray to get a darker pink into the inner edge of the petals and flick outward with the tip of the brush, creating short veins going from the center of the flower. Paint the buds with a pale wash of Opera Pink, then drop a darker pink at the base of each bud. Paint the center of the flower with a medium-value Quinacridone Rose. Let dry.

STEP THREE

Mix a large amount of Manganese Blue with water for a pale blue color and use a larger brush to paint the entire background except for the pink petals. Start from the bottom with the palest blue and end with a medium-value blue at the top, above the pink buds. Let dry.

STEP FOUR

Mix a medium value of Sap Green with a little Payne's Gray and use a small brush to paint some leaves and stems. Drop a darker value of the green mixture at the base of some of the leaves. Let dry.

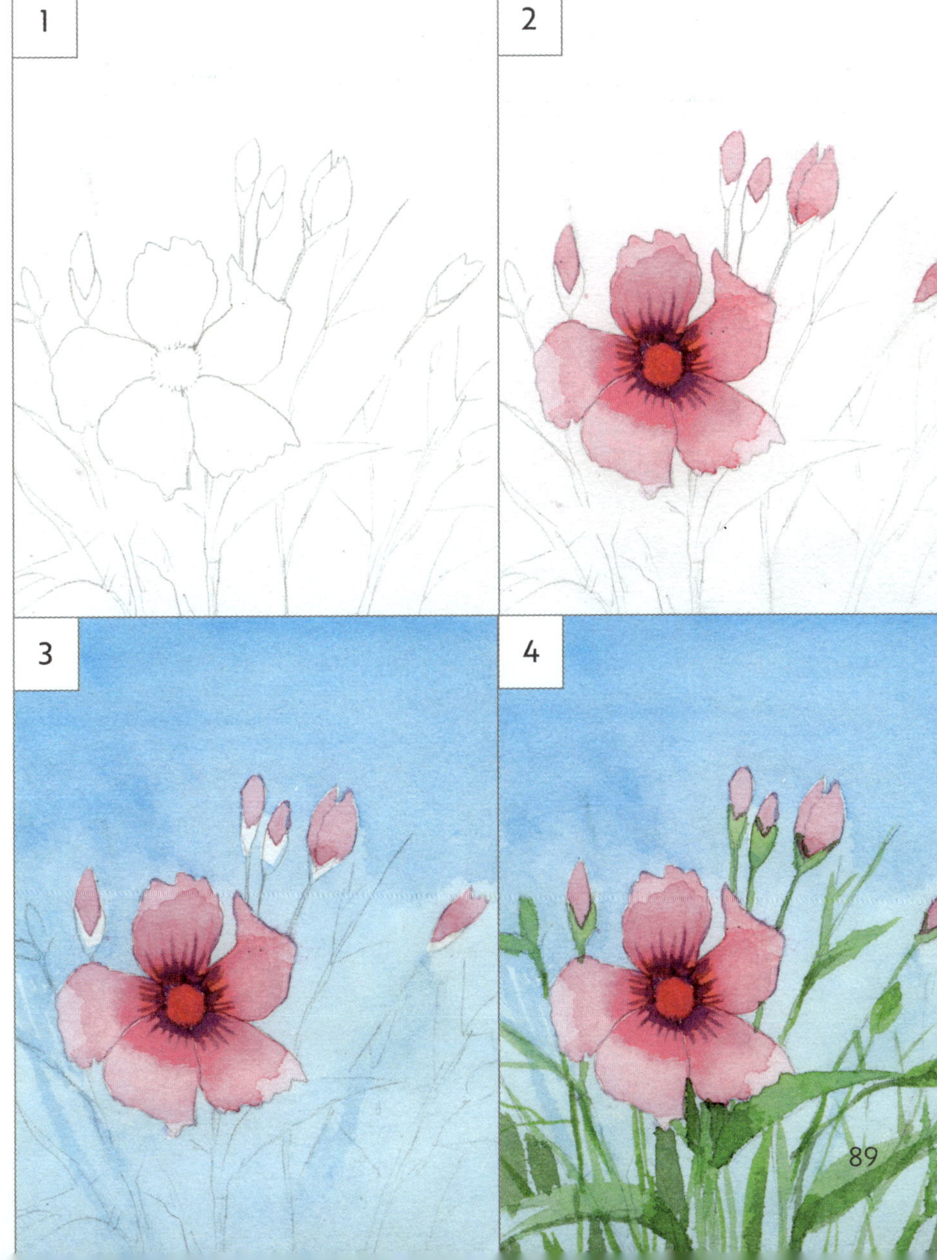

Mix a darker value of Sap Green with a little Manganese Blue and Payne's Gray and paint more areas in the leaves to create contrast in the leaves and stems, concentrating in the area below the flower.

Add a little Manganese Blue to the mix and use a fine-line brush to paint more stems. Let dry.

Mix a dark value of Quinacridone Rose with Payne's Gray and use a fine-line brush to paint details on the flower buds and the inside of the flower. Let dry.

Use a fine-line brush to paint the details in the center of the flower with white ink. Paint thin pale-pink lines on the petals with a fine-line brush. Let dry.

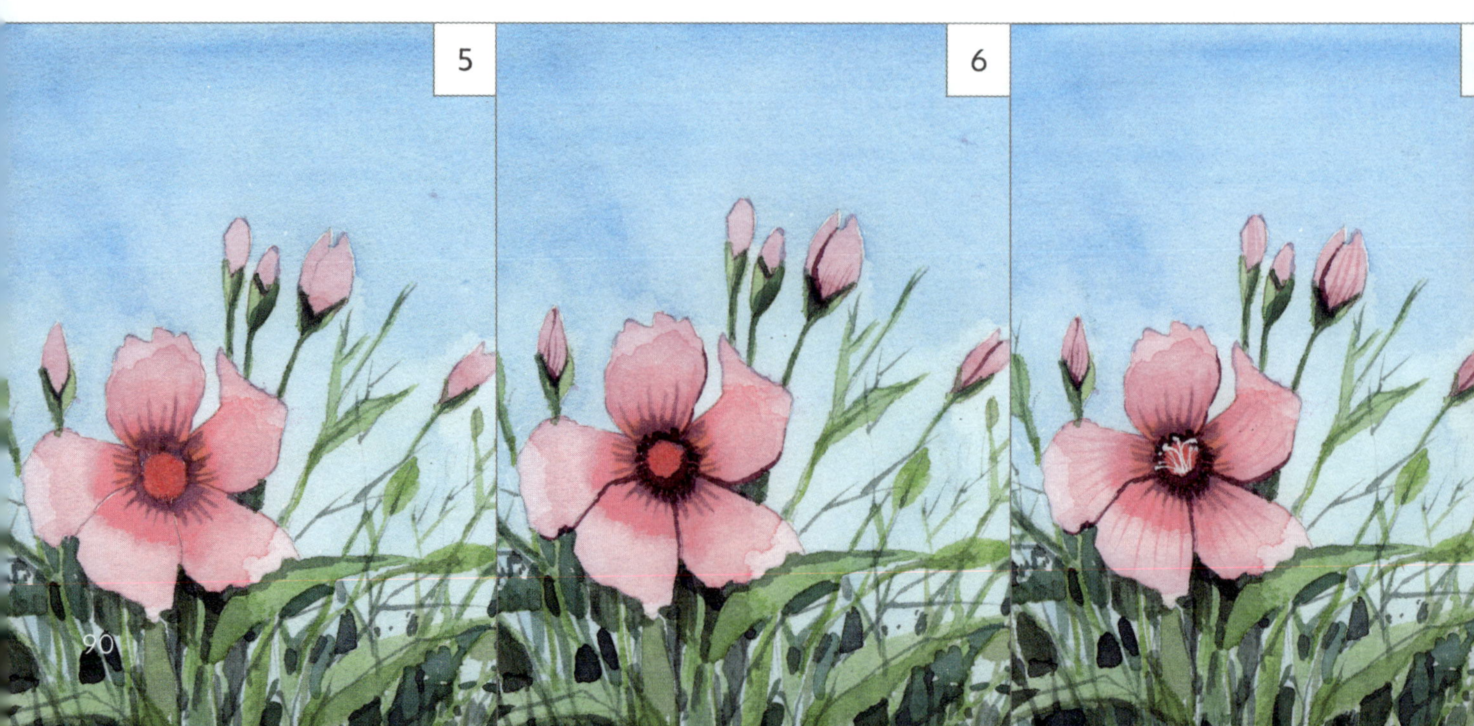

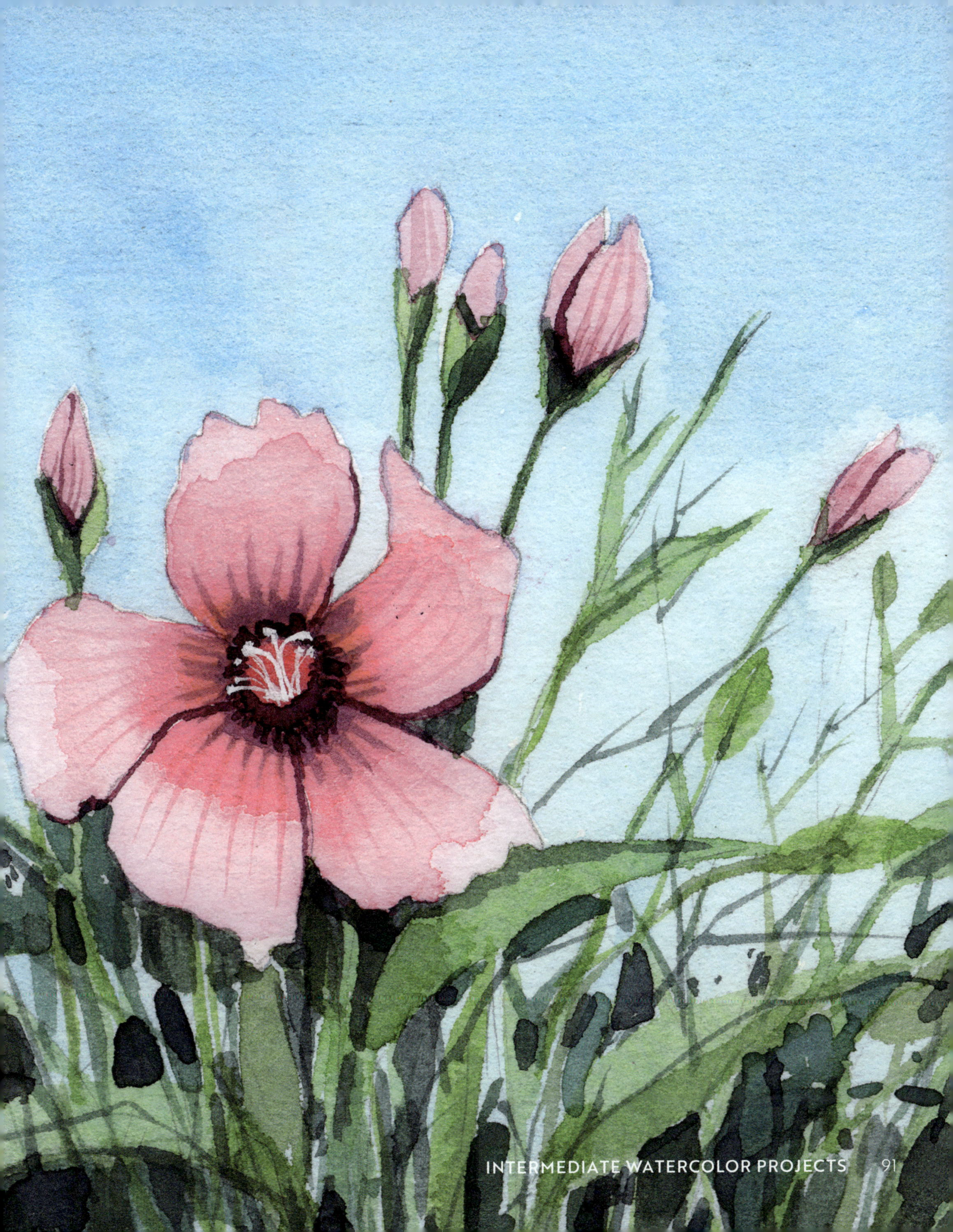

Monarch Butterfly and Flower

The Monarch butterfly is one of nature's most magnificent creatures. Its high-contrast color makes it fun and easy to paint once you break down the steps. The pink flower complements the orange, yellow, and black in the butterfly's wings.

COLORS

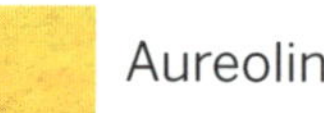 Aureolin

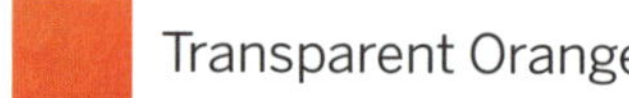 Transparent Orange

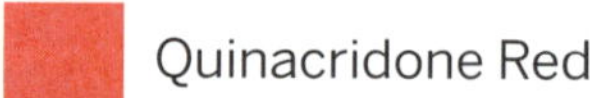 Quinacridone Red

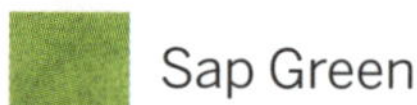 Sap Green

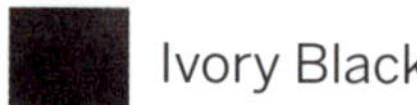 Ivory Black

TECHNIQUES

- Wet on dry
- Layering
- Masking
- Sketching

MATERIALS

- Watercolor paper, 5" × 7"
- 2H lead mechanical pencil
- Kneaded eraser
- Medium round watercolor brush
- Small round watercolor brush
- Fine-line brush
- Masking fluid or masking fluid pen
- Masking fluid eraser (optional)
- White ink (optional)
- Facial tissue

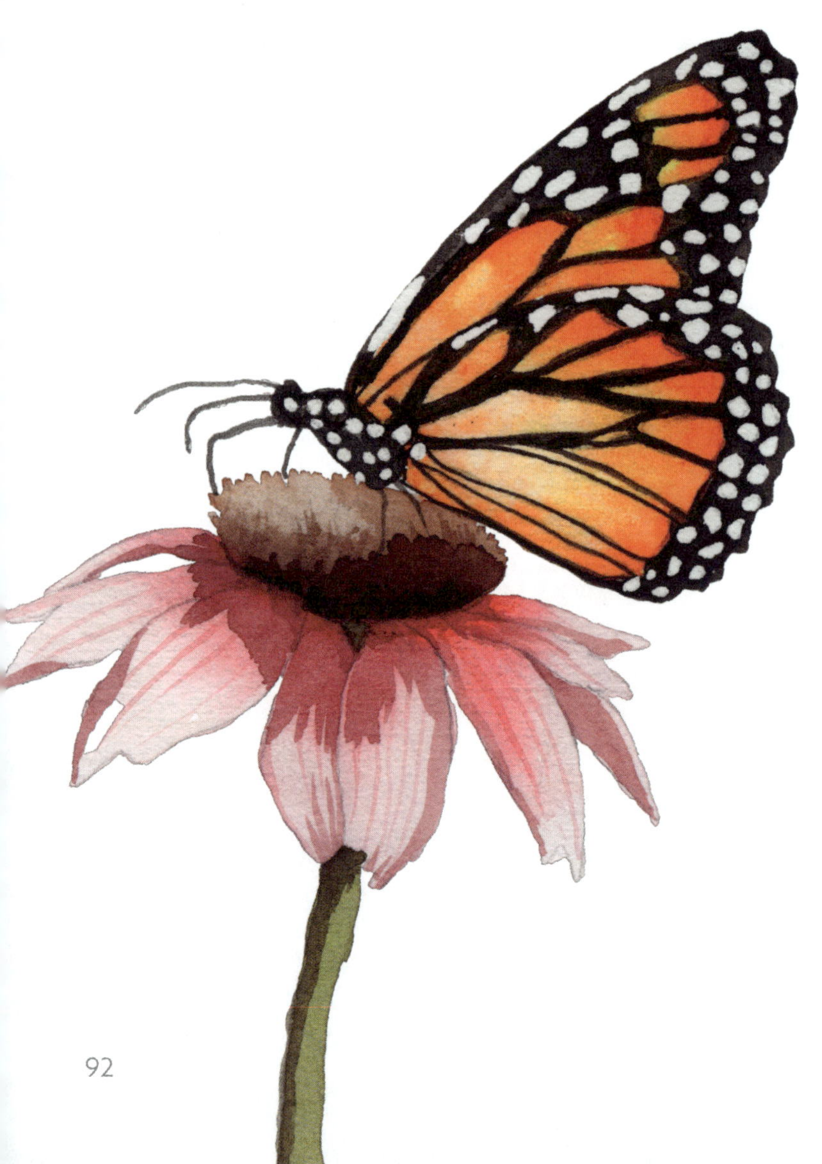

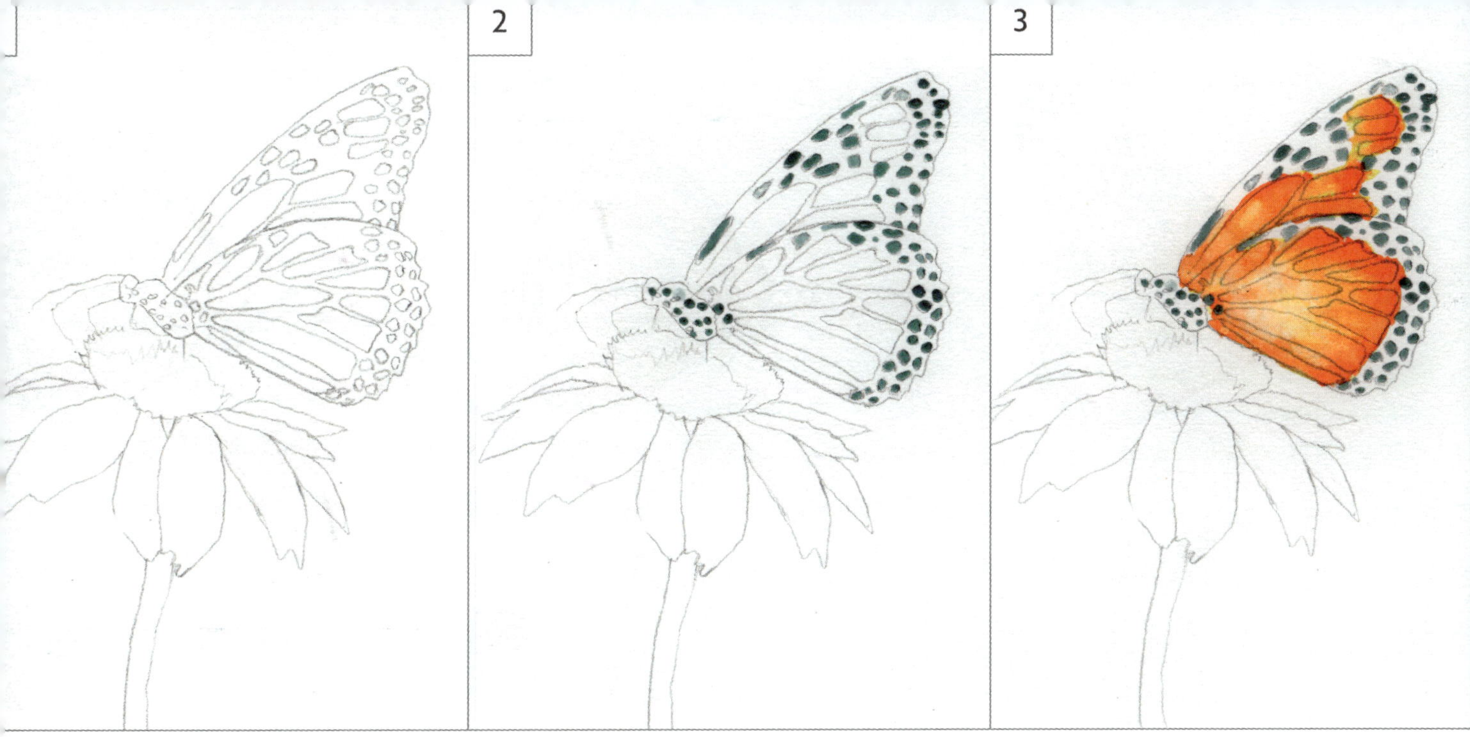

STEP ONE

Sketch the butterfly and flower on the paper with a mechanical pencil using a light touch.

STEP TWO

Apply a thin layer of masking fluid on the tips of the wings to preserve the white areas. Let dry.

OPTIONAL: Omit this step and use white ink to create details later.

STEP THREE

Mix a medium value of Aureolin (or any Transparent Yellow) with a little Transparent Orange and use a medium brush to paint in the wings closest to the body going all the way to the edges of the wings.

Drop in more Transparent Orange at the edges and let the color blend in. Blot with tissue to lighten areas in the wings. Let dry.

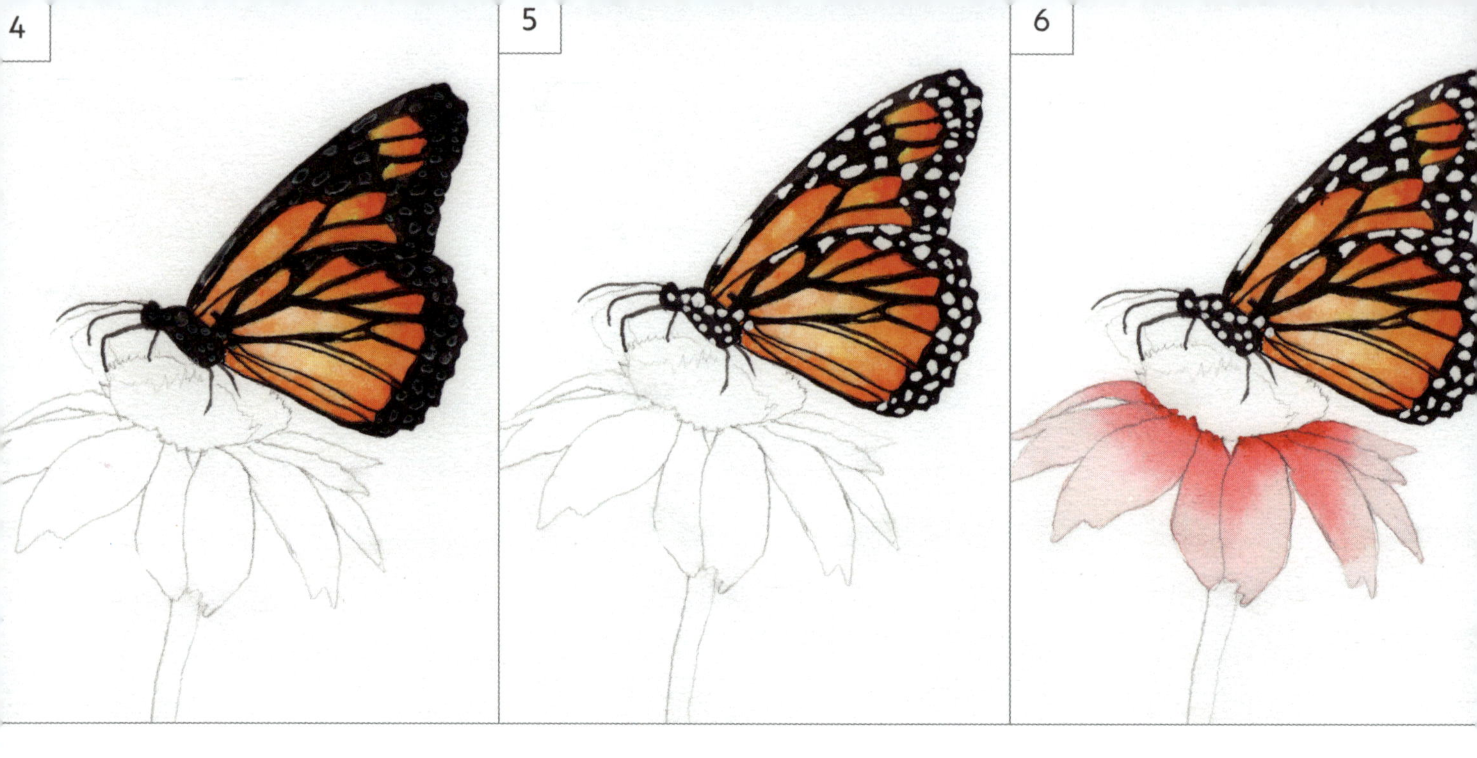

STEP FOUR

Mix a dark value of Ivory Black and use a small brush to paint the tips and the details of the wings as well as the body.

Use a fine-line brush to paint the antennae and legs. Let dry.

STEP FIVE

Carefully remove the masking fluid by rubbing it with your fingers, or use a masking fluid eraser.

STEP SIX

Paint a light wash of Quinacridone Red (palest pink) on the flower petals and drop a medium value of Quinacridone Red at the top of the petals. Drop a saturated value of Quinacridone Red at the very top of the flower while the petals are still wet. Let dry.

STEP SEVEN

Mix Transparent Orange and Ivory Black to create a medium-value warm brown. Paint the top area of the flower above the petals, and drop a darker value of the warm brown at the base.

Drop a saturated value of Quinacridone Red at the bottom edge closest to the petals. Blot the upper-left part of the top of the flower with a tissue to lighten it.

Add Sap Green to the brown mix and paint a medium-value wash on the stem. Let dry.

STEP EIGHT

Paint fine lines on the flowers and stem using the same value or a little darker value of the colors used on each part. Use a fine-line brush for details. Let dry. Erase any visible pencil lines with a kneaded eraser.

OPTIONAL: Write or stamp a sentiment or inspirational quote in the empty space below the flower.

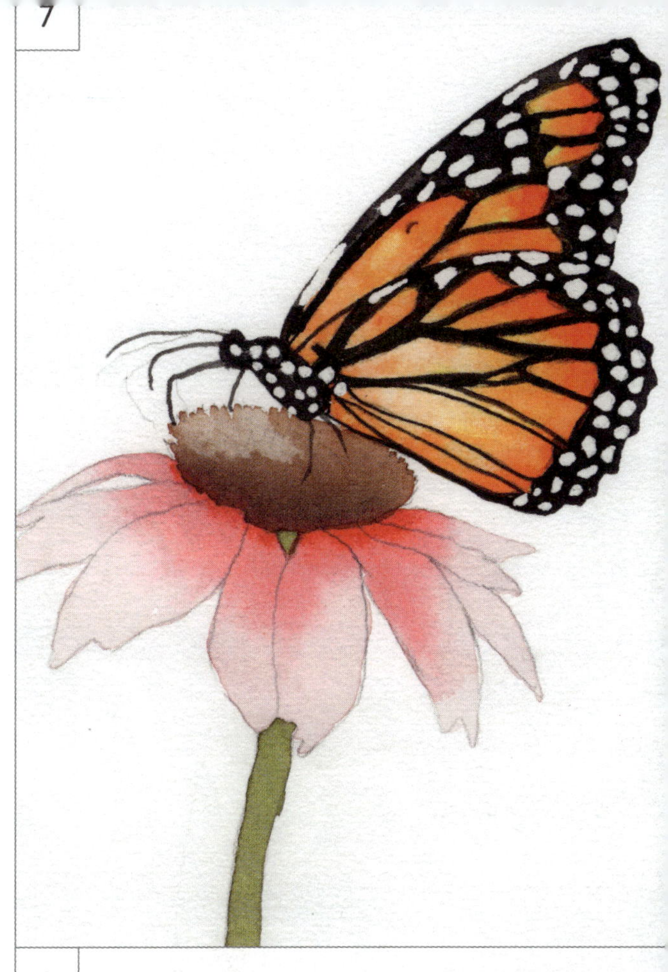

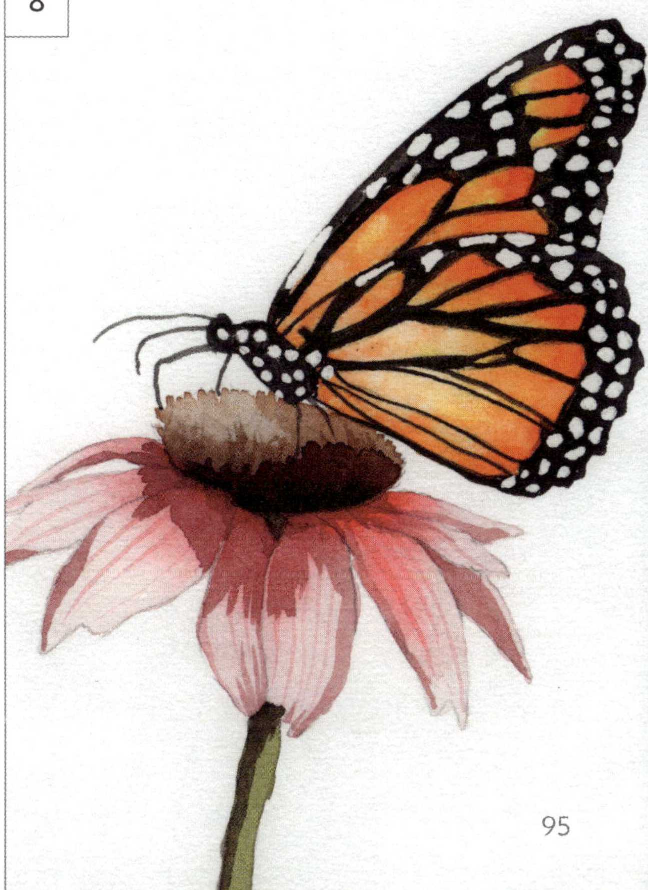

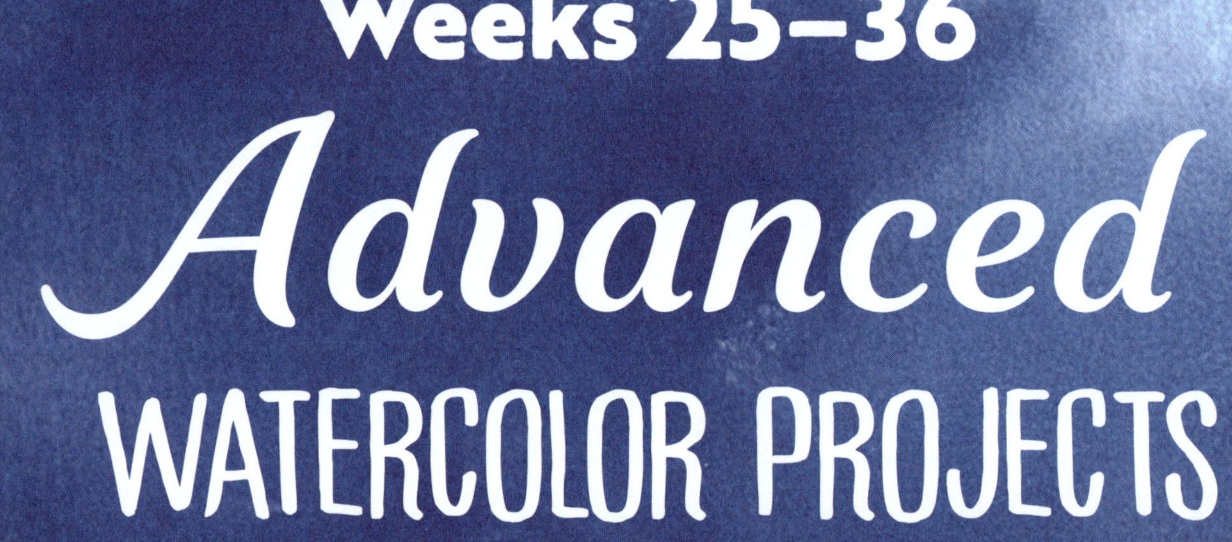

Advanced
WATERCOLOR PROJECTS

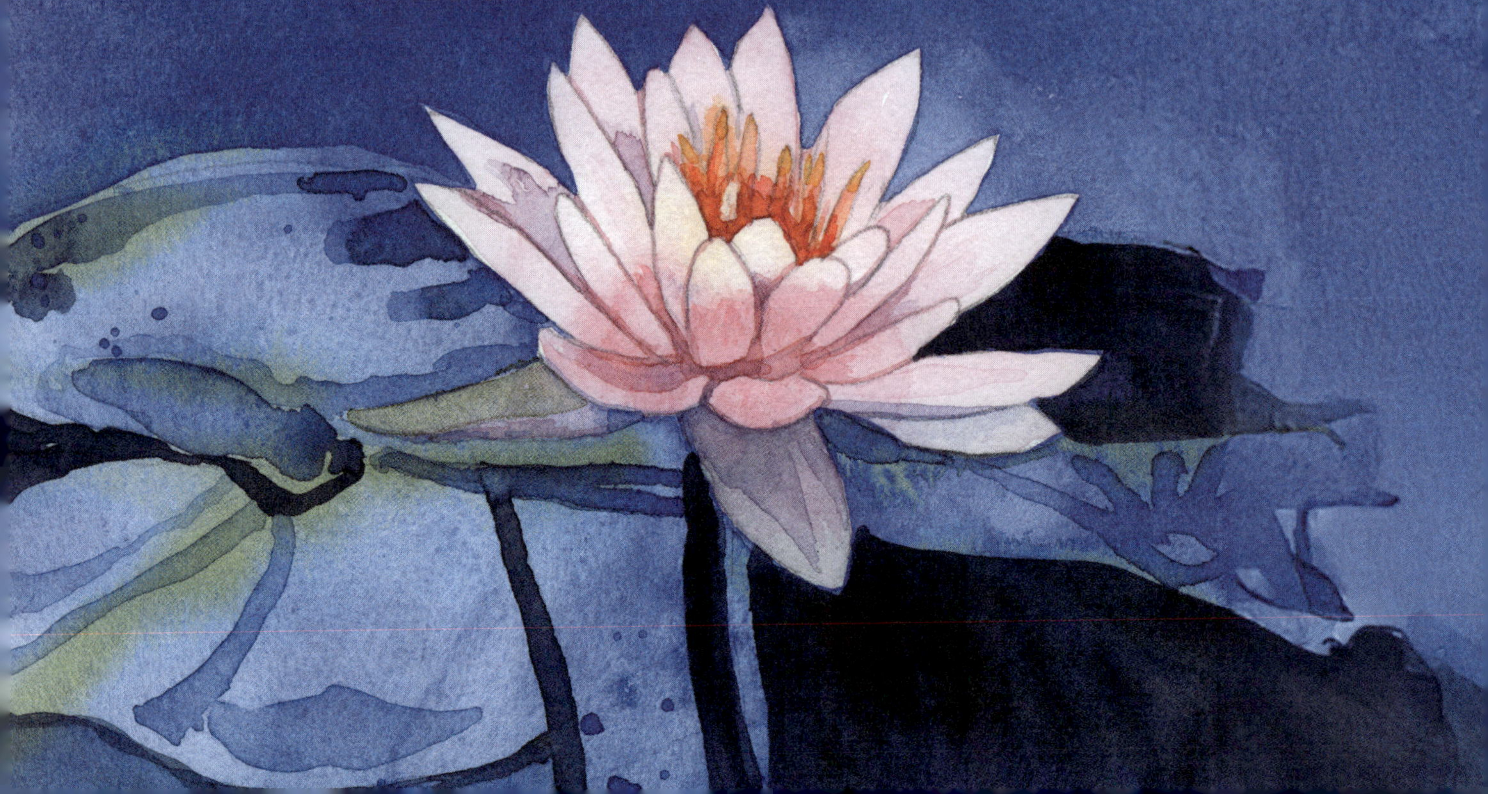

Congratulations on completing the intermediate projects! Take a moment to appreciate how far you have come since you started. Look at your earlier paintings and see the progress you've made. You should now feel more confident in your water handling, color mixing, sketching, and observation skills.

These final twelve projects are even more challenging, but by now you've acquired the skills to meet the challenge. You will also be adding a few more tools, tricks, and techniques to your watercolor practice. Let's get started!

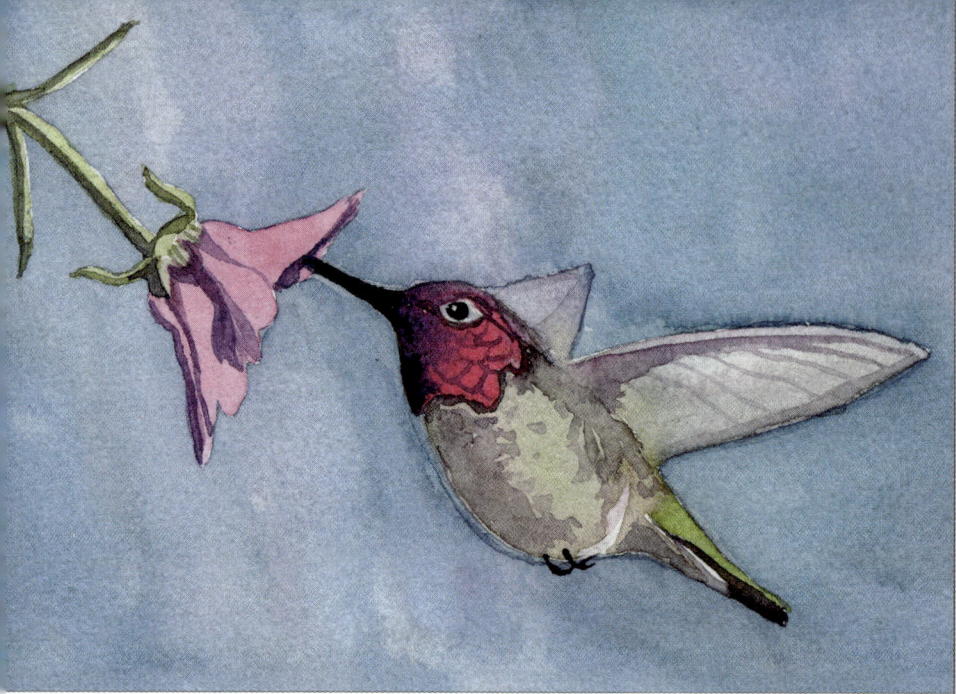

- Wet on wet
- Wet on dry
- Glazing
- Sketching

MATERIALS

- Watercolor paper, 6" × 8"
- Masking or washi tape
- Masonite panel
- 2H lead mechanical pencil
- Kneaded eraser
- Medium round watercolor brush
- Small round watercolor brush
- Fine-line brush
- White ink
- Masking fluid
- Masking fluid eraser (optional)
- Facial tissue

WEEK 25

Anna's Hummingbird

The Anna's hummingbird, originally native to California, is highly adaptable, which has enabled it to expand its range eastward to Arizona as it seeks exotic flowers in the open desert and urban gardens.

COLORS

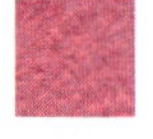 Quinacridone Magenta

 Opera Pink

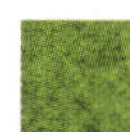 Sap Green

 Moonglow

 Payne's Gray

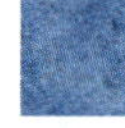 Cerulean Blue

 Prussian Blue

STEP ONE

Attach the paper to a board with masking or washi tape, creating a ½-inch border with the tape on all edges of the paper. The painting area will be 5 × 7 inches, which is perfect for framing or a greeting card.

Sketch the hummingbird and flower on the paper with a mechanical pencil. Erase any heavy or extra lines with a kneaded eraser, focusing the area on the wing tips so the lines are barely visible.

STEP TWO

Paint the flower and parts of the hummingbird with a thin layer of masking fluid. You will be painting the background first, so concentrate the masking on the outer edges of the flower and hummingbird. Let dry.

STEP THREE

Mix a light value of Cerulean Blue and use a medium brush to paint the background. While the background is still wet, drop a light value of Moonglow, Prussian Blue, and Quinacridone Magenta in random areas. Blot with a tissue to lift some color if needed. Let dry, then remove the masking fluid by rubbing it with your fingers, or use a masking fluid eraser.

STEP FOUR

Mix a dark value of Opera Pink and use a small brush to paint the area around the eye and neck of the hummingbird. Drop a small amount of Quinacridone Magenta and Prussian Blue near the beak and let it blend into the Opera Pink.

Mix a dark value of Payne's Gray and use a small brush to paint the beak. Mix a light value of Prussian Blue and Payne's Gray and paint the wings. Drop a small amount of Quinacridone Magenta at the tip of the top wing.

CONTINUED ➡

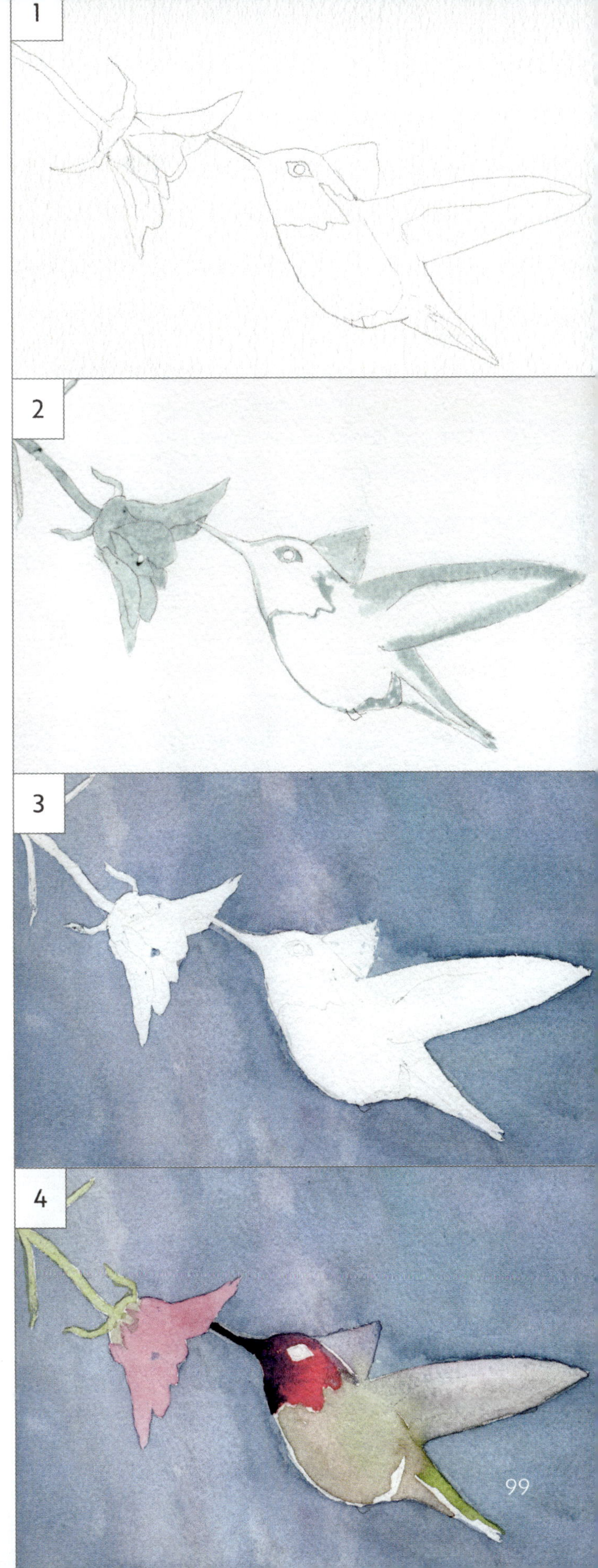

Mix a medium to light value of Sap Green and paint the top of the tail and belly area. Drop a light value of Quinacridone Magenta on the edges and let the colors blend together.

Mix a light to medium value of Opera Pink and Quinacridone Magenta and use a medium brush to paint the flower.

Mix a light value of Sap Green with a tiny amount of Quinacridone Magenta and paint the stem and leaves of the flower. Let dry.

STEP FIVE

Using the existing colors in your palette, use a small brush to paint details and shadows in the flower and stem with a medium value of the green mixture. Paint details and shadows in the wings and body using a light-value mix of Quinacridone Magenta and Moonglow.

Use a fine-line brush to make the feather shapes in the neck and feathers in the wings using the same color.

Mix a little Payne's Gray with Moonglow for a darker-value color and paint the tip of the tail and the feet. Soften the edges of the humming-bird with a line of light-value Prussian Blue.

Paint a tiny dot on the eye with white ink. Let dry, then carefully remove the masking tape.

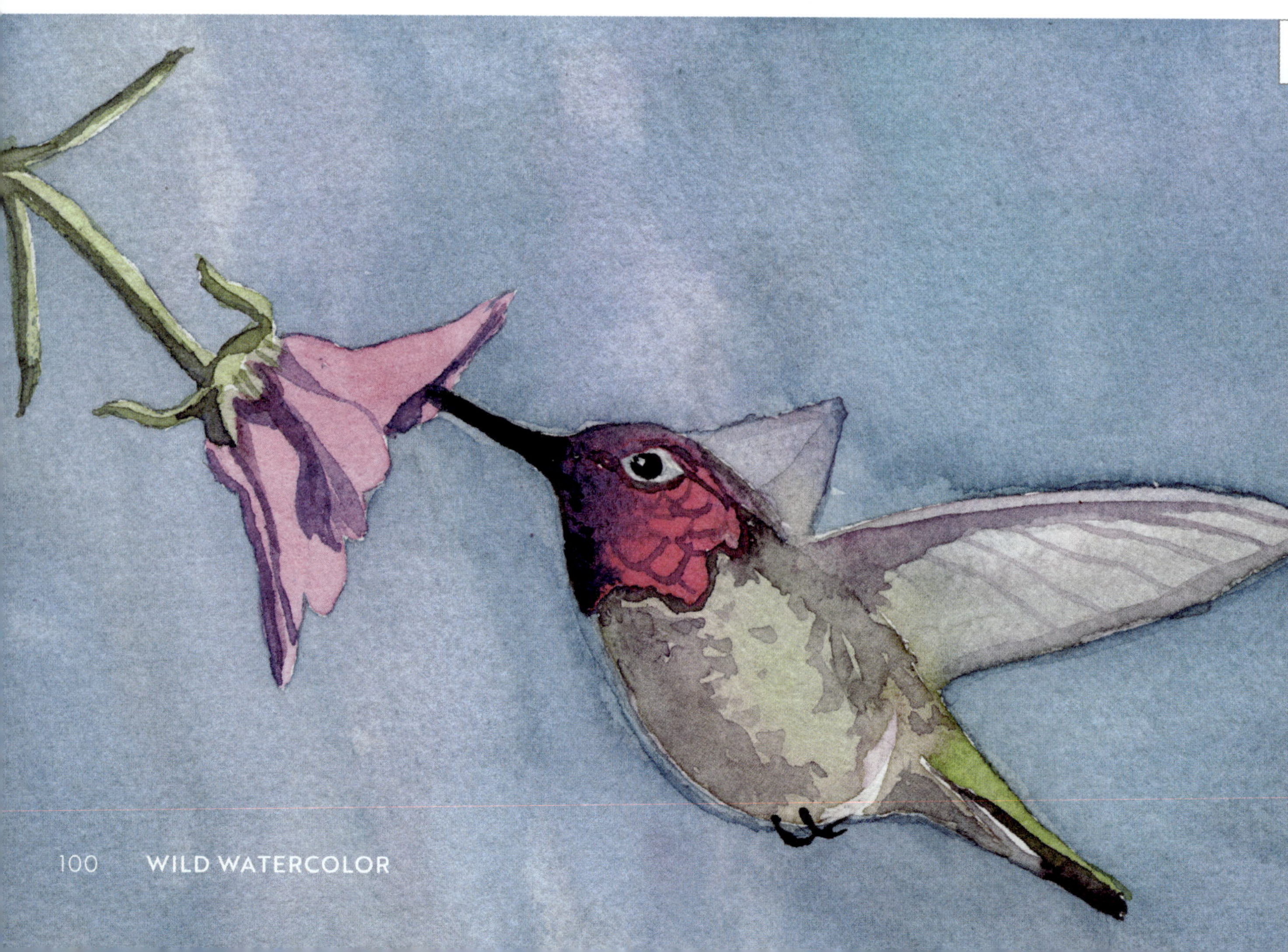

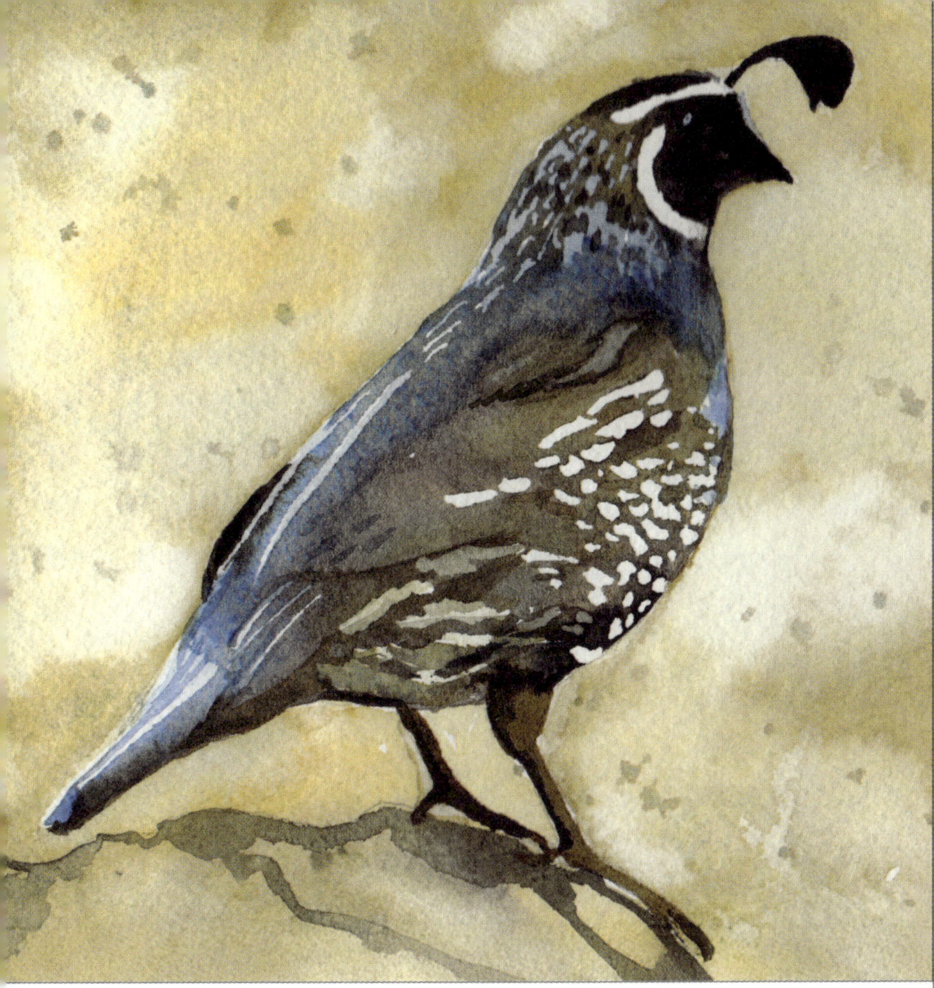

WEEK 26
Desert Quail

A cute topknot on the head easily distinguishes the quail, which we see running and hopping among the shrubs and trees in the desert instead of flying.

COLORS

 Quinacridone Gold

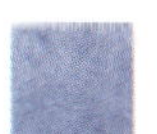 Ultramarine Blue

 Shadow Violet

 Payne's Gray

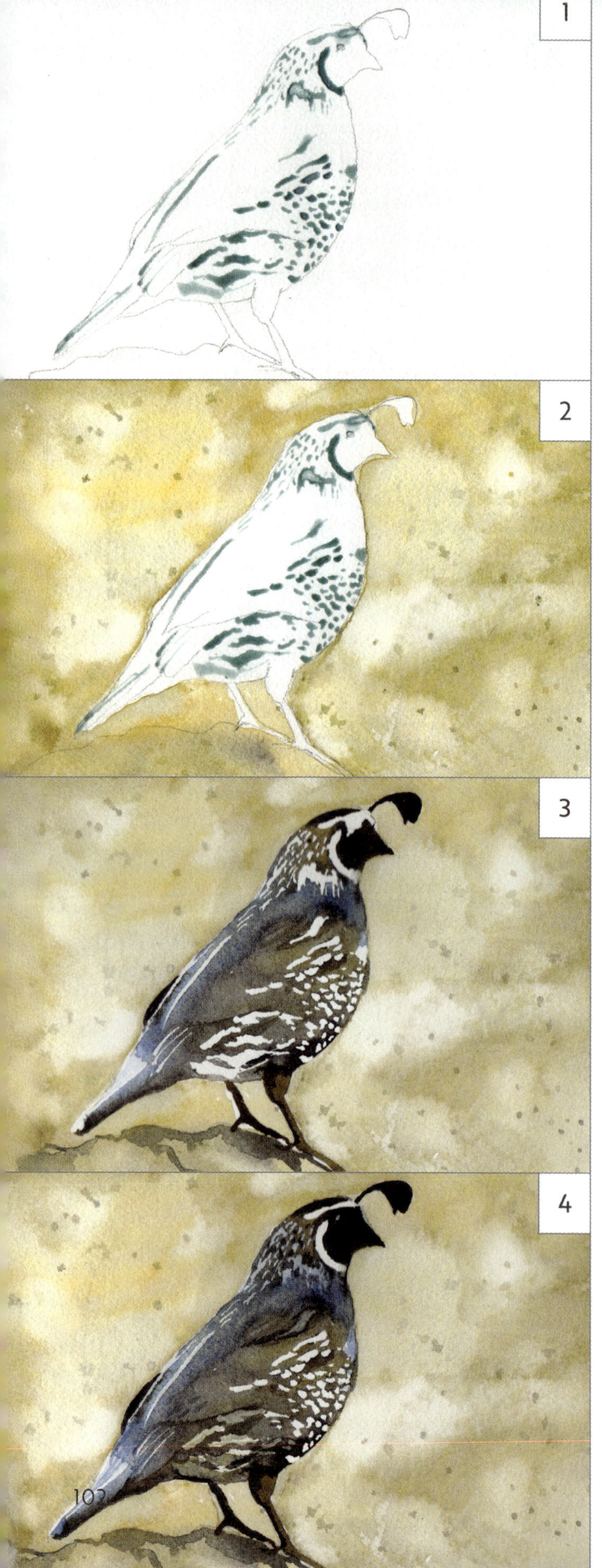

STEP ONE
Sketch the quail and rock shape on the paper with a mechanical pencil using a light touch. Draw the white areas with the masking fluid or masking pen on the head and body. Let dry completely.

STEP TWO
Mix a very light value of Quinacridone Gold and Shadow Violet and use a medium brush to paint the background with an even wash. Wet a brush with water and go back into the wash in areas with the tip of the brush and blot with tissue. The color will lift in the places touched with the wet brush, bringing out lighter areas, creating a mottled texture.

Splatter the background lightly with a light value of Shadow Violet. Blot with tissue as needed. Let dry.

STEP THREE
Mix a light value of Ultramarine Blue and paint the chest, back, and tail of the quail, then follow with a medium-value mix of Shadow Violet and Quinacridone Gold in the wing, tail, and belly, letting the warm color blend with the blue.

Mix a dark value of Payne's Gray and Shadow Violet. Using a small brush, paint the head, beak, topknot, tips of the wings, legs, and feet; drop some of the darker gray into the wing area.

Paint some shadows in the rock with the same mixture. Let dry completely, then carefully remove the masking fluid by rubbing it with your fingers, or use a masking fluid eraser.

STEP FOUR
Paint some details in the quail using a diluted wash of the colors already in your palette.

Soften the white masked areas around the neck, back, and tail with a light-value mix of Ultramarine Blue and Payne's Gray.

Soften the white areas under the body with a light-value mix of Shadow Violet. Mix a dark value of Payne's Gray and Shadow Violet to bring out details in the head and create shadows on the legs and feet. Mix some white ink with Ultramarine Blue to make a dot for the highlight in the eye. Let dry.

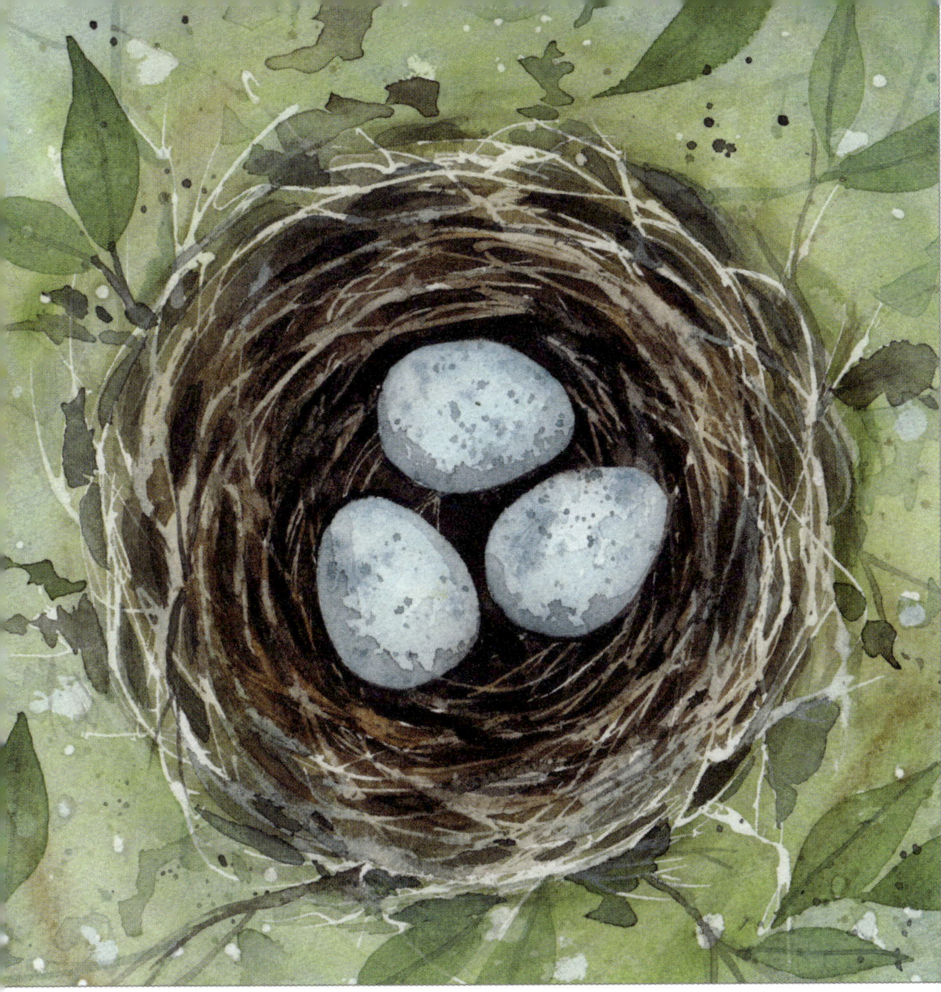

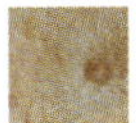
Raw Umber

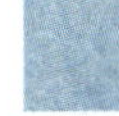
Cerulean Blue

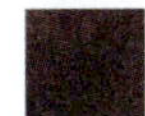
Sepia

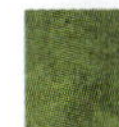
Sap Green

Payne's Gray

TECHNIQUES

- Wet on wet
- Value study
- Masking
- Layering
- Splattering
- Sketching

MATERIALS

- Watercolor paper, 8" × 8"
- Masking or washi tape
- Masonite panel
- 2H lead mechanical pencil
- Medium round watercolor brush
- Small round watercolor brush
- Masking fluid
- Making fluid pen
- Masking fluid eraser (optional)

WEEK 27

Bird's Nest with Spotted Eggs

A bird's nest is a fascinating wonder of creativity and engineering; it is much more than an egg container. The blue speckled eggs of a robin pop against the neutral colors of the nest. Painting a bird's nest with eggs is easy if you have the right tools and techniques.

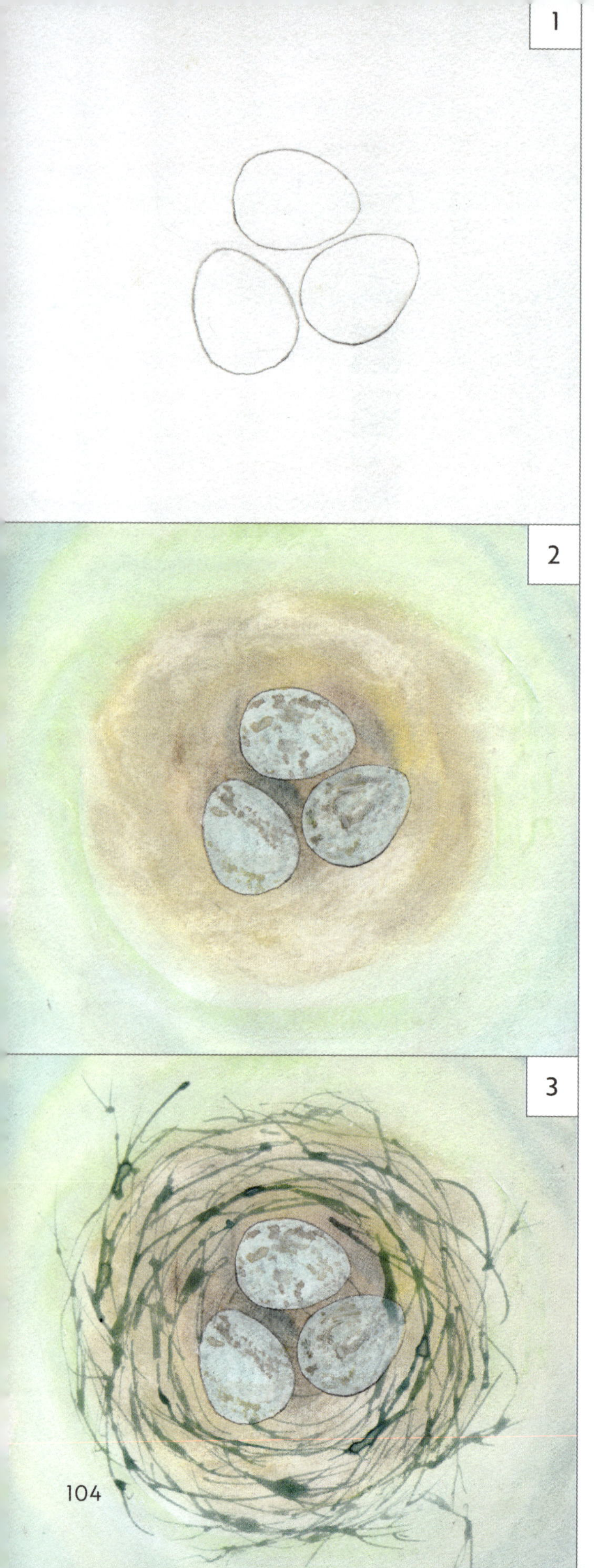

STEP ONE

Attach the paper to a board with masking or washi tape, creating a border with the tape around all edges of the paper. Sketch three egg shapes in the center of the paper with a mechanical pencil using a light touch.

Paint an even layer of masking fluid on the eggs and let dry. I prefer using Pebeo Drawing Gum because it brushes on easily and is tinted so you can see what you have masked off. I filled a fine-line pen with the drawing gum to make the fine lines.

OPTIONAL: Sketch the eggs on a separate sheet until you achieve the shape you want and then trace or transfer the egg drawing onto your watercolor paper before attaching it to the board.

STEP TWO

Make separate light-value puddles of Raw Umber, Cerulean Blue, Sap Green, and Sepia in your palette. Using a medium brush, paint a very-light-value loose wash over the masked eggs with Raw Umber and Sepia, starting at the center of the paper.

Follow with a very light wash of Sap Green, then Cerulean Blue to the edge of the paper, painting in a circular motion with your brush. Let dry.

STEP THREE

Draw thin, irregular lines representing twigs and the nest using a masking fluid pen or a fine-line brush loaded with masking fluid. Be generous with this step. It's better to have more masking fluid than not enough. Let dry.

STEP FOUR

Mix a medium-value Raw Umber and Sepia in your palette and loosely paint a wash, starting at the center, over the eggs and outward to the edge of the nest. Let dry, then draw more irregular lines in a circular direction with the masking pen. Splatter some masking fluid on the edge of the nest on all sides of the paper. Let dry.

STEP FIVE

Mix a dark-value Sepia and Payne's Gray in your palette. Brush this over the eggs and make short, irregular strokes to the edge of the nest. Mix a medium-value Sap Green and brush it around the nest, followed by a light wash of Cerulean Blue.

Drop a medium value of Raw Umber on the outer edges of the nest. Let dry, then carefully remove the masking fluid by rubbing it with your fingers, or use a masking fluid eraser.

STEP SIX

Paint shadows and details in the nest using a mix of Sepia and Payne's Gray. Drop some Raw Umber in the areas around the eggs. Keep painting layers, concentrating at the center of the nest in the area below the eggs, to achieve depth and contrast.

Paint branches and leaves with a mix of Sap Green and Cerulean Blue. Mix a light value of Cerulean Blue and paint an even wash on the eggs. Drop in a medium-value blue around the edges of the eggs to create a shadow and bring out the eggs' round shape. Mix a little Payne's Gray in the Cerulean Blue and splatter it on the eggs with a small brush. Let dry.

CONTINUED →

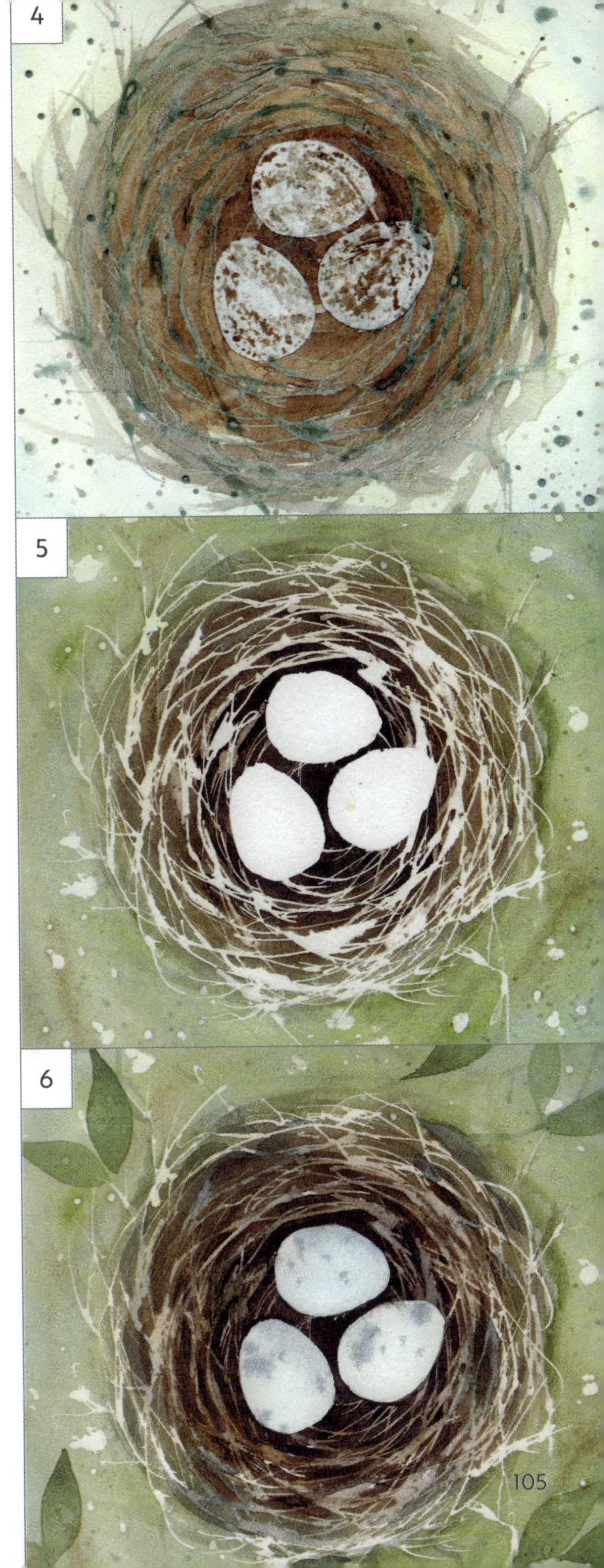

Create shadows on the eggs with a medium-value mix of Cerulean Blue and Payne's Gray. Splatter some of the blue mixture onto the eggs.

Paint more shadows using Sepia and Payne's Gray to bring out details in the nest.

Splatter the outside of the nest with pale mixtures of blue and Payne's Gray. Rotate the painting and bring out more details as needed with a small brush. Let dry, then carefully remove the masking tape.

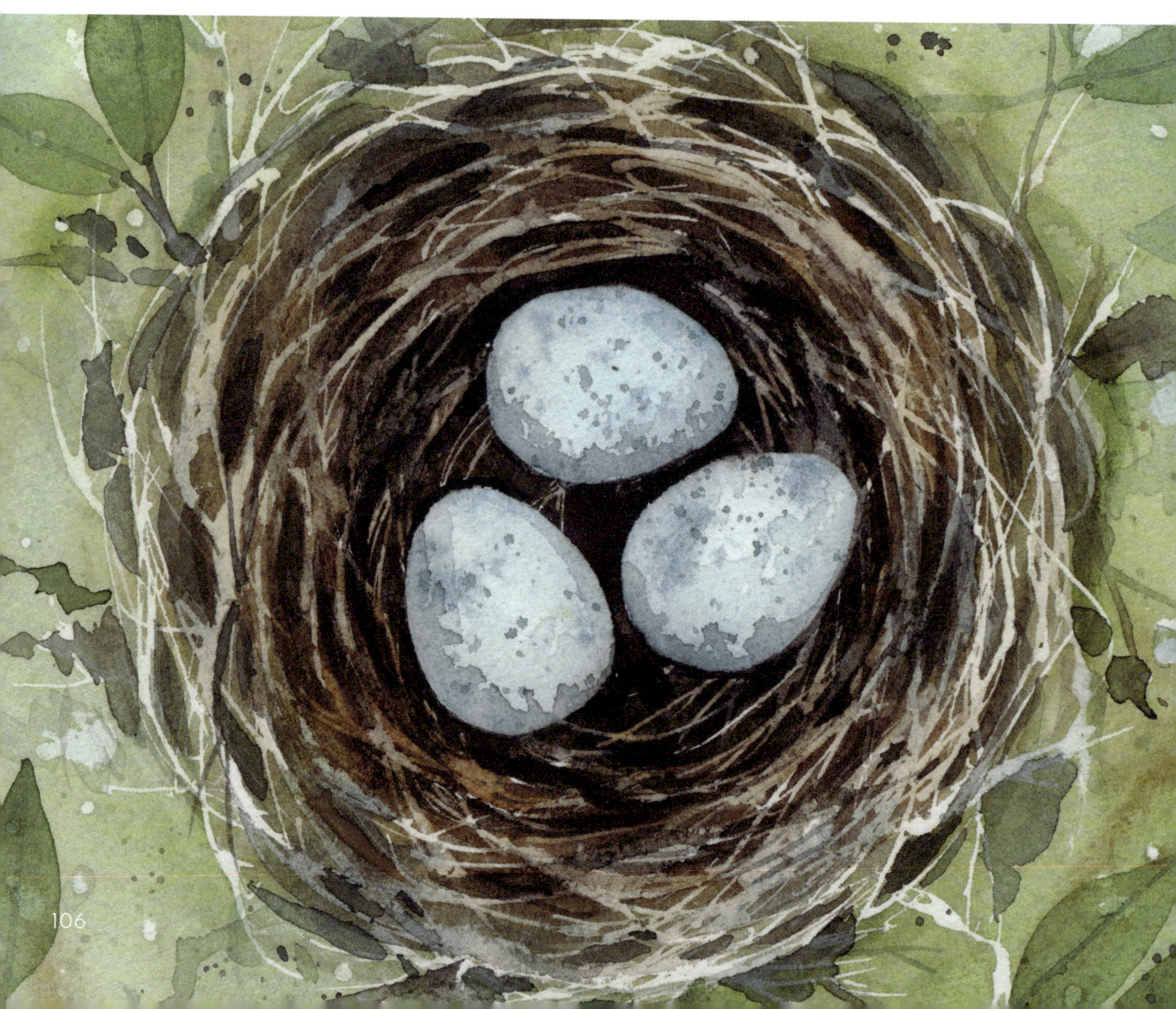

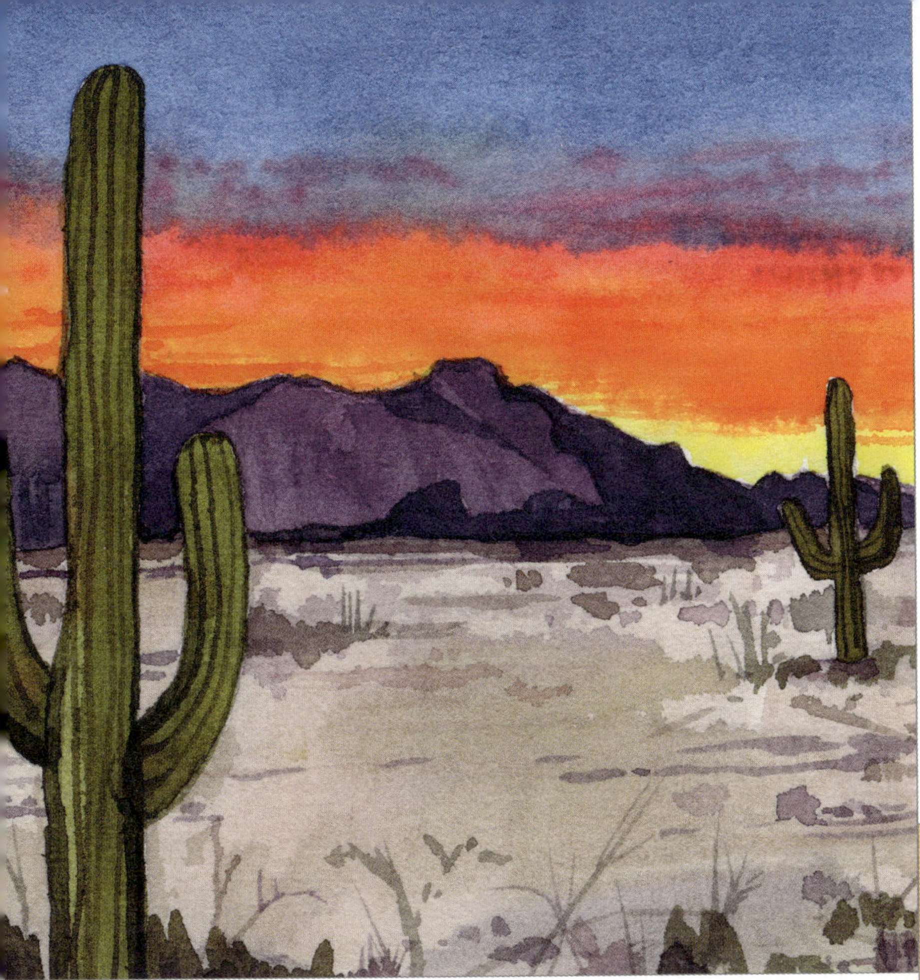

COLORS

Hansa Yellow

Transparent Orange

Quinacridone Magenta

Raw Umber

Sap Green

Payne's Gray

Phthalo Blue (Red Shade)

WEEK 28
Sonoran Sunset

The vibrant colors of a desert sky as the sun drops behind the mountains are beautiful and inspiring but more challenging to paint. You will learn to choose the right colors for wet-on-wet blending for a brilliant sunset, majestic mountains, and dramatic saguaro cactus silhouettes.

TECHNIQUES

- Wet on wet
- Layering
- Color mixing
- Sketching
- Perspective

MATERIALS

- Watercolor paper, 6″ × 6″
- Masking or washi tape
- Masonite panel
- 2H lead mechanical pencil
- Medium round watercolor brush
- Small round watercolor brush
- Fine-line brush
- Facial tissue

STEP ONE

Attach the paper to a board with masking or washi tape, creating a ¼-inch border with the tape on all edges of the paper. Sketch the mountains, horizon, and cactus shapes on the paper with a mechanical pencil using a light touch.

STEP TWO

Wet the sky area with clear water until it is shiny but not dripping wet. Load the medium round brush with an intense value of Hansa Yellow and drop it at the base of the sky on top of the mountains. The yellow will spread upward.

Load the brush with Transparent Orange and drop it right above the yellow area, followed by an intense value of Quinacridone Magenta. While still wet, load the brush with a medium value of Phthalo Blue (Red Shade) and brush it at the top edge of the paper. Blot any excess yellow moving into the blue area with a tissue to avoid a green sky. Finally, while the sky is still wet, load the tip of the brush with more Quinacridone Magenta and tap the color into the orange and blue areas and sweep lightly in a horizontal direction. Let the colors blend and dry.

STEP THREE

Mix Phthalo Blue (Red Shade) and Quinacridone Magenta into a medium-value purple and load the medium brush with the mixture. Paint an even wash on the mountains.

Load the brush with Payne's Gray and paint the mountain shadows. Let dry.

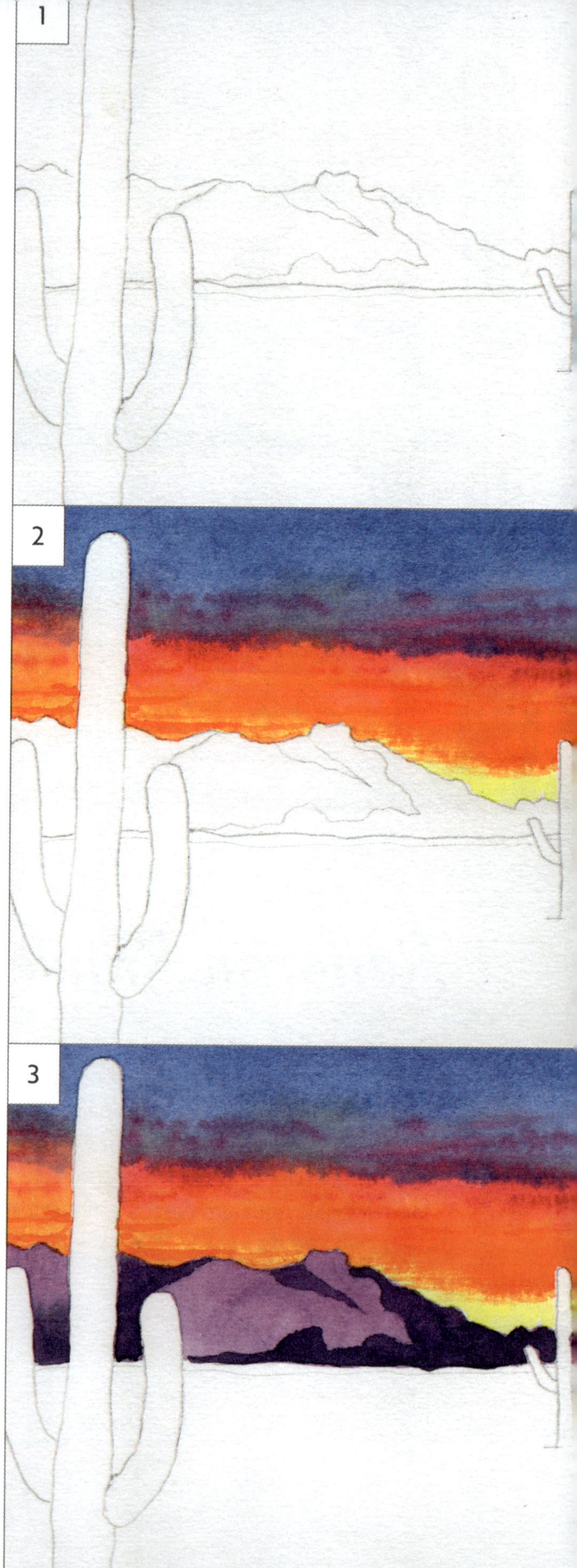

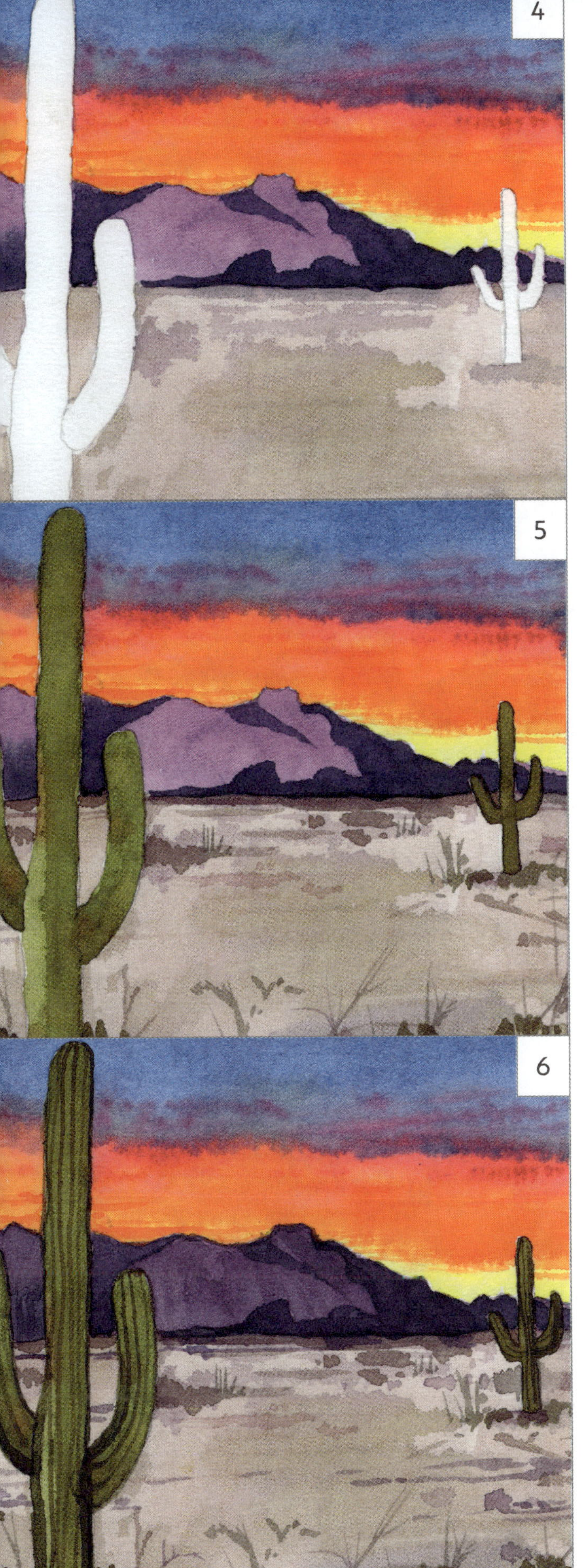

STEP FOUR

Mix Raw Umber with a tiny amount of Sap Green, making a light-value neutral sand color. Brush this evenly onto the ground under the mountains and horizon.

Drop a tiny bit of the purple mixture from the mountains into the area just below the mountains and some areas of the foreground. Do this while the sand color paint is still damp so it spreads.

Mix a small amount of light-value Sap Green and drop it into random areas of the sand color while it's still damp. Let dry.

STEP FIVE

Mix Sap Green and Raw Umber for a medium-value green and paint the large cactus starting with the body of the cactus, then the arms. Drop a small amount of medium-value Transparent Orange and Hansa Yellow in a couple areas of the cactus while still damp.

Add a little Payne's Gray to the green mixture and paint the smaller cactus a little darker than the larger one.

Mix a little water with the colors already in the palette and use a small brush to paint loose details representing rocks and twigs in the sand-colored foreground. Drop some diluted purple mixture into some of the areas as well.

Use a fine-line brush to paint thin strokes of green mixed with a small amount of magenta to represent dry grasses and twigs. Let dry.

STEP SIX

Add a little Payne's Gray and Transparent Orange to the green color and paint details in the cactus using a fine-line brush.

Paint loose details representing rocks and twigs in the foreground area using the dark-green mix. Add more details with small, loose brush strokes as needed. Paint more details in the mountains with the purple mixture and add some in the foreground to finish. Let dry, then carefully remove the masking tape.

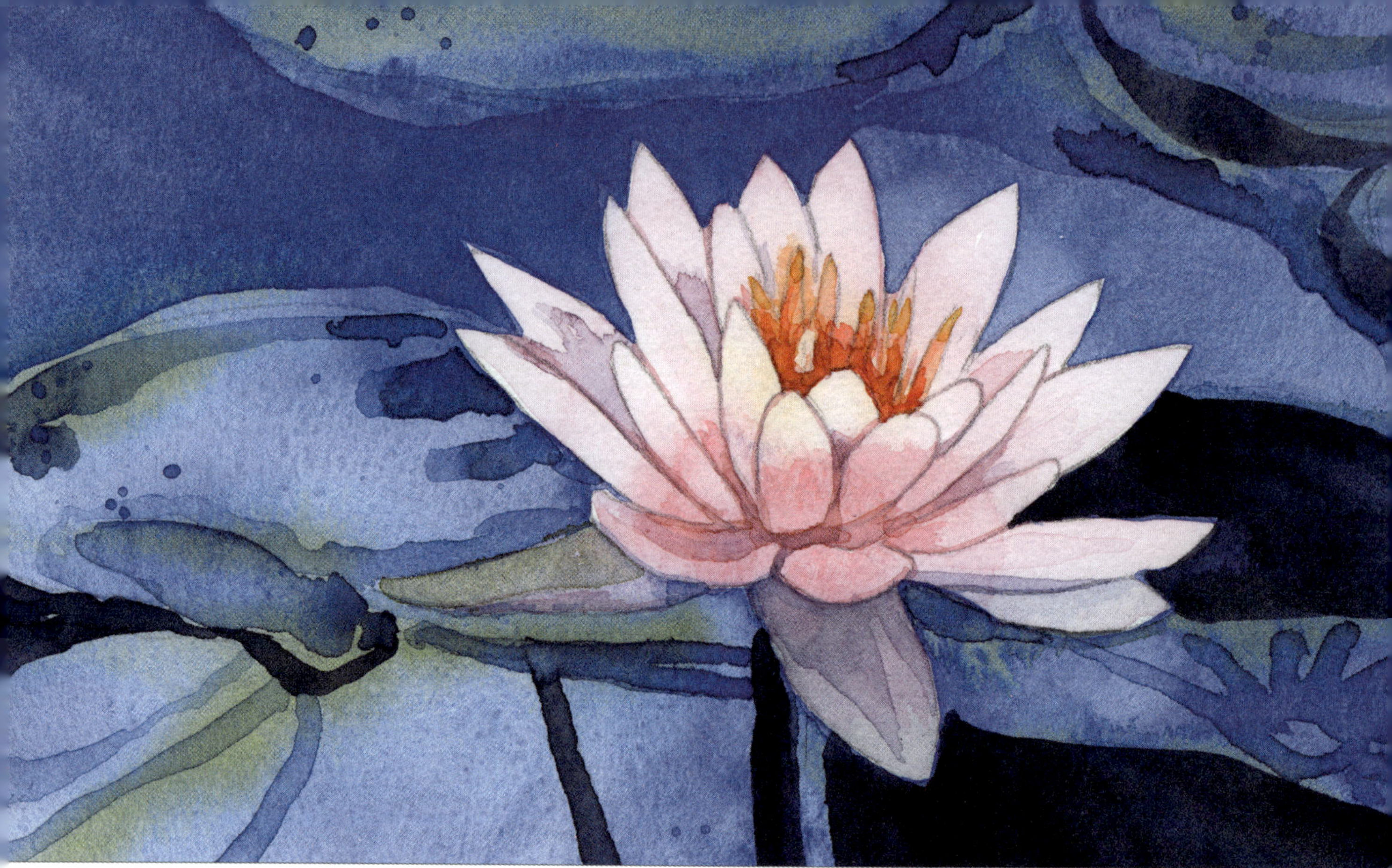

WEEK 29
Water Lily

Water lilies are beautiful flowering aquatic plants that thrive on lakes and in still fresh waters and they have inspired artists for centuries. In this lesson, you will paint a dramatic, saturated background first, then the delicate petals of the lily.

COLORS

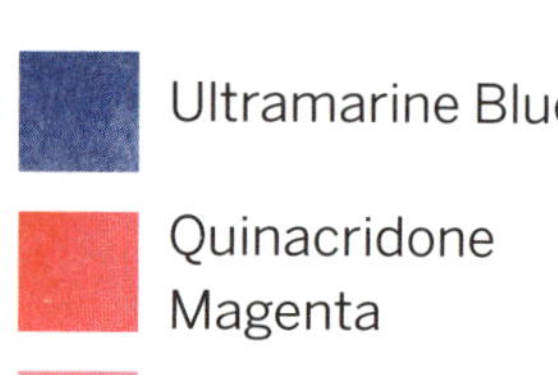

- Ultramarine Blue
- Quinacridone Magenta
- Opera Rose

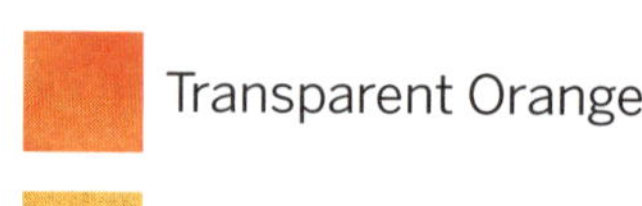
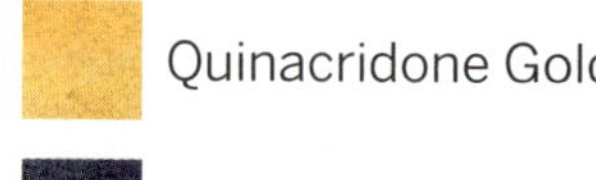

- Transparent Orange
- Quinacridone Gold
- Payne's Gray

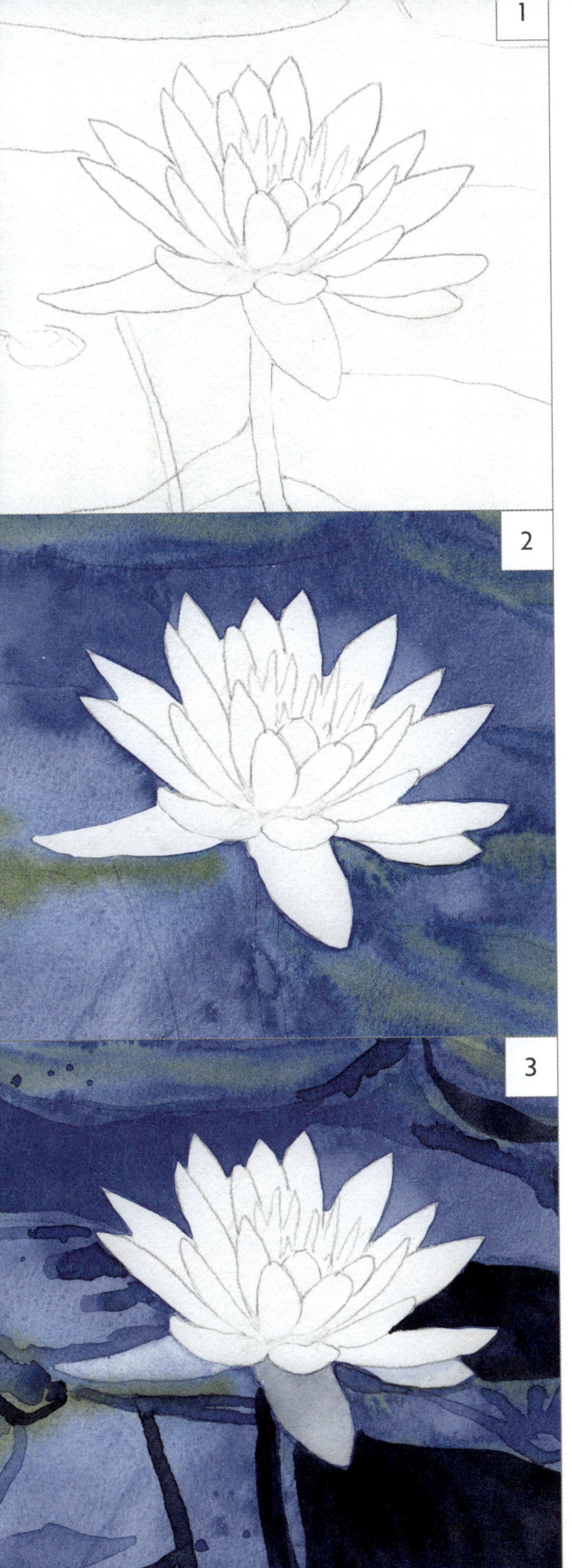

STEP ONE

Sketch the lily and basic lily pad shapes on the paper with the mechanical pencil using a light touch. Soften heavy lines with a kneaded eraser.

STEP TWO

Prepare a generous mix of medium- to dark-value Ultramarine Blue in your palette. Using a medium brush, apply a fairly even wash around the lily. It is easier to start with the tip of your brush and move outward from the flower.

While the wash is still wet, brush a light value of Quinacridone Gold in the lily pad shapes. Ultramarine Blue is a granulating color so it will have an interesting texture when it dries. Watch the Quinacridone Gold push the blue and spread into soft green-yellow values. Let dry.

STEP THREE

Mix Ultramarine Blue with Payne's Gray for a dark-value color and paint an even wash of dark in some areas under the lily pad shapes. Paint the stems under the lily and some details on the lily pads.

Splatter some medium-value Ultramarine Blue on a few small areas of the lily pads being careful not to splatter it on the lily. Thin the blue-gray mixture with water and paint a light wash on three of the lower petals. Let dry.

STEP FOUR

Mix a very light value of Quinacridone Rose and Opera Pink and paint a very pale wash inside the petals of the lily.

Drop a medium value of Quinacridone Magenta and Opera Rose into the base of the petals and in the center of the flower. Drop a little Quinacridone Gold in the center stamen area of the flower. Let dry.

STEP FIVE

Paint details in the flower with a light-value mix of Quinacridone Magenta and Opera Rose.

Drop a medium value of the pink mix at the base of each area just painted.

Add a small amount of light-value Ultramarine Blue in some of the areas just painted while they're still wet. Let dry.

STEP SIX

Using a fine-line brush, paint thin, delicate lines with a light-value pink mixture along the visible pencil lines to create details around the edges of the petals and stamen. This will create more definition and contrast.

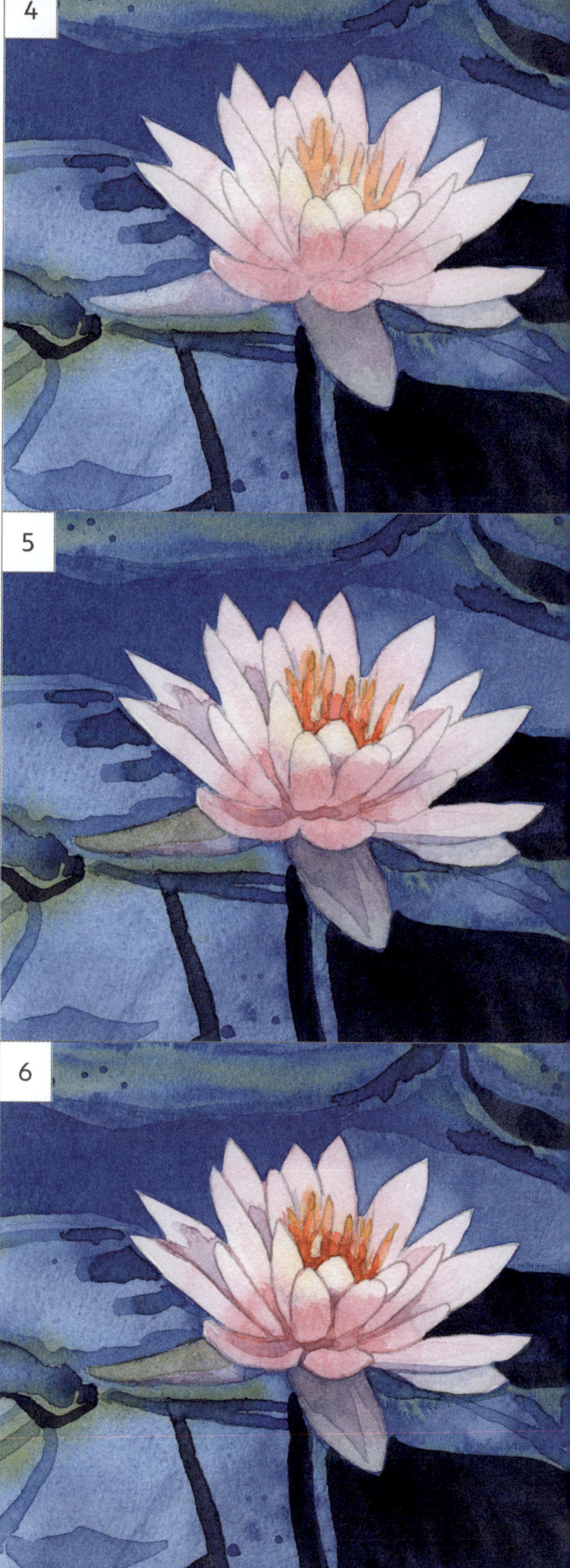

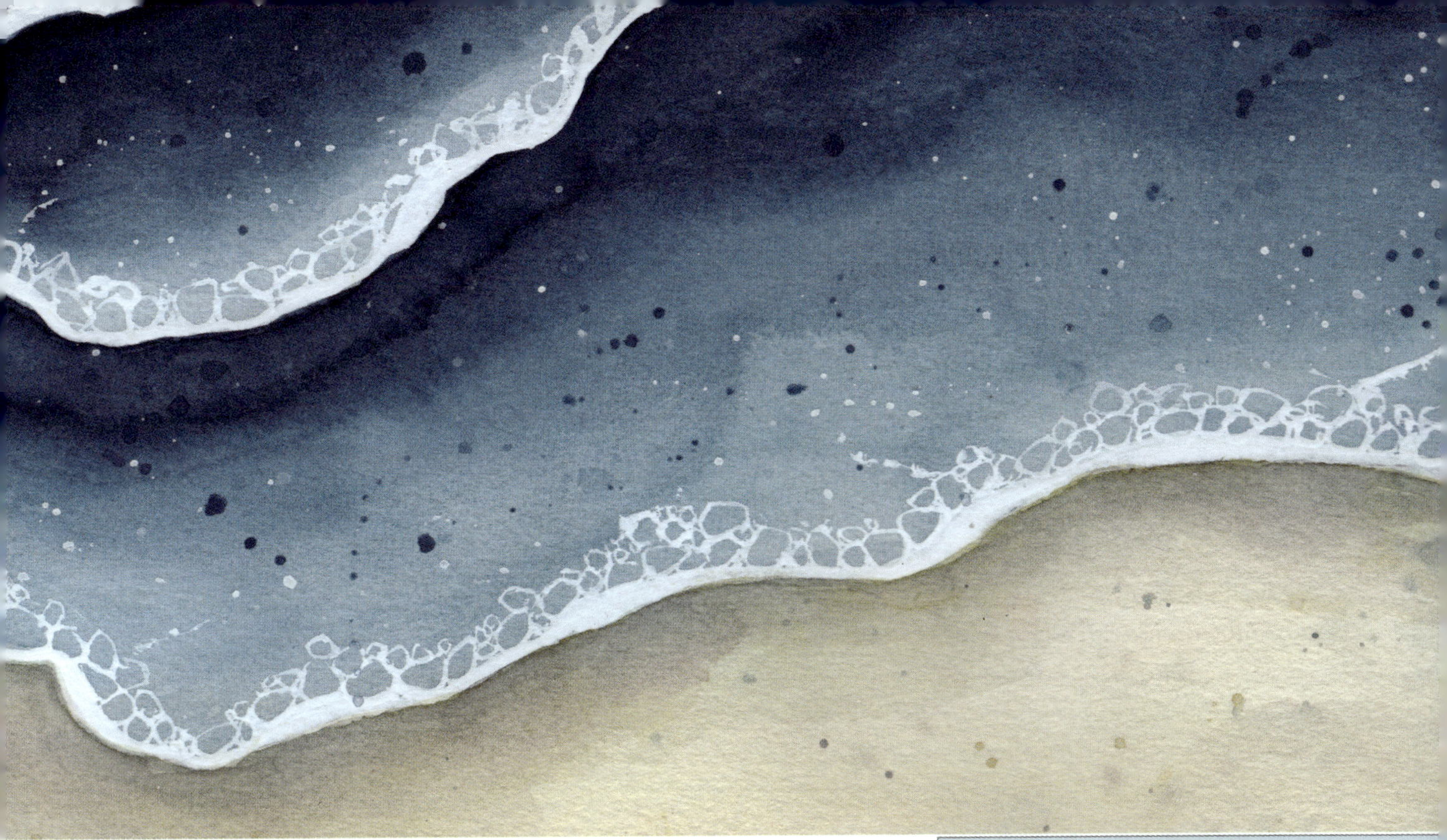

Seagull's Beach View

Imagine a seagull flying low over the shoreline watching the waves crash onto the soft sand. This watercolor painting project evokes memories of the ocean's calming colors, scents, and sounds.

COLORS

 Moonglow

 Burnt Slenna

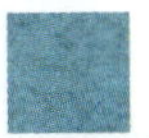 Phthalo Turquoise

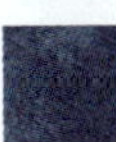 Indigo (or a mix of Phthalo Blue, black, and magenta)

TECHNIQUES

- Wet on wet
- Wet on dry
- Glazing
- Highlighting
- Splattering

MATERIALS

- Watercolor paper, 5" × 7"
- Masking or washi tape
- Masonite panel
- 2H lead mechanical pencil
- Medium round watercolor brush
- Fine-line brush
- White ink
- Facial tissue

STEP ONE

Attach the paper in landscape orientation to a board with masking or washi tape, creating a thin border with the tape around all edges of the paper. Draw three curvy "wave break" lines on the paper with a mechanical pencil.

STEP TWO

Using a medium brush loaded with clear water, wet the paper evenly. The paper should have a satin sheen but not be too shiny.

Mix a small amount of Burnt Sienna with lots of water for a very pale yellow. Starting at the bottom of the paper, brush the yellow watercolor close to the first wave break line.

Load the brush with a light value of Phthalo Turquoise and paint just above the first wave break line, going all the way to the top of the paper.

Load the brush with a light value of Indigo and paint above and just below the first two wave break lines. The colors will blend together for a soft blended wash. Let dry.

STEP THREE

Load the brush with a dark value of Indigo mixed with Phthalo Turquoise and paint at the very top left edge of the paper.

Load the brush with clear water and blend the dark color toward the first wave break line. You want the top of the wave break shape to be darker and lighten toward the bottom of the line. Use a tissue to blot the lighter area if needed. Let dry.

STEP FOUR

Load the brush with a dark value of Indigo mixed with a small amount of Phthalo Turquoise and paint a thick line at the top of the wave break.

Load the brush with clear water and blend the dark-value blue by brushing across and downward toward the next wave break line.

Drop more dark-value blue at the very top for an intense dark value. Blend with clear water going toward the next line. Blot the lighter area with tissue if needed.

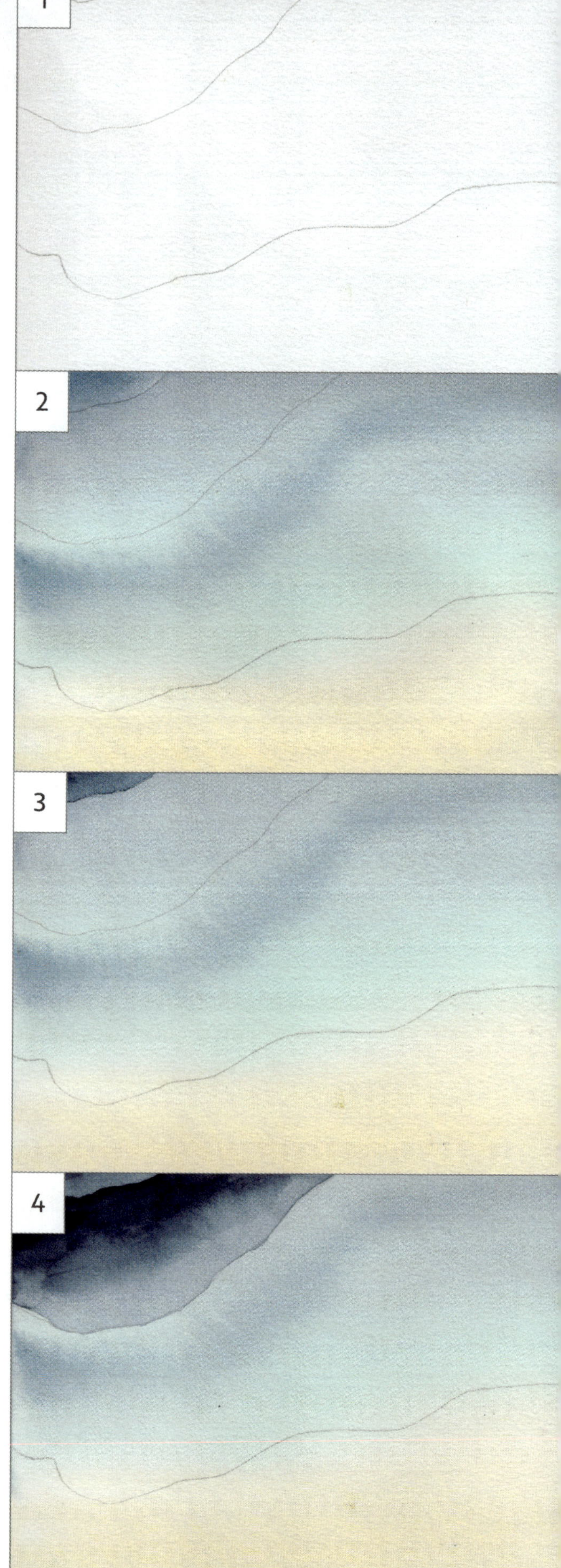

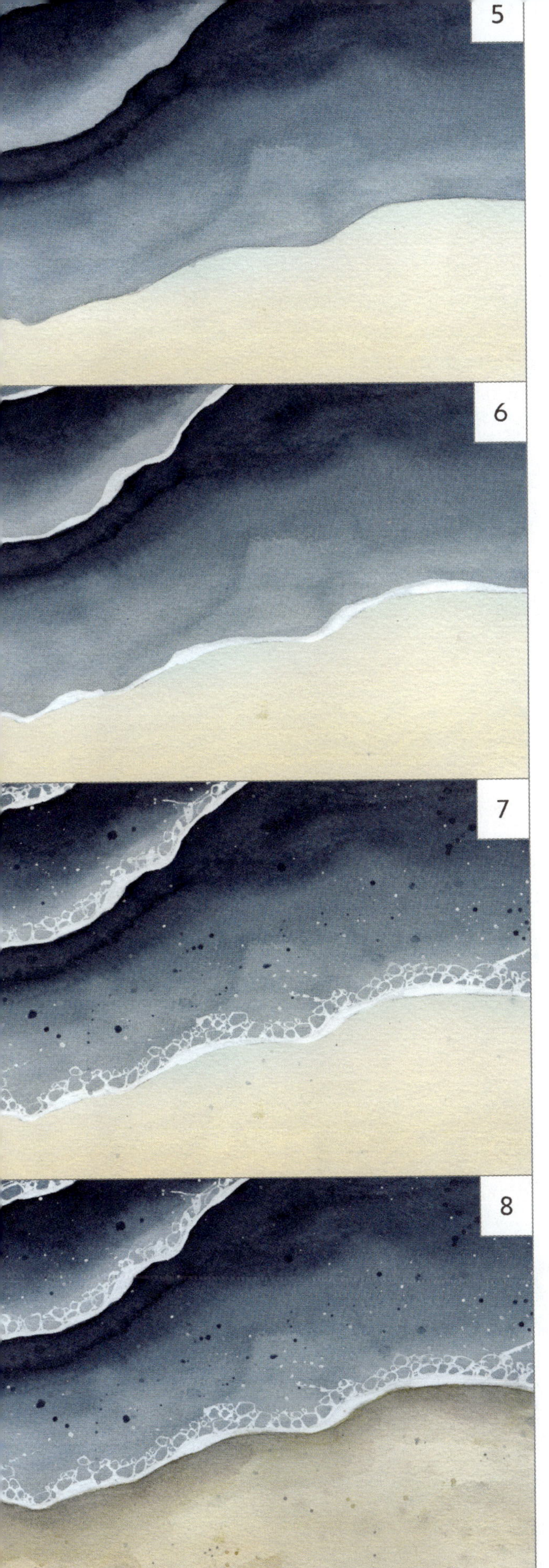

STEP FIVE

Load the brush with a dark value of Indigo mixed with a small amount of Phthalo Turquoise and paint a thick line at the top of the next wave break, just like step 4.

Load the brush with clear water and blend the dark-value blue by brushing across and down toward the last wave break line.

Drop more dark-value blue at the very top for an intense dark value. Blend with clear water going toward the next line. Blot the lighter area with tissue if needed.

STEP SIX

Load a fine-line brush with white ink and paint an irregular line along the edge of each wave break line. Make the areas thin and thick for a more realistic look.

STEP SEVEN

Use a fine-line brush to paint small, irregular cell shapes with white ink to represent sea foam along the white lines of each wave break.

Splatter the white ink lightly by loading the brush with white ink and tapping on it gently. Try to avoid the darker parts of the water and blot excess splatters with a tissue.

Load a medium round brush with a medium-value Indigo-Turquoise mixture and splatter it lightly on the water areas. Avoid the sandy beach if possible and blot with a tissue if needed. Let dry.

STEP EIGHT

Load a light value of Moonglow on a medium round brush and paint the area directly under the bottom wave break area.

Load the brush with clear water and blend the shadow into the sand. Splatter with Moonglow for texture. Let dry, then carefully remove the masking tape.

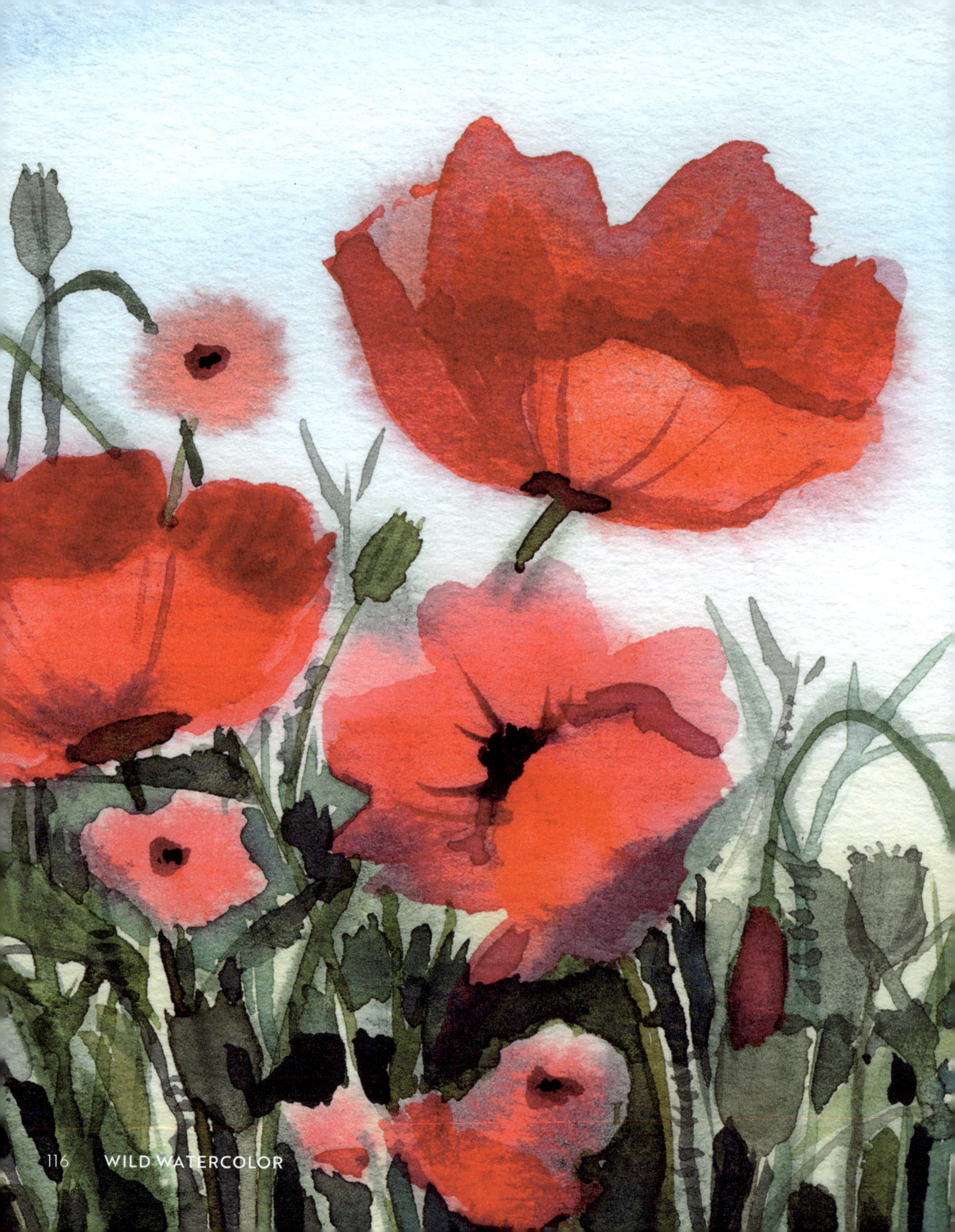

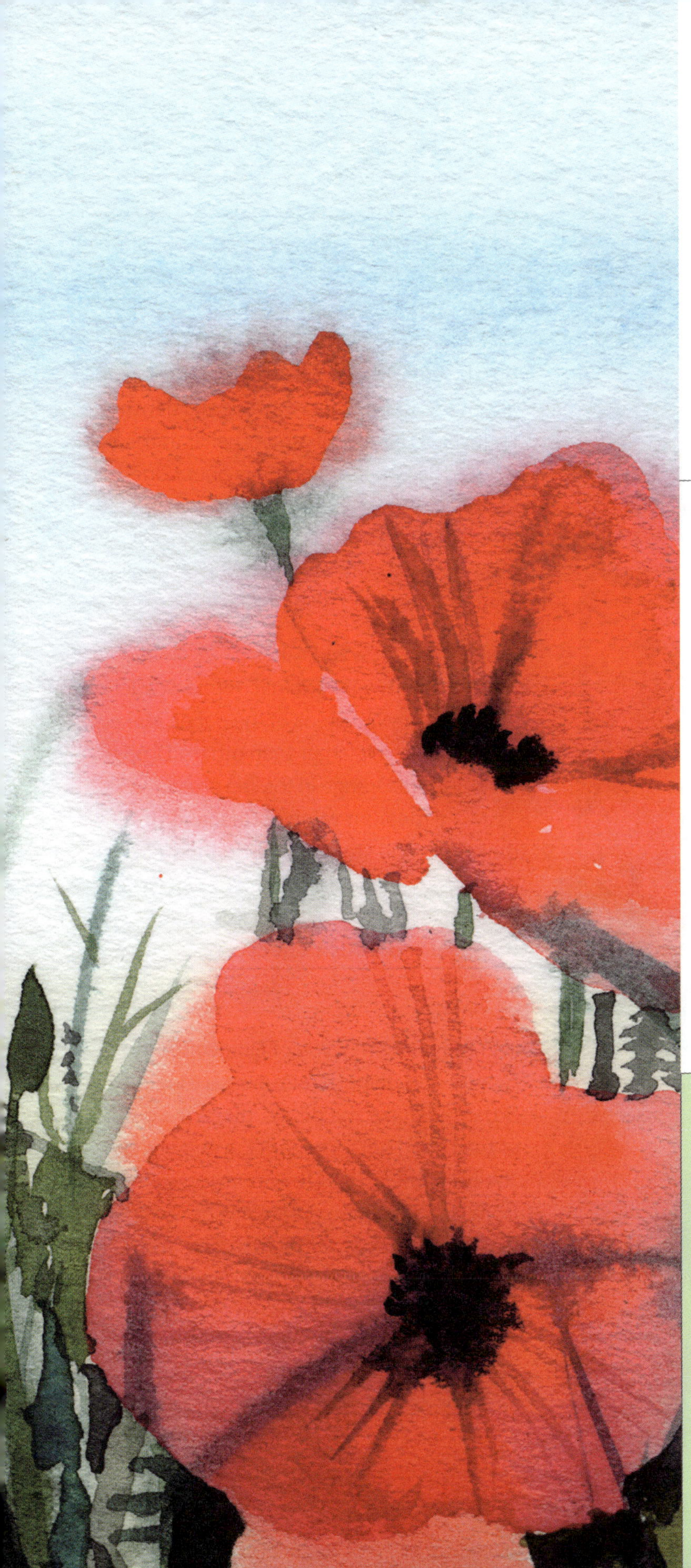

Poppy Field

The poppy is not only a beautiful and fragrant flower with medicinal properties, but it is also deeply symbolic. An image of a vibrant poppy field stretching as far as the eye can see evokes feelings of prosperity, hope, and abundance.

COLORS

- Quinacridone Scarlet
- Brilliant Orange
- Aureolin
- Cascade Green
- Cerulean Blue
- Sap Green
- Payne's Gray

TECHNIQUES

- Wet on wet
- Wet on dry
- Glazing
- Layering

MATERIALS

- Watercolor paper, 5" ×7"
- Masking or washi tape
- Masonite panel
- Large round watercolor brush
- Medium round watercolor brush
- Fine-line brush

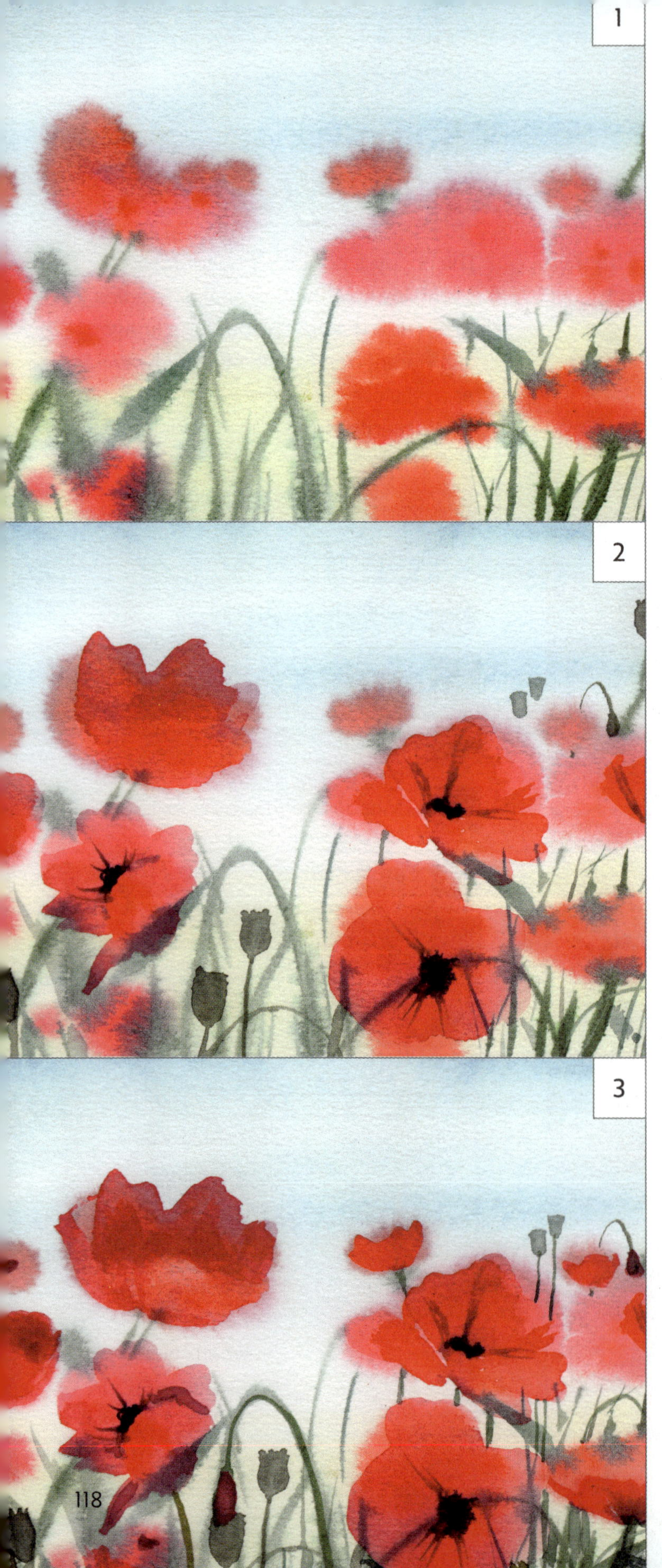

STEP ONE

Attach the paper to a board with masking or washi tape, creating a ¼-inch border with the tape around all edges of the paper. Load a medium or large round brush with clear water and wet the paper until glossy but not dripping wet. Tilt the paper to check for dry spots and brush on water as needed.

Mix a light value of Cerulean Blue and brush across the top of the paper horizontally about one-third of the way down. Then, mix a light value of Aureolin and brush it at the bottom of the paper horizontally about one-third of the way up the paper. Avoid an unwanted green color by keeping the blue and yellow washes away from each other. The middle of your paper should be nearly white.

While the paint is still wet

Mix a medium-value Quinacridone Scarlet and drop it in random areas of the paper. Make some areas a bit larger than others. Drop a little Brilliant Orange in the red areas.

Mix a medium value of Cascade Green and make leaf and stem shapes in the wet background. Mix a medium value of Sap Green and make more stems and leaf shapes with the tip of your brush. Let dry.

STEP TWO

Use the medium value of Quinacridone Scarlet and paint petals using a medium brush. To make the petals, place the point of the brush onto the paper and move the "belly" of the brush (the curved underside) from side to side to create a wider stroke.

Load the brush with the greens from step 2 and paint small bell-shaped heads in a few areas on the paper. Paint the stems with the same color. Then mix a medium to dark value of Payne's Gray and Quinacridone Scarlet and paint a few of the flowers' centers with it.

STEP THREE

While the paint in the center of the flowers is still wet, drag some of the dark centers outward with the tip of your brush, creating lines going to the edges of the petals. Let dry.

STEP FOUR

Bring out the petals in some of the flowers using a medium round brush to paint a wash of Quinacridone Scarlet mixed with Brilliant Orange. Leave some of the lighter red areas alone for contrast. Paint leaves and stems with shades of green, creating depth in the bottom area of the foreground. Let dry.

STEP FIVE

Paint in between stems with a saturated green mixture connecting the poppy flowers to the bottom of the page. Paint more details in the foreground with different shades of green. While those areas are still wet, drop in a little Cerulean Blue and Payne's Gray. Keep building layers with the colors in this palette until you reach a contrast of dark and light. Be careful not to overwork this step. Just work on small areas, concentrating on the bottom half of the painting. Let dry.

STEP SIX

Load a fine-line brush with a darker value of scarlet and paint more details in some of the flowers. Use a mix of greens for the leaves and stems.

Add Payne's Gray to green and paint small, dark areas in the foreground to bring out the shapes of the stems and leaves.

With the tip of a fine-line brush, make short horizontal marks with a mix of green on some of the stems to finish. Let dry, then carefully remove the masking tape.

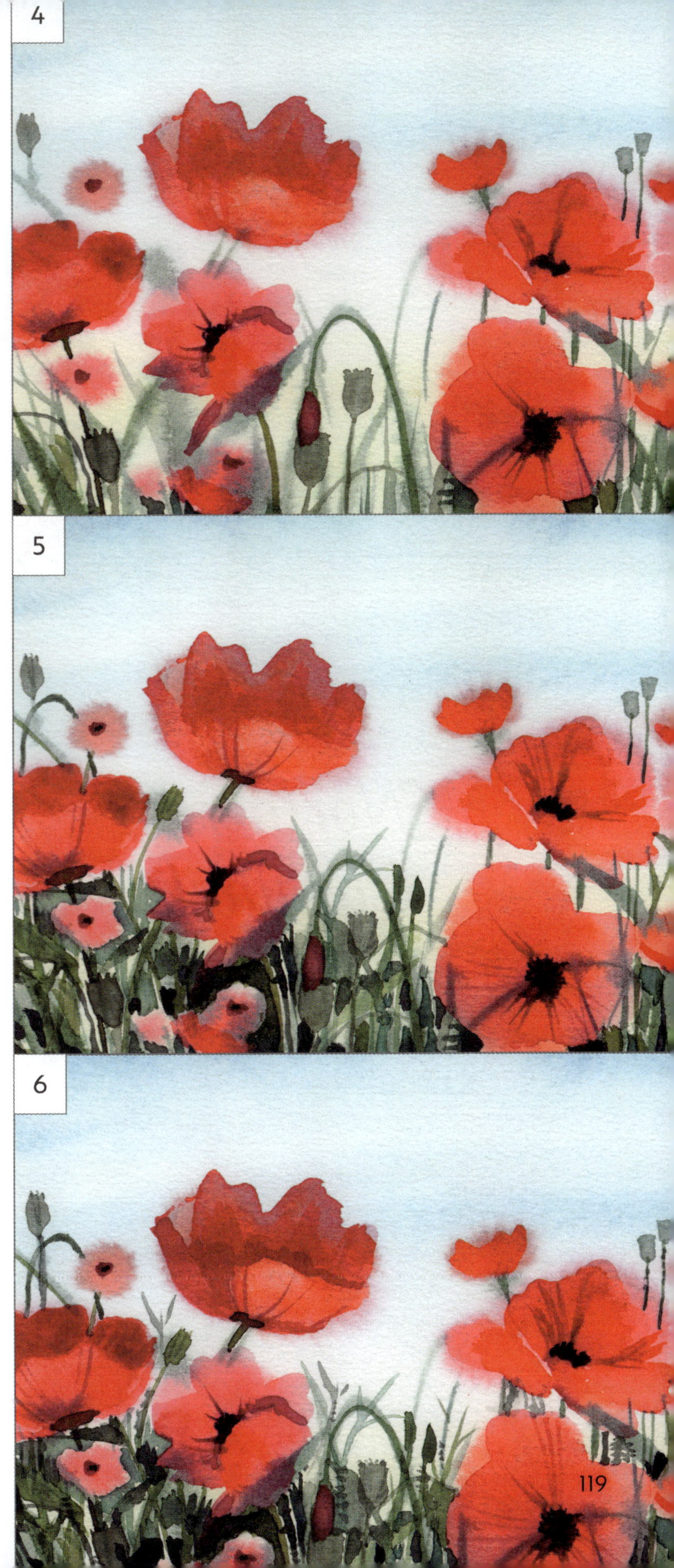

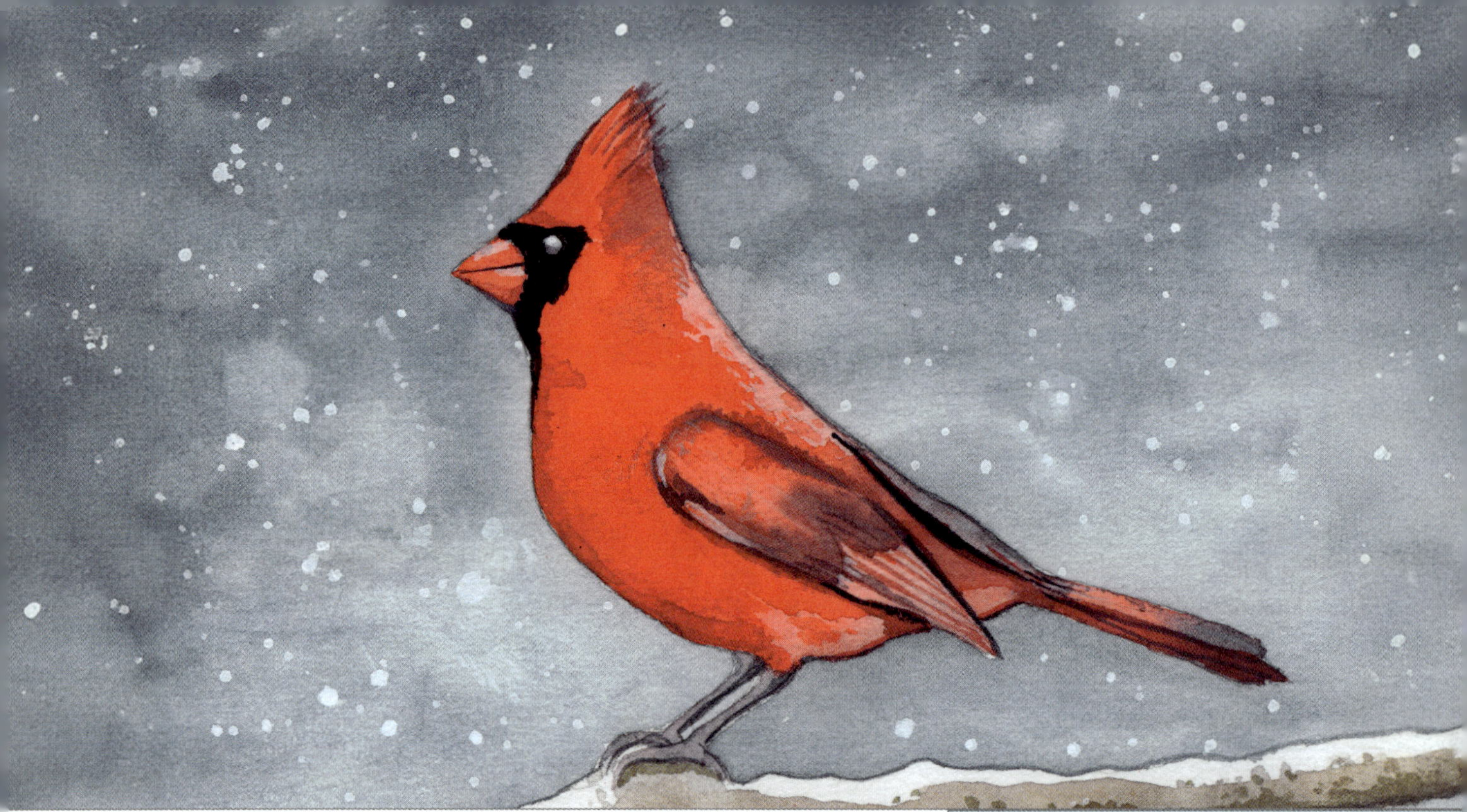

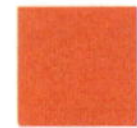

WEEK 32
Northern Cardinal

The vibrant male cardinal is a striking sight in winter with its brilliant red color. A pair of cardinals has made a home in my backyard for a couple of years now, and their sweet song brings joy to my heart.

COLORS

Pyrrole Red Light

Anthraquinone Red

Payne's Gray

Raw Sienna

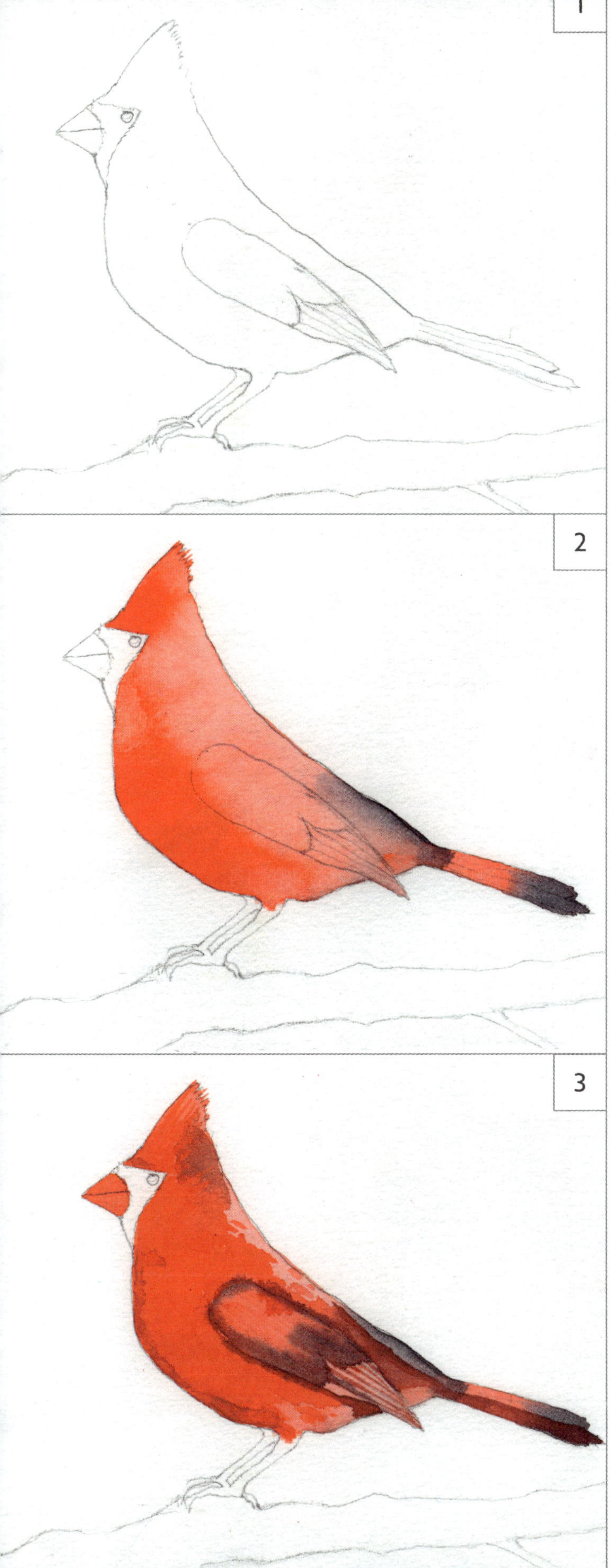

STEP ONE

Sketch the cardinal and the branch on the paper with a mechanical pencil. Erase any extra lines or marks with a kneaded eraser.

STEP TWO

Mix saturated values of Pyrrole Red Light and Anthraquinone Red in separate puddles in your palette. Using a medium round brush loaded with clean water, dampen the body, wing, and tail of the cardinal so it is shiny but not dripping wet.

Brush a saturated amount of Pyrrole Red Light at the belly, around the beak at the forehead, then move the brush to the wing, tail, and back to create a smooth graded wash.

Drop a saturated value of Anthraquinone Red at the edge of the belly and forehead while the first wash is still damp. Use the tip of your brush to make feathers at the top of the head.

While the wash is still wet, drop a medium value of Payne's Gray at the tip of the tail and the lower back. Let dry.

STEP THREE

Paint the beak with the Pyrrole Red Light mixture and, with the tip of the brush, paint a small amount of Anthraquinone Red to create shadows on the beak.

Paint another layer of Pyrrole Red Light on the body, concentrating the color on the belly. Use the tip of the brush to make small marks representing feathers and shadows on the back, belly, tail, and below the wing.

Add a medium-value Payne's Gray into the wet areas below the wings, tail, and belly to create a blended shadow. Let dry.

STEP FOUR

Mix a very dark value of Payne's Gray and paint the area around the beak and eye. Mix a light value of Payne's Gray and paint the legs and feet.

Drop a light value of Anthraquinone Red into the wet areas of the legs and feet. Let dry.

STEP FIVE

Using the pointed end of a cotton swab or a small brush dipped in clean water, make a small circle in the eye area and blot with a tissue to lift the color. Repeat until the eye is visible.

Mix a light value of Raw Sienna and Payne's Gray and paint the underside of the branch, leaving white areas at the top.

Drop a light value of Payne's Gray at the bottom of the branch in random areas. Let dry.

STEP SIX

Using a larger round brush, dampen the entire background with clear water.

Mix a medium value of Payne's Gray and brush it onto the paper, starting at the top and working your way down. The wash will be darker at the top and lighter at the bottom of the paper. Immediately blot areas with a tissue to lighten the wash and create texture. Let dry.

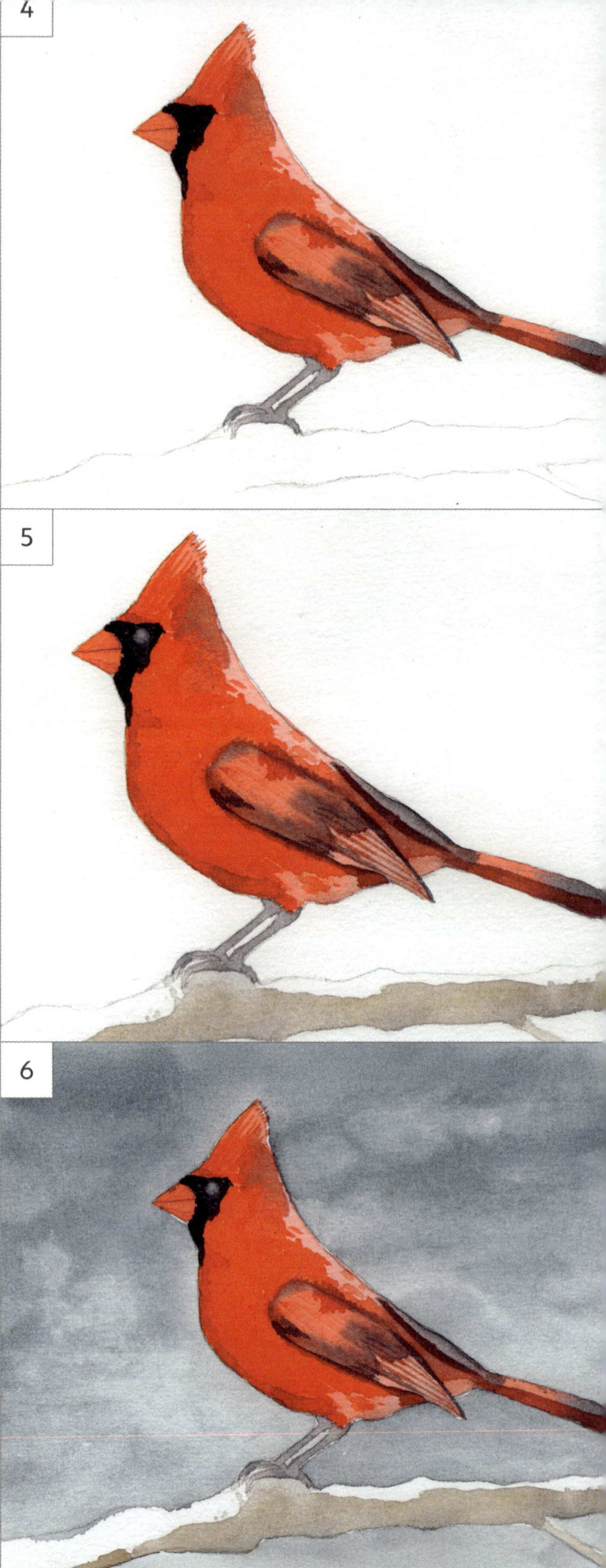

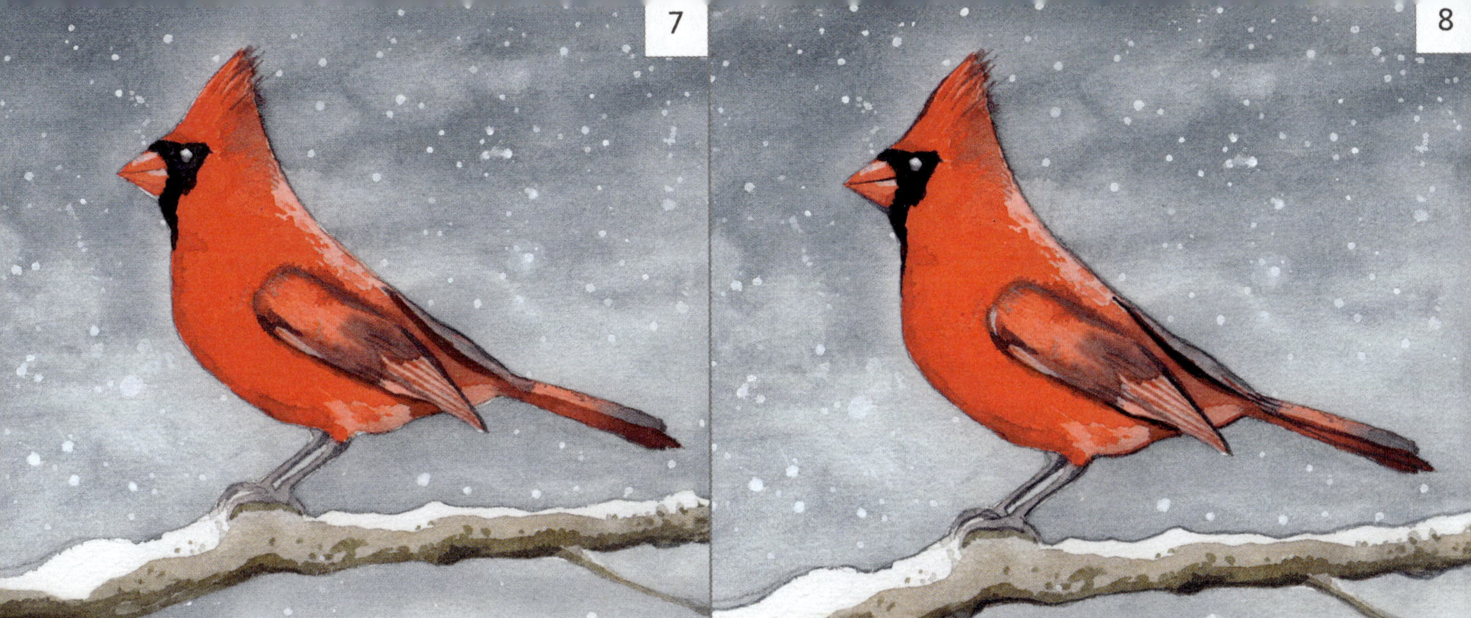

Mix a medium value of Payne's Gray, Raw Sienna, and Pyrrole Red Light and brush it along the bottom of the branch. Make little marks with the same mixture to create texture in the branch.

Mix white ink with a small amount of Pyrrole Red Light and use a small brush to paint highlights on the beak and wing. Thin the white ink with water and paint a small dot in the eye.

Thin the white ink with water again and use a medium round brush to splatter the background, being careful to avoid splattering the bird.

NOTE: For best results, hold the brush loaded with white ink and tap it on your fingers about 4 inches above the paper.

Continue splattering until you are satisfied with the results. Blot areas with tissue to remove unwanted splatters. Let dry.

With a small brush, paint fine details in the beak, crown, wings, and under the branch with a medium-value mixture of Payne's Gray and a small amount of Anthraquinone Red.

Paint a thin line of medium-value Payne's Gray at the bottom of the belly behind the legs and on the lower top part of the back to finish. Let dry.

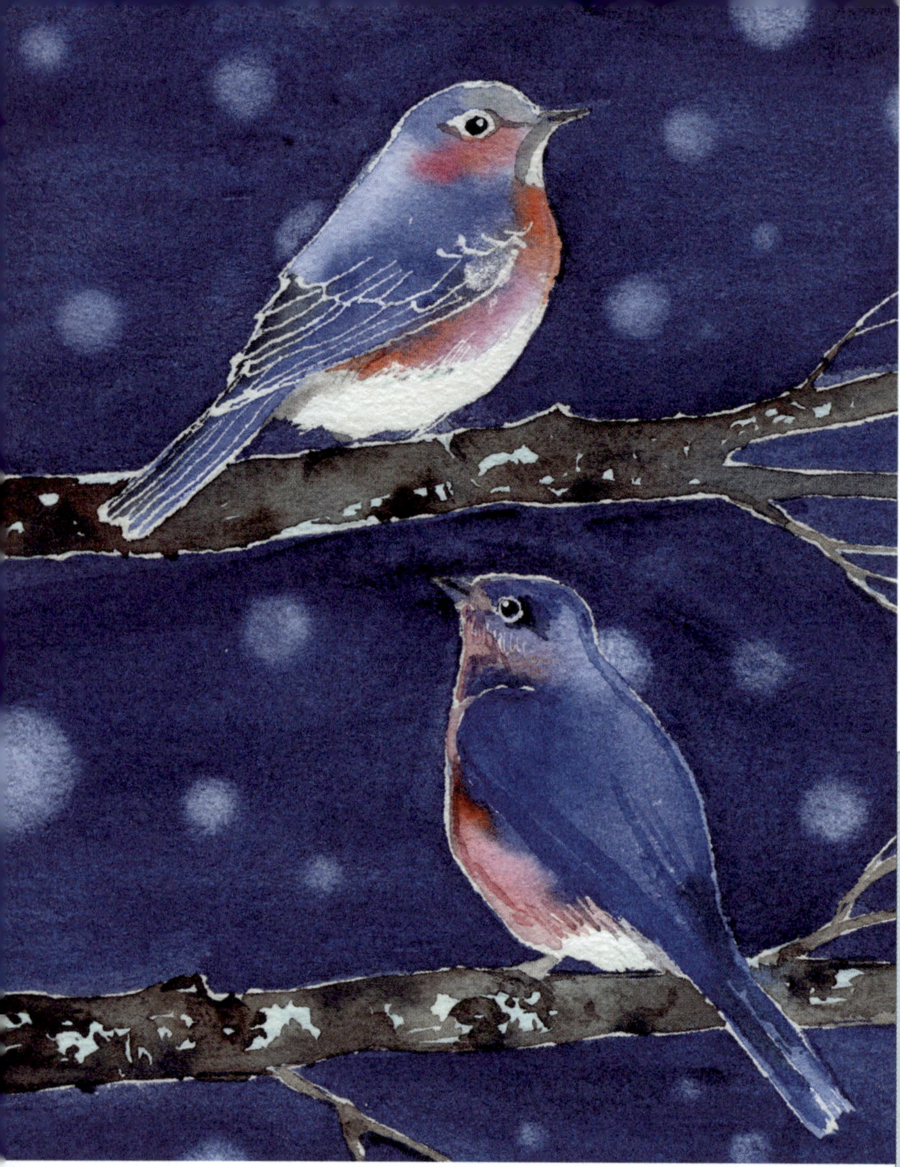

COLORS

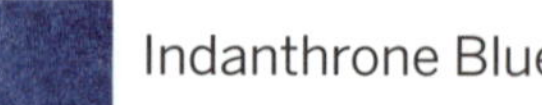 Indanthrone Blue

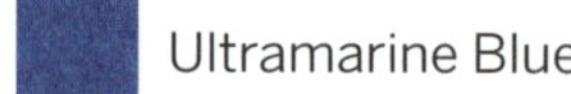 Ultramarine Blue

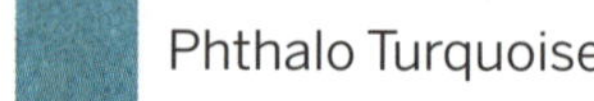 Phthalo Turquoise

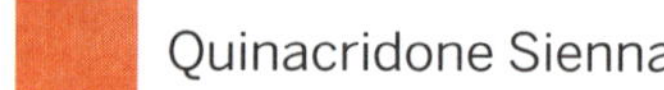 Quinacridone Sienna

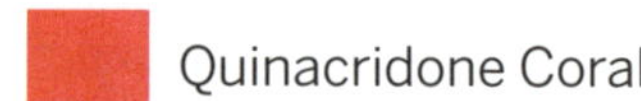 Quinacridone Coral

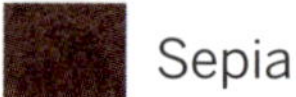 Sepia

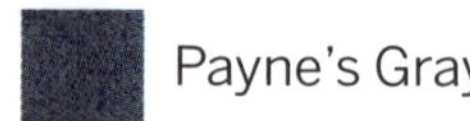 Payne's Gray

WEEK 33

Songbirds

After the sun sets, birds gather in a tree just outside my window. I can't see them underneath the foliage, but they group in large numbers, making the tree's leaves move and rustle. They chirp and sing to each other before settling down for a silent night of sleep.

TECHNIQUES

- Wet on wet
- Color lifting
- Wet on dry
- Glazing
- Sketching

MATERIALS

- Watercolor paper, 6" × 8"
- Masking or washi tape
- Masonite panel
- 2H lead mechanical pencil
- Kneaded eraser
- Medium round watercolor brush
- Small round watercolor brush
- Fine-line brush
- Masking fluid pen
- Masking fluid eraser (optional)
- White gel pen
- Facial tissue

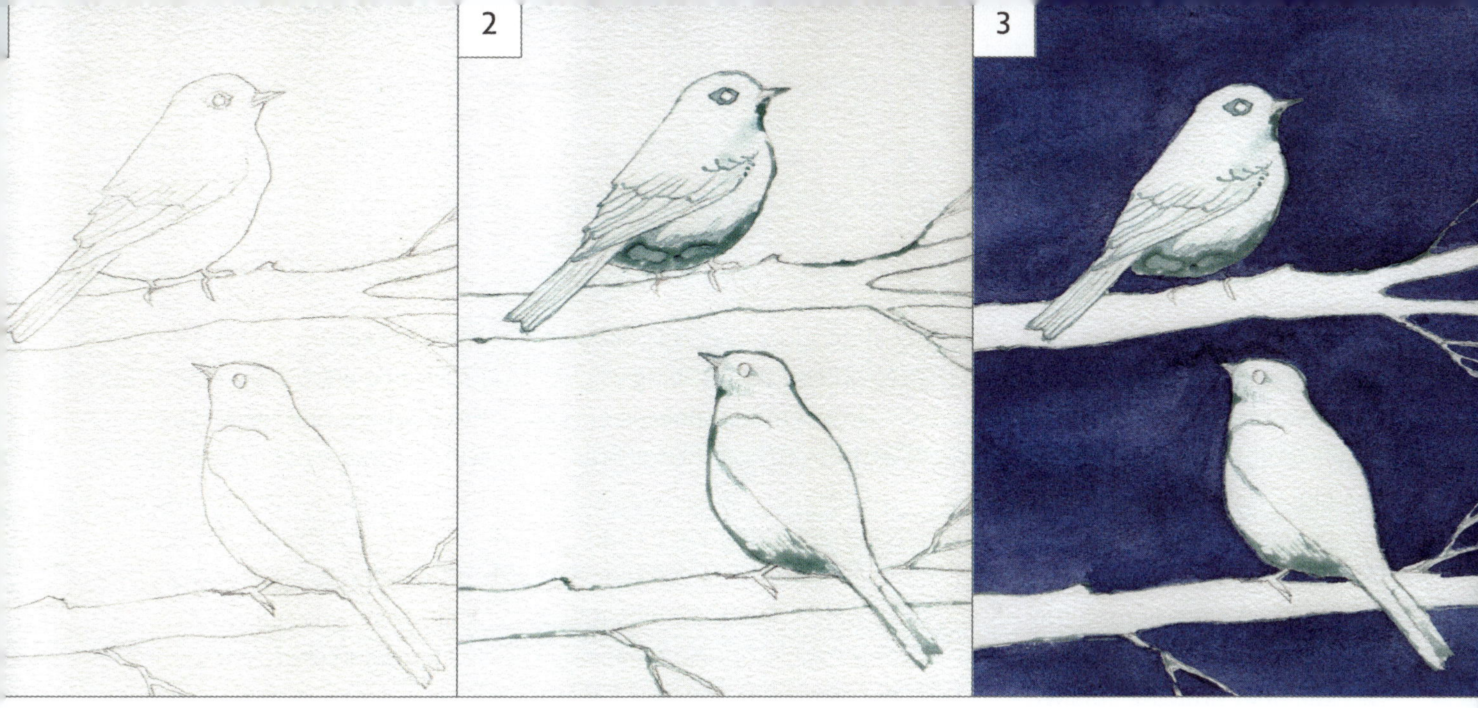

STEP ONE

Attach the paper to a board using masking or washi tape, creating at least a ¼-inch border with the tape around all edges of the paper. Sketch the birds on branches on the paper with a mechanical pencil. Erase any extra or heavy lines with a kneaded eraser.

STEP TWO

Mask the sketched lines on the branches, the birds' wings, and other areas of the birds with the masking fluid pen. Let dry.

STEP THREE

Mix a medium to dark value of Indanthrone Blue in your palette and use the medium brush to paint a wash in the background area behind the birds and the branches. Let dry.

STEP FOUR

Load a medium or small round brush with clear water and make small circular strokes in the blue wash, then blot with a clean tissue to lift the color. This will create a beautiful bokeh effect, which looks like lights in the distance.

Vary the sizes of the circle shapes by gently "scrubbing" the small areas and blot with a clean, dry tissue. Remember, this technique works with non-staining colors only, so always test the lifting properties of any color on a separate sheet of paper first. Let dry.

STEP FIVE

Mix a very light value of Phthalo Turquoise and paint the branches.

Wet the bottom bird with clear water, then drop a dark value of Ultramarine Blue in the wing area and on the head.

Drop a medium value of Quinacridone Coral in the belly area and follow with a small amount of Quinacridone Sienna.

Drop a medium value of Payne's Gray in the tail area.

Wet the top bird with water and drop a medium value of Ultramarine Blue in the wing and tail area.

Drop a medium value of Quinacridone Coral and Quinacridone Sienna bellow the eye and under the wing.

Drop a medium value of Payne's Gray on the tail area.

The colors will blend together beautifully. Let dry, then carefully remove the masking fluid by rubbing it with your fingers, or use a masking fluid eraser.

STEP SIX

Mix a medium value of Sepia and use a small brush to paint areas in the branches, leaving some of the turquoise color showing. Use clear water in your brush to spread the color around.

Drop a dark value of Sepia and Payne's Gray into other areas for contrast. Use a small brush to paint details in the birds' wings, bodies, and eyes with the same colors used for the body. Paint the eyes with a dark value of Payne's Gray.

Paint to the edge of the white-masked areas to thin out the lines and sharpen them.

Paint small shadows below the wings and eyes with a light value of Payne's Gray.

Use a white gel pen to dot a highlight on the eyes. Let dry, then carefully remove the masking tape.

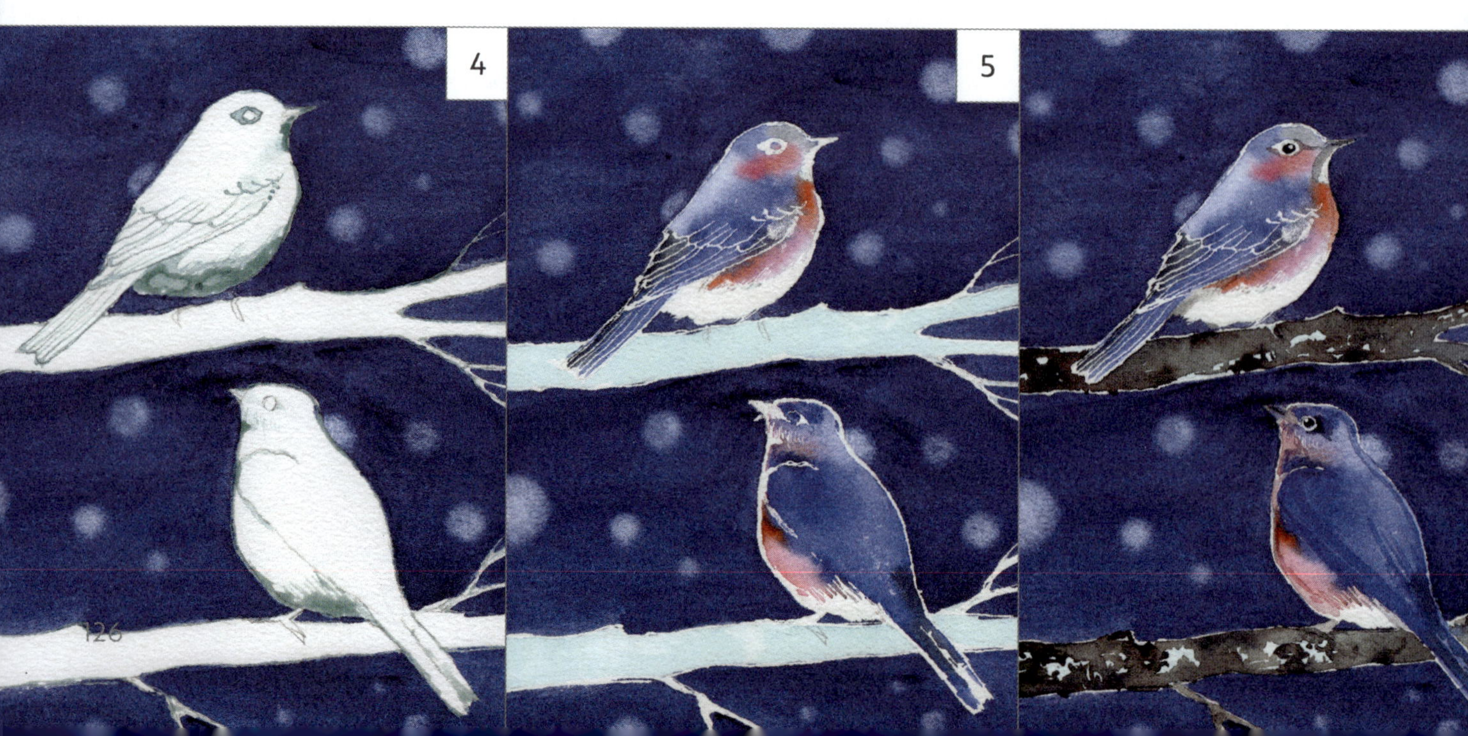

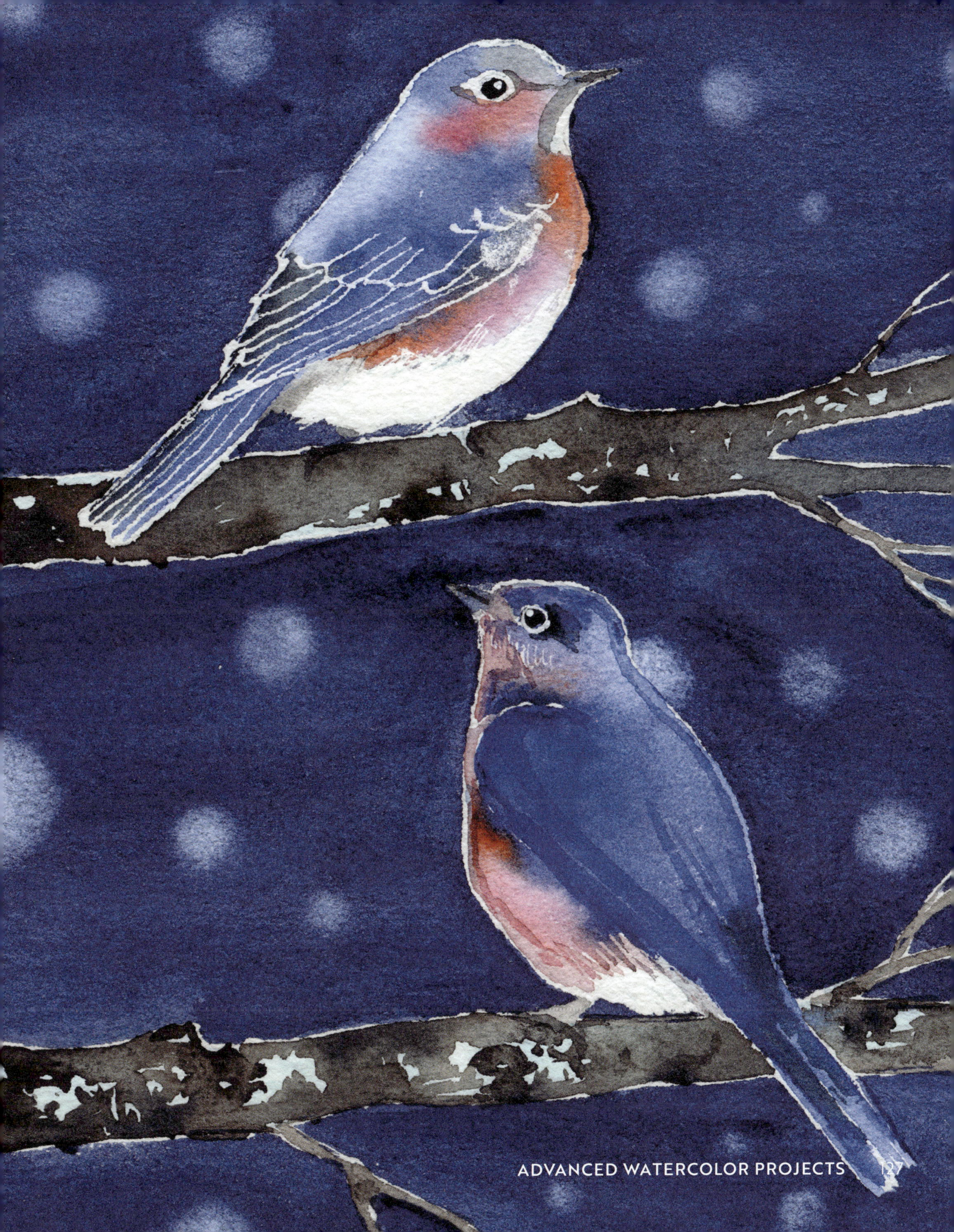

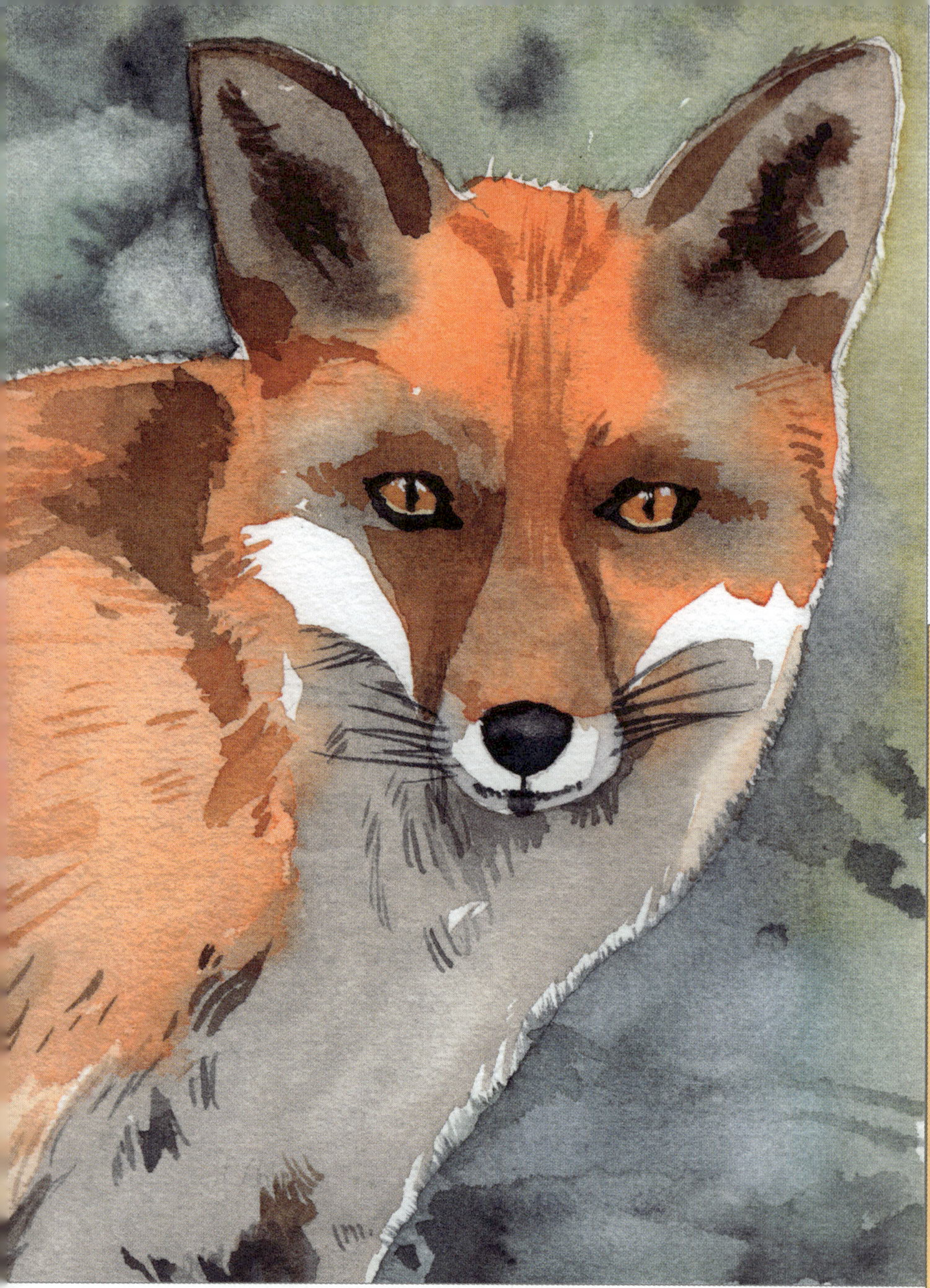

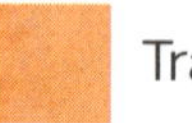

COLORS

- Transparent Orange
- Payne's Gray
- Quinacridone Gold
- Cerulean Blue
- Permanent Brown

Red Fox

The adorable red fox, despite its small size,
is a highly resilient and adaptable survivor,
able to thrive in various habitats.

TECHNIQUES

- Wet on wet
- Wet on dry
- Glazing
- Dry brush
- Sketching

MATERIALS

- Watercolor paper, 5" × 7"
- 2H lead mechanical pencil
- Kneaded eraser
- Medium round watercolor brush
- Small round watercolor brush
- ¼" soft-hair flat brush
- Fine-line brush
- White ink
- Cotton swabs
- Facial tissue

STEP ONE

Sketch the basic shapes of the fox on the paper with a mechanical pencil. Concentrate on the eyes and nose as they will be the focal point of the painting. Erase any heavy lines with a kneaded eraser.

STEP TWO

Mix medium values of Payne's Gray, Quinacridone Gold, and Cerulean Blue in separate puddles in your palette.

   Paint the background with a medium brush, letting all three colors blend together. While the background is still wet, push the wet paint along the edges of the fox with a dry, flat brush in short strokes. Blot any dark areas or puddles with tissue. Let dry.

CONTINUED ➜

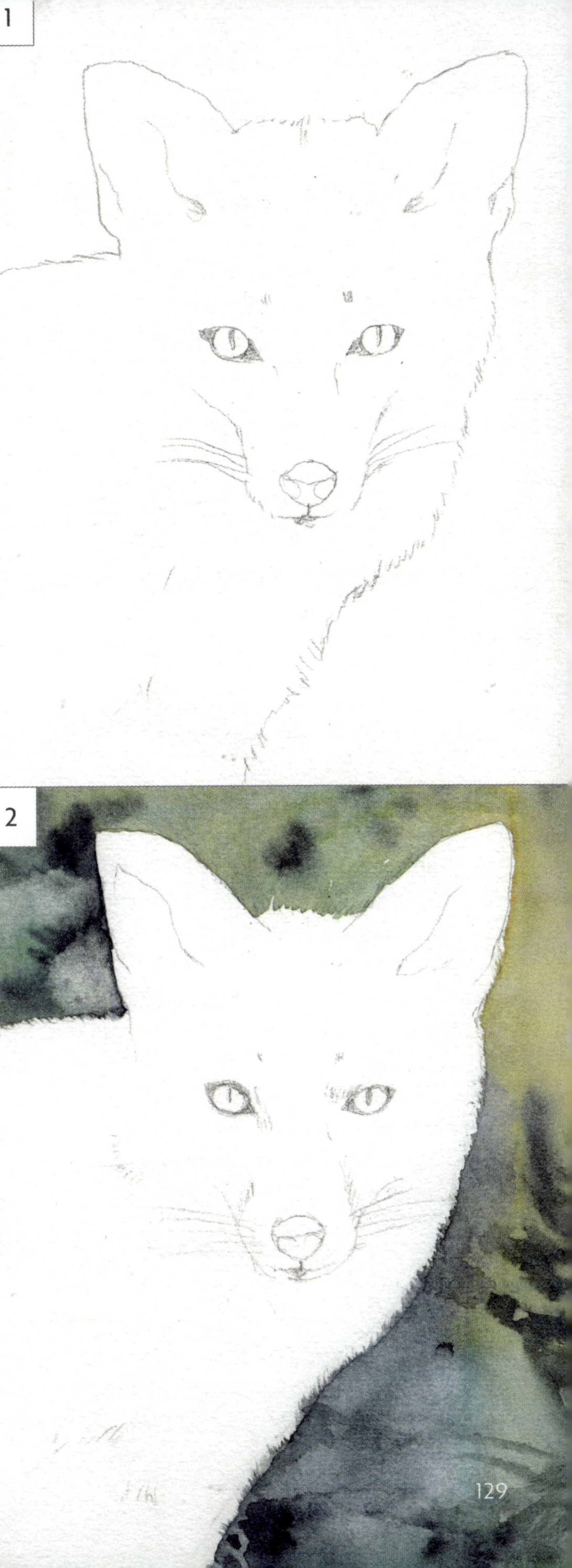

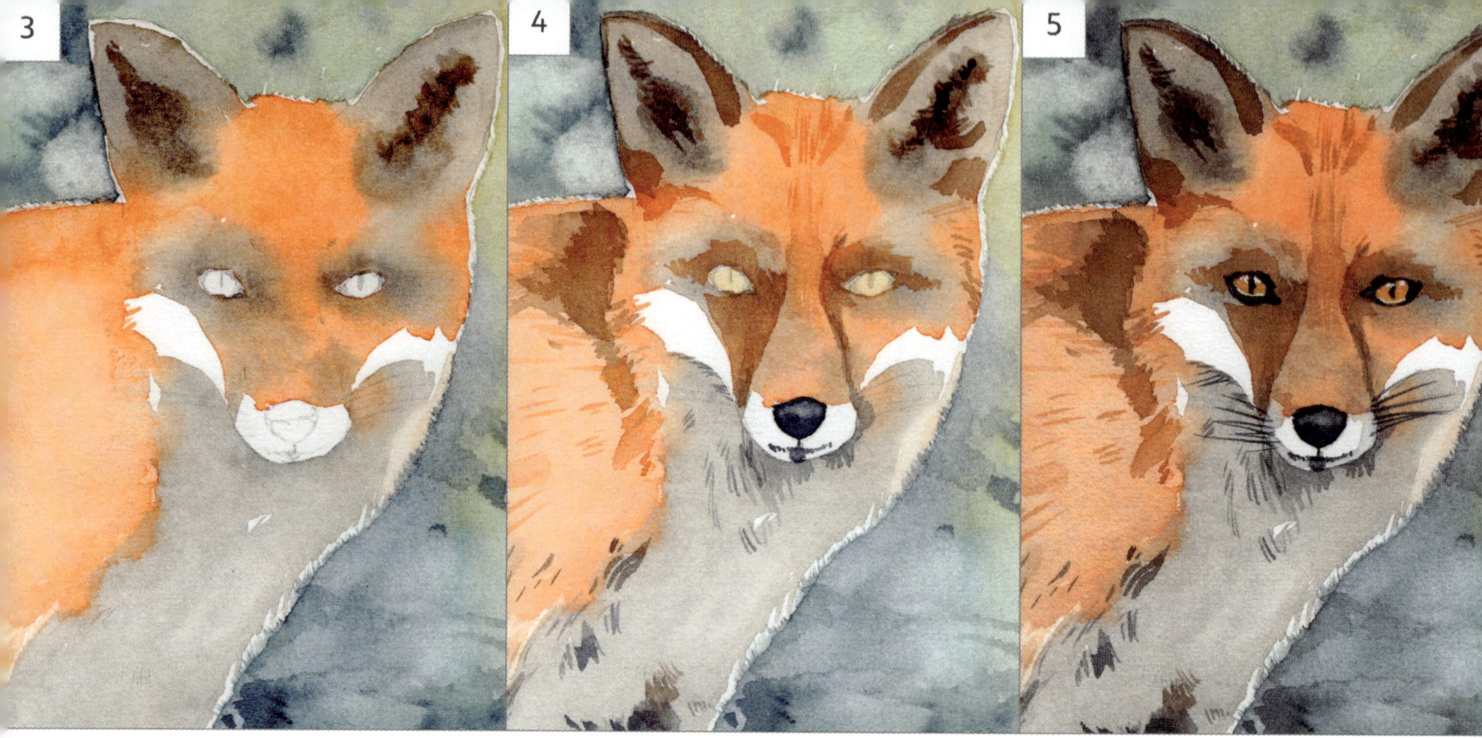

STEP THREE

Mix medium values of Transparent Orange, Permanent Brown, and Payne's Gray in separate puddles in the palette.

Using a medium round brush loaded with clear water, wet the body, face, and ears. Drop Transparent Orange on the head and upper body and around the eyes. While the paint is still wet, drop Permanent Brown and Payne's Gray in the ears.

Mix a light value of Payne's Gray and paint the chest area. Avoid painting the chin and cheek areas.

Drop a darker value of Payne's Gray and Permanent Brown in the center of the ears. Use a dry, flat brush to soften the edges and make short strokes for hair. Let dry.

STEP FOUR

Mix a dark value of Payne's Gray and use a small brush to paint the nose and mouth. Blot the upper part of the nose with a dry cotton swab to lift some of the color.

Mix a very light value of Quinacridone Gold and use a small brush to paint the eyes.

Mix a medium value of Payne's Gray and use a small brush to paint details in the fur on the chest, body, and ears. Let dry.

STEP FIVE

Mix a dark value of Payne's Gray and use a fine-line brush to paint the area around the eyes, pupils, and whiskers.

Mix a light value of Transparent Orange and paint the eyes, leaving a small amount of the gold at the bottom of the eyes. Dilute some white ink and dot the areas in the eye for highlights. Let dry.

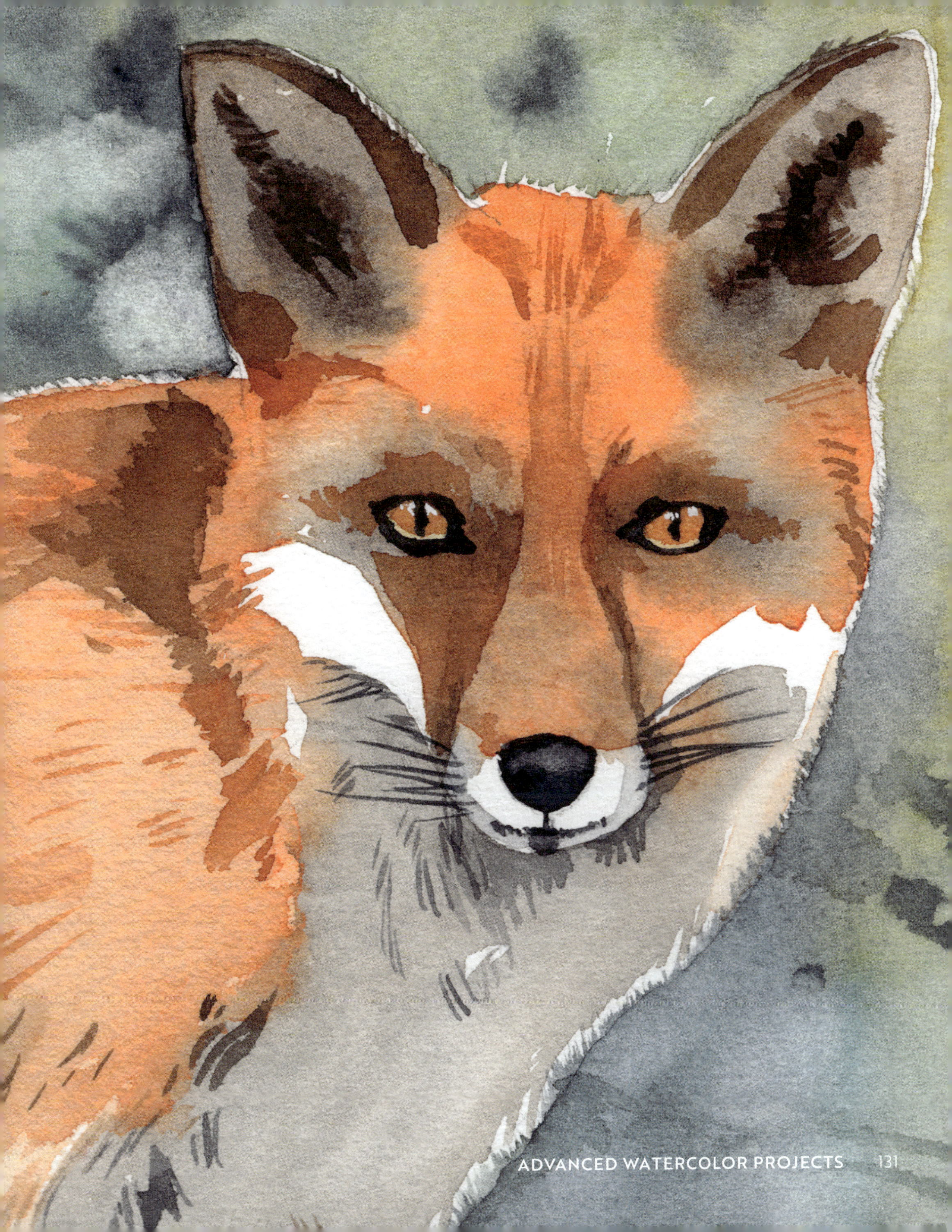

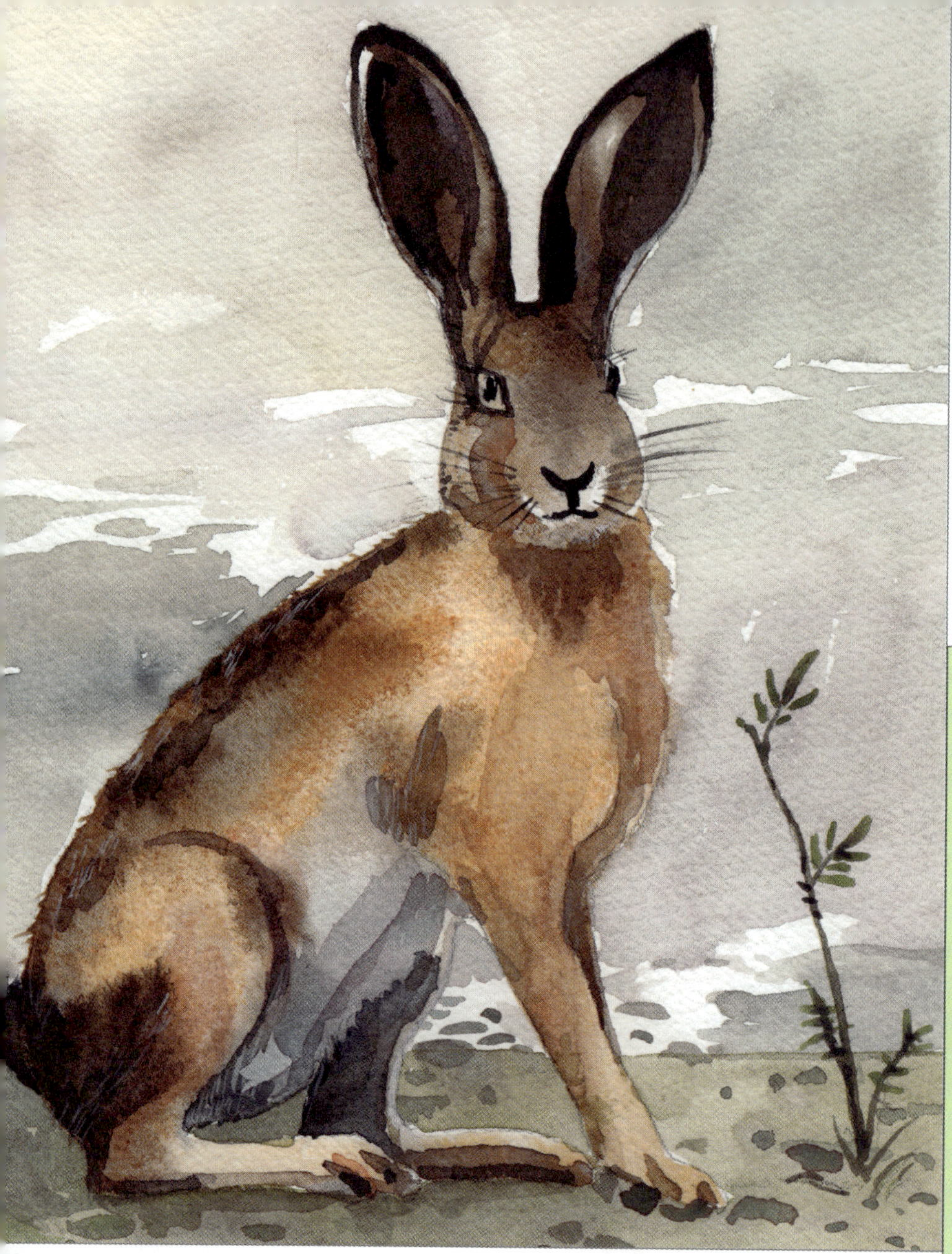

WEEK 35

Jackrabbit

The jackrabbit can be recognized by its large ears, which are tipped with black fur. They help release heat, which helps regulate their body temperature in the desert heat.

STEP ONE

Attach the paper to the board with masking or washi tape, creating a ¼-inch border with the tape around all edges of the paper. Sketch the jackrabbit, ground, and a small shrub on the paper with a mechanical pencil. Erase any heavy or excessive lines with a kneaded eraser.

STEP TWO

Mix a medium value of Raw Umber in a puddle in your palette. Using a medium brush loaded with clear water, wet the body, then paint the center of the chest and the legs with Raw Umber. Drop a medium value of Sepia on the back and tail area.

Paint a very light value of Payne's Gray in the belly area while it is still wet. Paint the ears with a darker value of Sepia and drop a medium value of Raw umber in the face area. While the paint is still wet, use a dry, flat brush at the edge of the back, below the tail, and in the chest area to make very short strokes going outward in the angle of hair growth. Drop a light value of Moonglow in the area above the nose and in the chest. You may be tempted to use the brush to move the colors around but let them blend together naturally as they dry.

STEP THREE

Mix very light values of Sap Green, Raw Umber, and Payne's Gray in separate puddles in your palette.

Paint the background with all three colors, leaving some white areas. Mix darker values of Sepia and Payne's Gray and paint details in the rabbit. Paint the inside of the eyes with a light value of Raw Umber. Let dry.

STEP FOUR

Mix a dark value of Payne's Gray and use a fine-line brush to paint the whiskers and eyelashes.

Dilute white ink and paint highlights on the eyes, and paint fur on parts of the body using the fine-line brush.

Mix a medium value of Moonglow and Sap Green and use a small brush to paint the shrub stem.

Mix a medium value of Sap Green and use a small brush to paint the leaves.

Drop in a medium value of Moonglow at the base of the leaves.

Brush a few more details in the background area with a light to medium value of the left-over colors in the palette. Let dry, then carefully remove the masking tape.

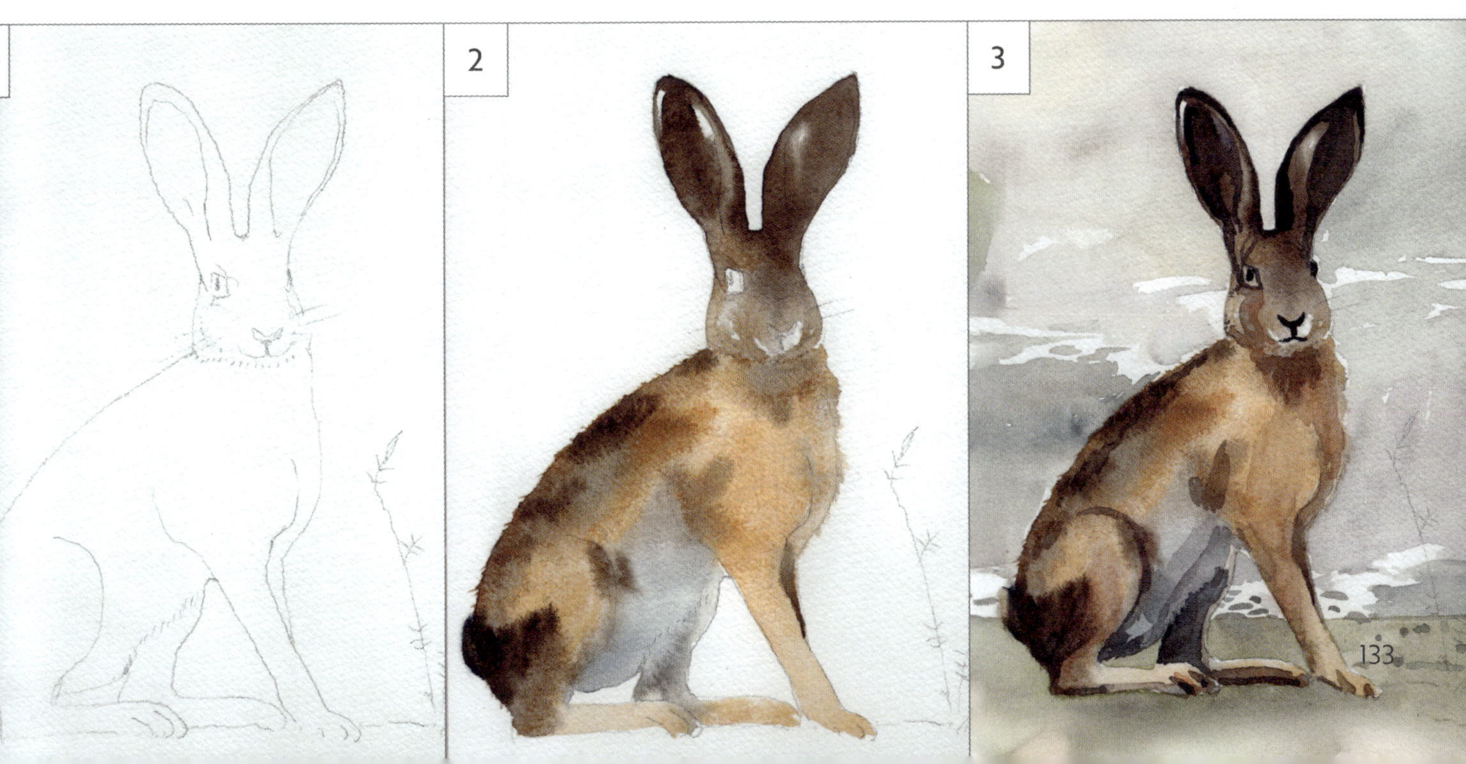

133

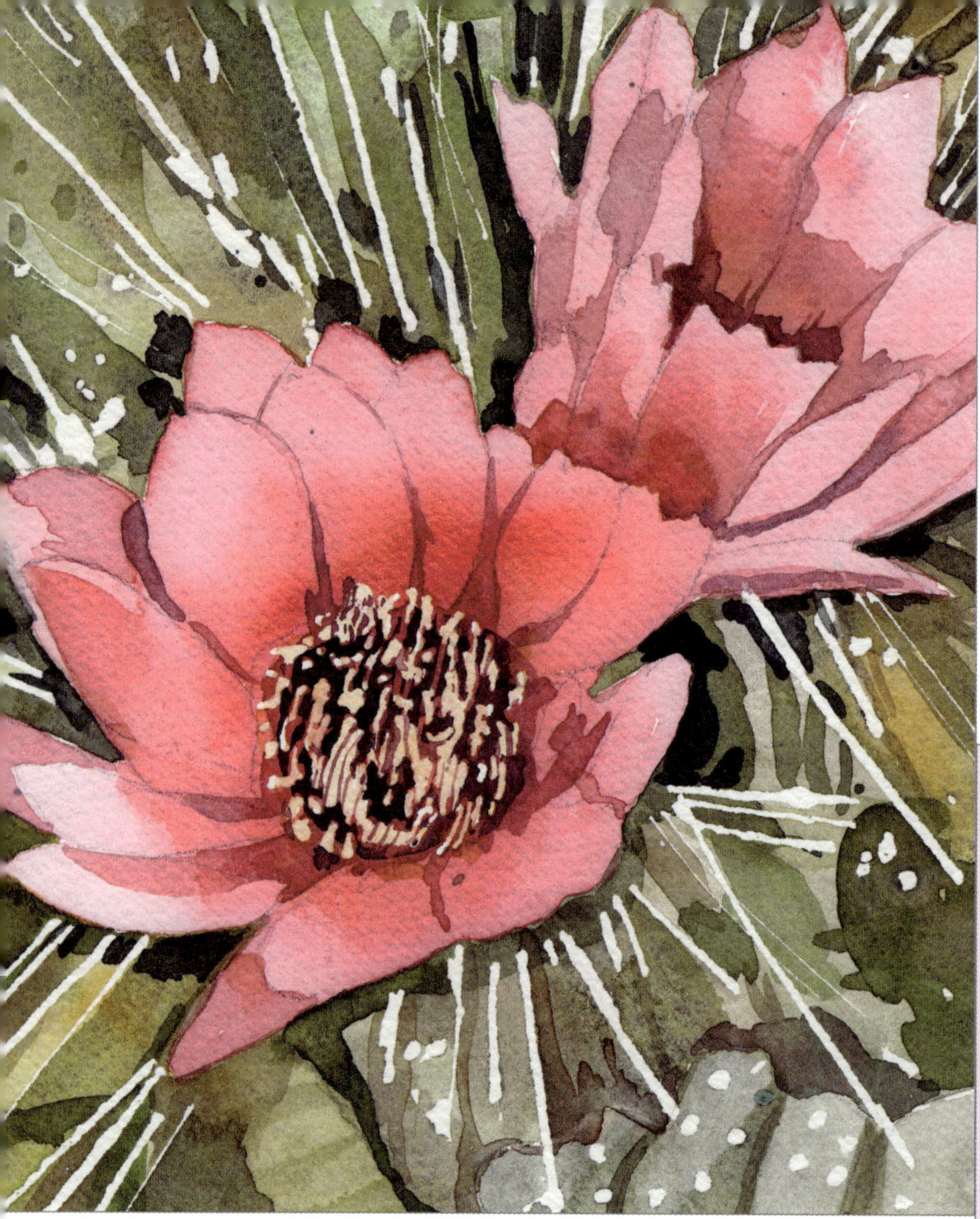

Prickly Pear Cactus Flower

The prickly pear cactus is a bountiful source of food and hydration for desert wildlife. In spring, the plant produces beautiful, delicate flowers, with most blooms ranging in color from white to yellow to fuchsia.

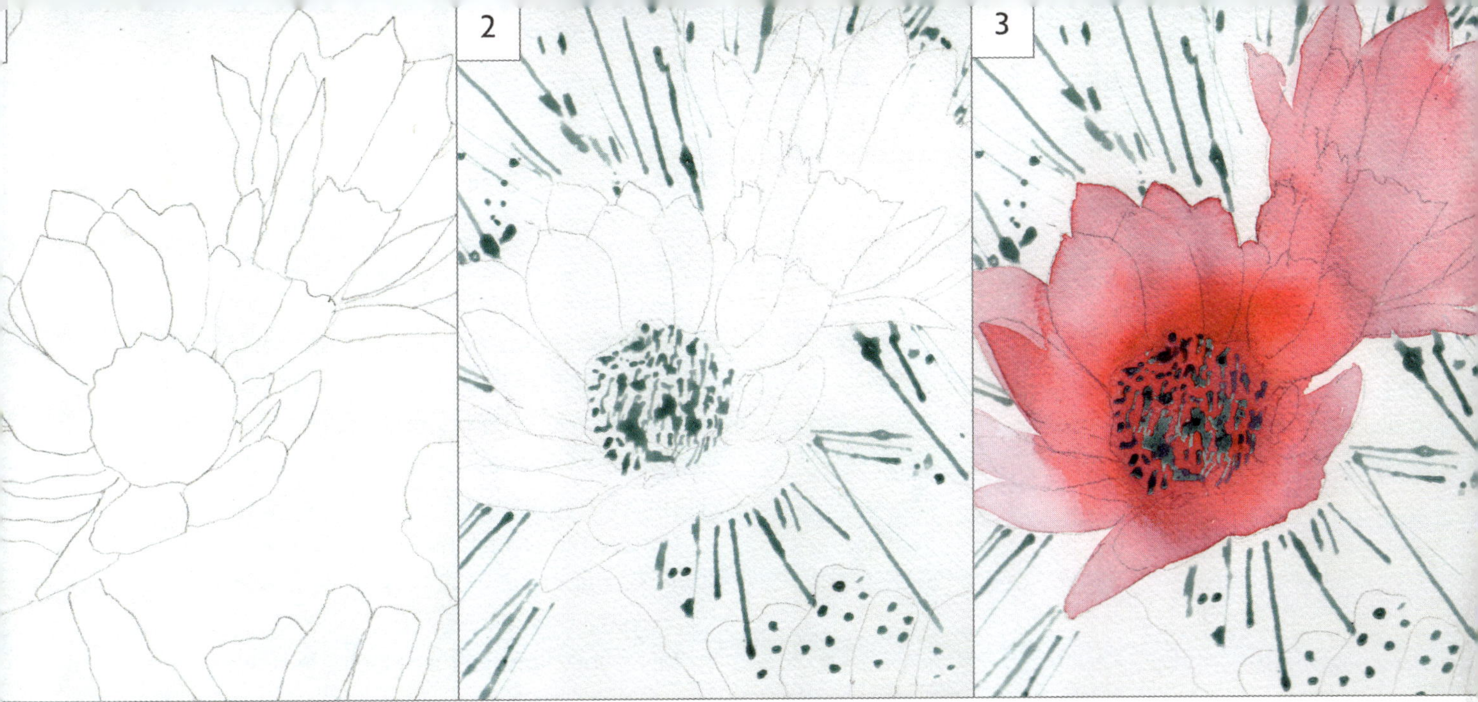

STEP ONE

Attach the paper to a board with masking or washi tape, creating a ½-inch or wider border with the tape around all edges of the paper. Sketch the flowers and basic shapes on the paper with a mechanical pencil, then erase any heavy or extra lines with a kneaded eraser.

STEP TWO

Use a masking fluid pen to draw small, random marks close to the center of the open flower on the bottom left and draw straight lines going away from the flower to represent the cactus spines. Make small, random marks in the background with the masking fluid pen. Let dry.

STEP THREE

Mix a light to medium value of Quinacridone Red and Opera Pink. Paint the flower petals all the way to the tips with a medium round brush.

Mix a dark value of Purple Magenta and Opera Pink and drop it in the center of the lower flower. Drop an intense value of Opera Pink just around the center edges of the lower flower and on the tip of the upper flower. Let dry.

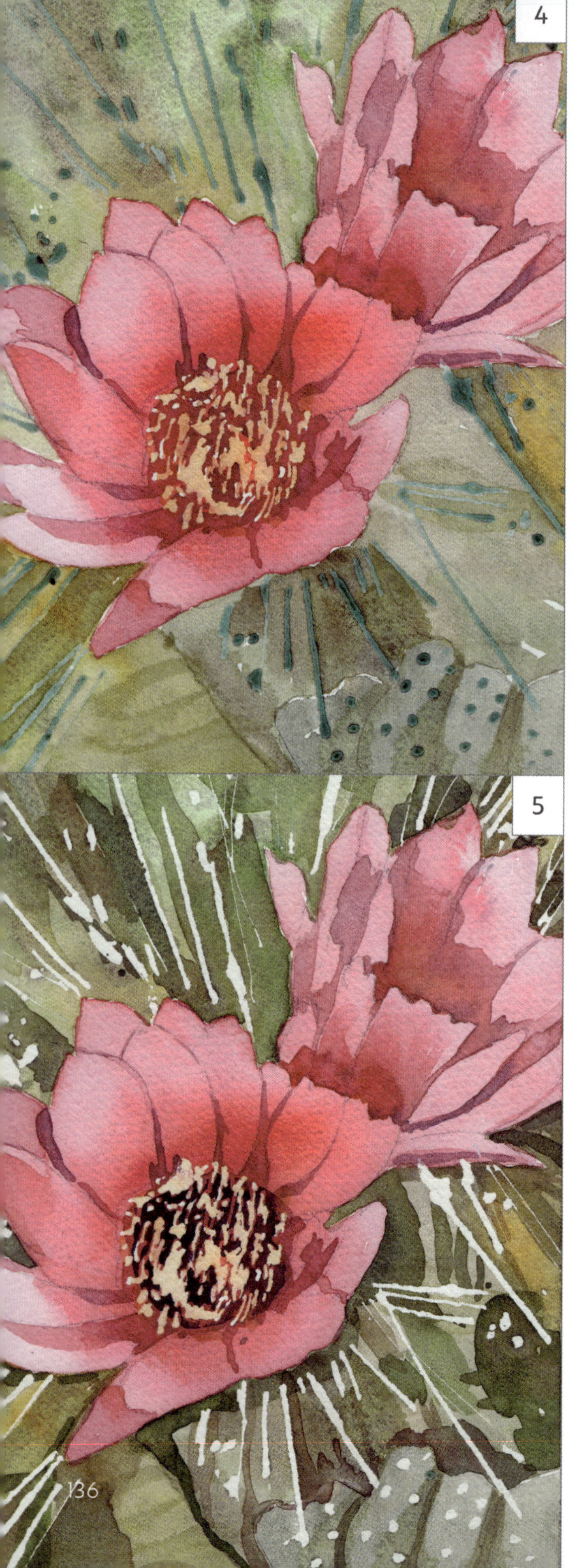

STEP FOUR

Mix a darker value of Opera Pink and Purple Magenta and paint details on the flower petals to bring out the individual petal shapes.

Mix a light to medium value of Green Apatite Genuine and paint the background. While the background is still wet, drop in a medium value of Quinacridone Gold in random areas. Then, drop a light value of Payne's Gray and Purple Magenta in random areas in the background while it is still wet.

Remove the masking fluid in the center of the lower flower only by rubbing it with your fingers, or use a masking fluid eraser.

Mix a very light value of Quinacridone Gold and use a small brush to paint the white areas. Let dry.

STEP FIVE

Mask the center area of the flower over the yellow with the masking pen. Let dry.

While the masking fluid is drying in the flower, paint loose details in the background with a medium- to dark-value mix of Green Apatite Genuine and Payne's Gray. Drop a medium value of Quinacridone Gold in areas while they are still wet. Drop a medium value of Purple Magenta in the wet areas as well. Let dry.

Mix a dark value of Quinacridone Red and Purple Magenta and paint the area of the flower in the masked areas to darken the center. Let dry. Remove the masking fluid on the entire painting by carefully rubbing it with your fingers, or use a masking fluid eraser.

STEP SIX

Using the colors in your palette, and a medium to dark value of Payne's Gray, paint shadows in the background to add contrast.

Paint details in the flowers with a small brush loaded with Purple Magenta, Quinacridone Red, and Payne's Gray. Let dry, then carefully remove the masking tape.

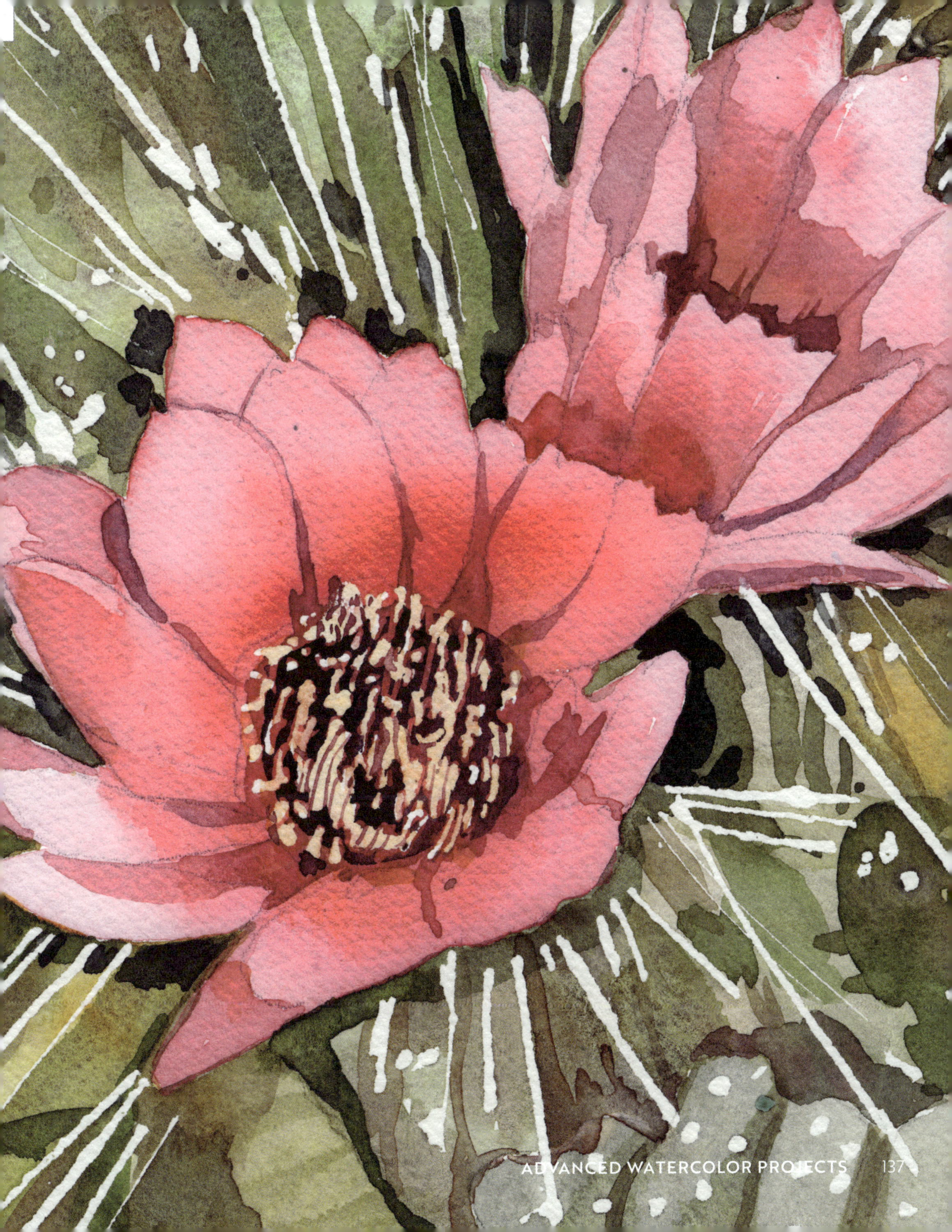

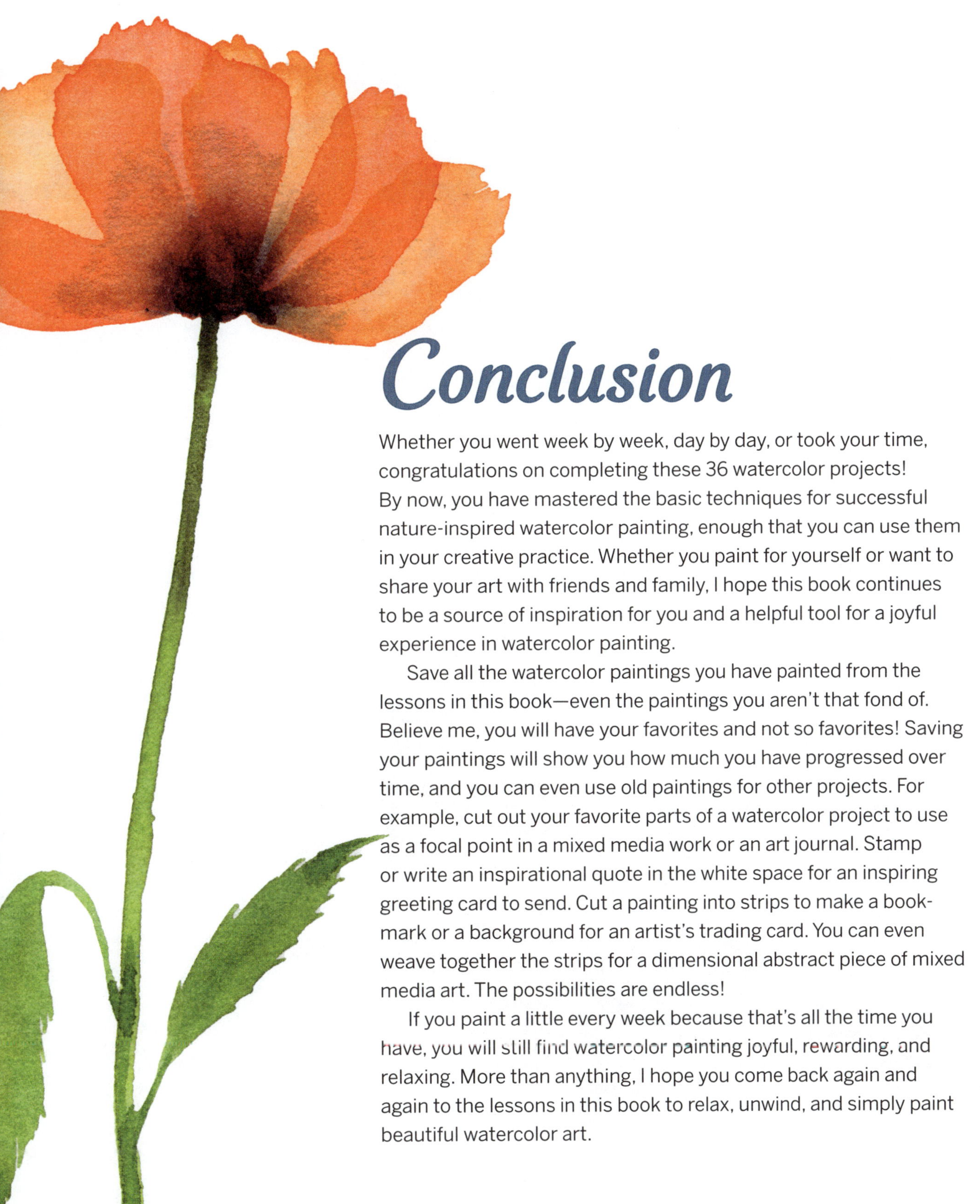

Conclusion

Whether you went week by week, day by day, or took your time, congratulations on completing these 36 watercolor projects! By now, you have mastered the basic techniques for successful nature-inspired watercolor painting, enough that you can use them in your creative practice. Whether you paint for yourself or want to share your art with friends and family, I hope this book continues to be a source of inspiration for you and a helpful tool for a joyful experience in watercolor painting.

Save all the watercolor paintings you have painted from the lessons in this book—even the paintings you aren't that fond of. Believe me, you will have your favorites and not so favorites! Saving your paintings will show you how much you have progressed over time, and you can even use old paintings for other projects. For example, cut out your favorite parts of a watercolor project to use as a focal point in a mixed media work or an art journal. Stamp or write an inspirational quote in the white space for an inspiring greeting card to send. Cut a painting into strips to make a book-mark or a background for an artist's trading card. You can even weave together the strips for a dimensional abstract piece of mixed media art. The possibilities are endless!

If you paint a little every week because that's all the time you have, you will still find watercolor painting joyful, rewarding, and relaxing. More than anything, I hope you come back again and again to the lessons in this book to relax, unwind, and simply paint beautiful watercolor art.

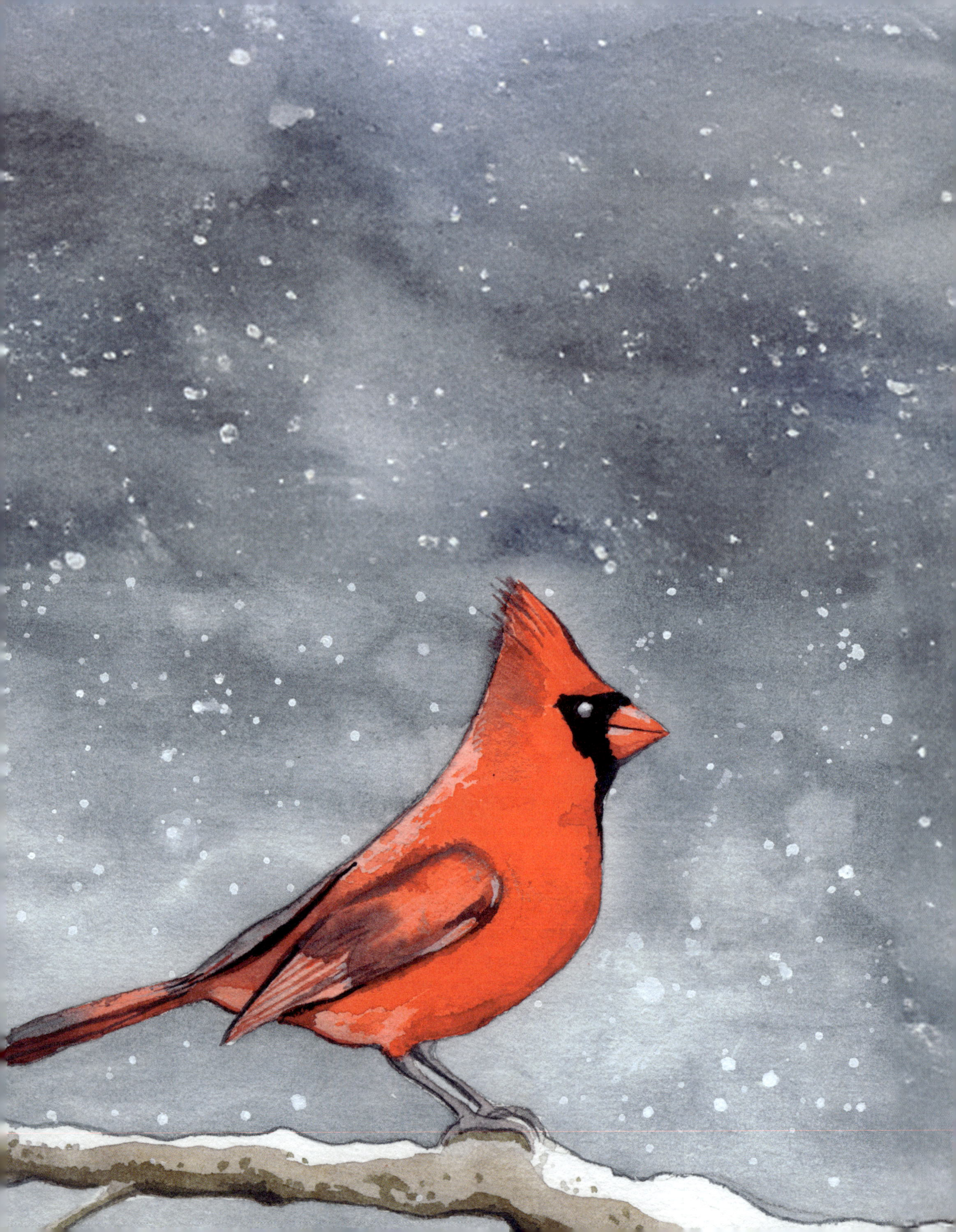

Acknowledgments

I want to express my heartfelt gratitude to the people I have worked with in the art supply industry, especially Dan Egusa, my former employer and owner of Yasutomo and Company. His unwavering support and the numerous opportunities he has given me have been instrumental in my growth as an artist, teacher, and ambassador for the art materials industry.

I am deeply grateful to my three best friends, Lea, Linda, and Sharon. Each has played a unique role in my journey, from being my cheerleaders to reminding me of life's preciousness and brevity, and I cherish their presence in my life.

My sincere thanks to the ladies of the Creative Collective. Their trust in me to test my teaching skills, their valuable feedback, and their constant encouragement have been invaluable in my professional development.

Lastly, I want to thank my husband, Dale, for being patient and supportive and feeding me during all the long hours I put into my work and play as an artist.

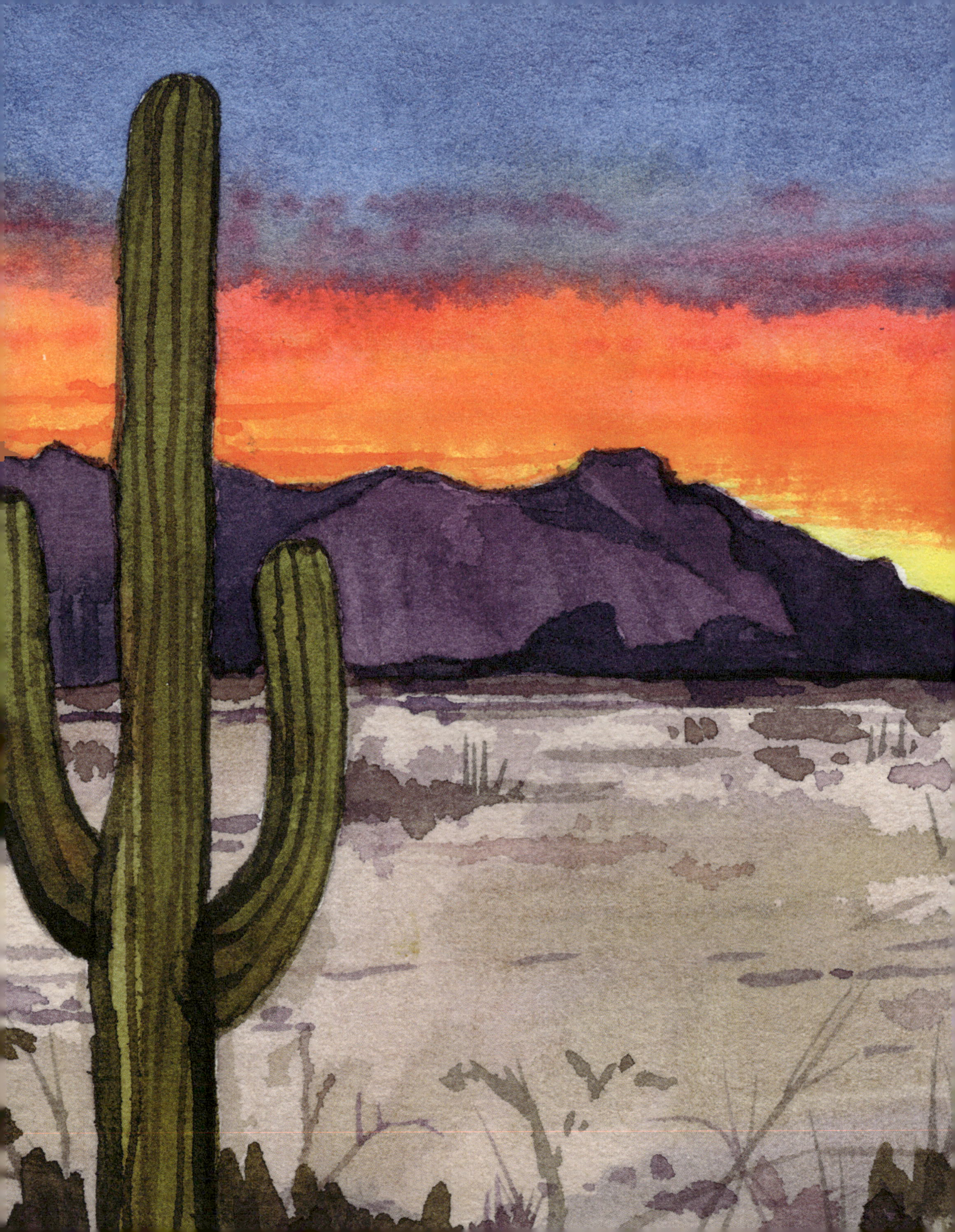

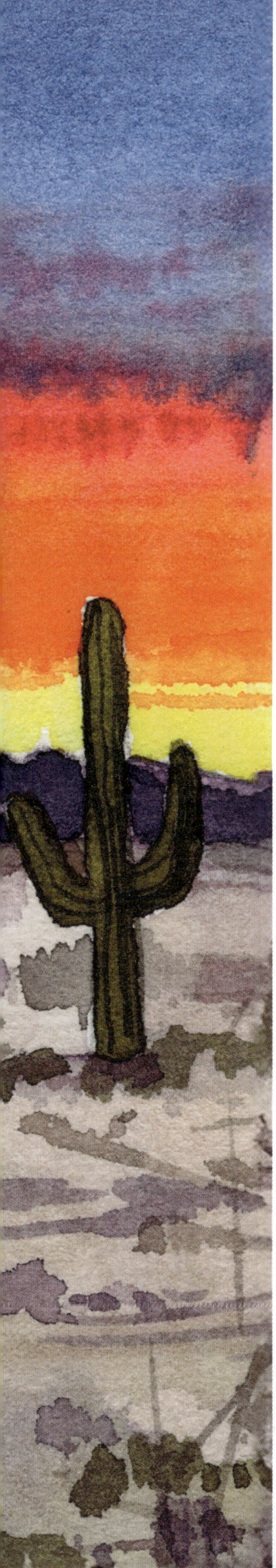

About the Author

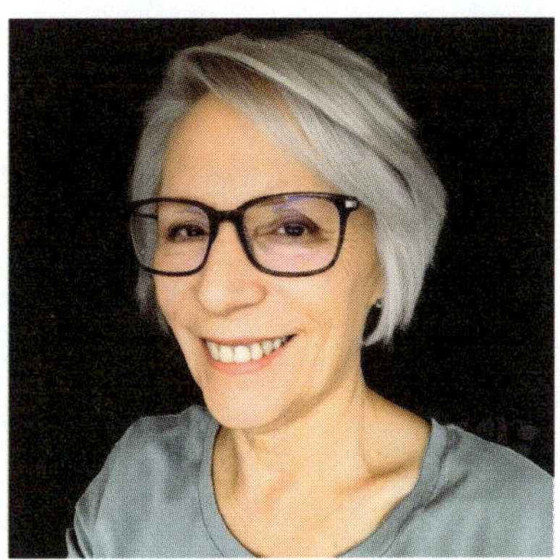

KAREN ELAINE is an artist, author, and teacher passionate about watercolor and paper crafting. Her lifelong mission is to encourage creativity to help people navigate life's joys, complexities, and challenges. Originally from Southern California, she lives and creates in her home studio near Sedona, Arizona. As the founder of Kumomi Studio, a creative consulting and design company, Karen Elaine has taught various online art and crafts classes and has developed creative products for the art materials industry for over three decades. Her innovative product development and generous teaching style have left indelible marks on the industry. A two-time breast cancer survivor, Karen has used her art and creativity for healing, inspiration, and empowerment.

WEBSITE: karenelaine.com

INSTAGRAM: @karenelainecreative

YOUTUBE: youtube.com/@KarenElaine

FACEBOOK: facebook.com/karenelaineartist

Hi there,

We hope you enjoyed *Wild Watercolor*. If you have any questions or concerns about your book, or have received a damaged copy, please contact customerservice@penguinrandomhouse.com. We're here and happy to help.

Also, please consider writing a review on your favorite retailer's website to let others know what you thought of the book!

Sincerely,

The Zeitgeist Team